—

WHO REALLY DROVE THE
ECONOMY INTO THE DITCH?

WHO REALLY DROVE THE ECONOMY INTO THE DITCH?

JOSEPH FRIED

Algora Publishing
New York

Library of Congress Cataloging-in-Publication Data —

Fried, Joseph.
  Who really drove the economy into the ditch? / Joseph Fried.
    p. cm.
  Includes bibliographical references and index.
  ISBN 978-0-87586-942-1 (soft cover : alk. paper)—ISBN 978-0-87586-943-8 (hbk. :
alk. paper)—ISBN 978-0-87586-944-5 (ebook : alk. paper) 1. United States—Economic
conditions—2001-2009. 2. United States—Economic policy—2001-2009. 3. Financial
crises—United States—History—21st century. 4. Recessions—United States—
History—21st century. 5. Global Financial Crisis, 2008-2009. I. Title.
  HC106.83.F73 2012
  330.973'0931—dc23
                        2012032065

Printed in the United States

For Floyd Fried and Eric Kurzdorfer
Two fine men who left us much too soon

Acknowledgments

This book would not have been possible without the love and support of my dear wife, Nina, and son, David.

David deserves special thanks for the hours he spent editing the book and for the valuable advice and encouragement he provided.

TABLE OF CONTENTS

PREFACE: WHO REALLY DROVE THE ECONOMY INTO THE DITCH?

> In the 15 years preceding the financial crisis of 2007/08 United States regulators were primarily concerned with the expansion of housing — particularly "affordable housing." They showed zero concern with regard to the financial health of banks.
>
> What if these regulators had used their time and resources to ensure prudent lending standards? Suppose that government auditors randomly test-checked bank loan files to make sure down payments were no less than 10 percent, borrowers had employment, and credit (FICO) scores were at least 660. Assume that banks could be sued and their expansion plans blocked if lending standards were found to be deficient. What would have happened? Nothing. There would have been no financial crisis.

Republicans as well as Democrats supported liberal housing and lending policies that led to the collapse of loan underwriting standards. The disintegration of lending standards set the stage for the creation of millions of loans to subprime borrowers — at all levels of income and for homes big and small. This was the primary cause of the financial crisis, and it has led to a new era of class warfare politics.

President Barack Obama would have us believe that the financial crisis of 2007 and 2008 was caused by cutting "taxes for millionaires," "eight years of Republican deregulation," and Republican deficit spending. After reviewing all aspects of the crisis, I believe that the President's words are nonsense. This crisis was chiefly caused by aggressive and persistent governmental intrusions into America's private lending system and by the consequences of those intrusions.

The primary cause of the financial crisis was the government's effort to promote affordable housing through the modification of loan underwriting standards. That effort soon led to a weakening of underwriting standards for most residential housing loans.

Title XIII of The Housing and Community Development Act of 1992 created an affordable housing mandate for Fannie Mae and Freddie Mac, and authorized their primary regulator, HUD, to monitor their success in implementing the mandate. Two and a half years later, in May 1995, HUD, Fannie, Freddie, and a vast network of state, local and nonprofit "partners" unleashed a comprehensive and detailed "affordable housing" *Strategy* that encouraged and sometimes required lenders to use lax automated appraisal and underwriting systems, to reduce or eliminate documentation requirements, and to tolerate third-party "gifts" and "silent second" mortgages designed to undermine down payment and closing cost requirements. This affordable housing *Strategy* went far beyond the requirements of that much-discussed red herring, the Community Reinvestment Act (CRA). Because the changes to underwriting standards could not be limited to certain neighborhoods or to low-income borrowers, the entire housing market was affected.

The secondary cause of the crisis was also a creation of government: After the 911 terrorist attacks the Federal Reserve sharply lowered the short-term borrowing rate of financial institutions, effectively giving banks a free source of funds. This motivated banks to make as many mortgage loans as feasible. At the same time it forced investors to look for higher yield and riskier investments — such as mortgage-backed securities and derivatives.

The Fed's low-interest policies greatly accelerated a housing boom that was already underway as a result of a maturing tech bubble and the new, anything-goes loan underwriting standards. Millions of subprime loans were created, enmeshed into complex securities (largely by private investment banks), and sold world-wide. When this subprime housing bubble could no longer be sustained, the result was the financial crisis.

There were other factors that contributed to the financial crisis, many of which were rooted in private enterprise. These factors and most aspects of the crisis are reviewed in *Who Really Drove the Economy Into the Ditch?* — a comprehensive review of all major financial crisis issues. However, there are 3 indirectly-related factors that are not addressed in the book: a so-called world-wide savings glut, the collapse of the NAS-

DAQ stock bubble in 2000, and U.S. tax policy that provides a deduction for interest on home-related debt but not on other forms of personal debt.

The causes and major factors that affected the financial crisis of 2007/08 are discussed in the first 4 parts of the book. Part Five outlines and analyzes the Obama Administration's alternative theories and the class warfare rhetoric that has emerged since the crisis. It can be shown that the crisis was not caused by "tax breaks for millionaires," deficit spending, or the deregulation of banks.

There are two addenda: The first comprises a general overview of the financial crisis. In that addendum (and other parts of the book) you will find a graphic flowchart of causes and other factors related to the financial crisis (Figure 23, on page 312). The major parts of the flowchart coincide with the first four parts of the book. Addendum B contains a summary of common myths concerning the crisis.

This book is written primarily from a United States perspective, and any honest review of the subprime mortgage crisis has to show that, in the U.S., most governmental "screw-ups" were bi-partisan in nature. Although the policies and practices that got us into the jam were more liberal than conservative, these initiatives were often espoused by Republicans, as well as Democrats. In this book, names and party affiliations are given as fairly and consistently as possible.

There are frequent references to Fannie Mae and Freddie Mac. Sometimes I call them "Fannie and Freddie," and at other times they are simply "F&F" or "the GSEs," which stands for government sponsored enterprises.

Finally, the reader should know that my personal political ideology is generally conservative. That said, I am not necessarily a small-government conservative: I feel that government has an important role to play in regulating the free enterprise system. When it does this, however, it must do so efficiently, effectively, with respect for the Constitution, and with extreme caution with regard to social agendas. Despite my conservative leanings I believe that all relevant facts have been presented fairly and accurately, and the conclusions reached are reasonable and logical.

Wouldn't it be nice if all authors writing on politically sensitive topics disclosed their ideological leanings?

PART ONE: TWO GOVERNMENTAL POLICIES CAUSED THE CRISIS

Part One comprises 9 chapters, the first 8 of which pertain primarily to government policies designed to expand home ownership. These polices, often referred to as "affordable housing" policies, were the principal cause of the financial crisis of 2007/08.

The federal government, several state and local governments, community activists, and the government sponsored enterprises (GSEs), known as Fannie Mae and Freddie Mac, waged war on common-sense lending standards. The weapons used included "silent second" loans, easy-to-qualify automated underwriting systems, Zillow-like computerized appraisal systems, specially-designed loan products with no down payments, arm twisting, threats, financial inducements, vast subprime purchases, promotion of shady mortgage brokers over community banks, the Community Reinvestment Act (CRA), and "voluntary" agreements for lenders not formally subject to the CRA..

Although the government's goal was to help 8 million tenants become homeowners, the means used (the degrading of loan underwriting standards) affected nearly every borrower in the market. Many prime borrowers effectively became subprime borrowers as they utilized the new, easy standards to help them stretch for bigger homes. The fuse was lit.

Chapter 9 addresses the secondary cause of the crisis: the Federal Reserve's error in keeping interest rates too low for too long. Those low rates, in combination with decimated underwriting standards, fueled a huge housing bubble, financed with millions of shaky loans.

These two causes of the crisis are represented by the shaded boxes in Figure 1, which provides a flow chart of elements related to the crisis. The flow chart is further described in Addendum A.

Figure 1 – A model of the causes and other factors affecting the financial crisis of 2007/08 (The shaded boxes pertain to Part One.)

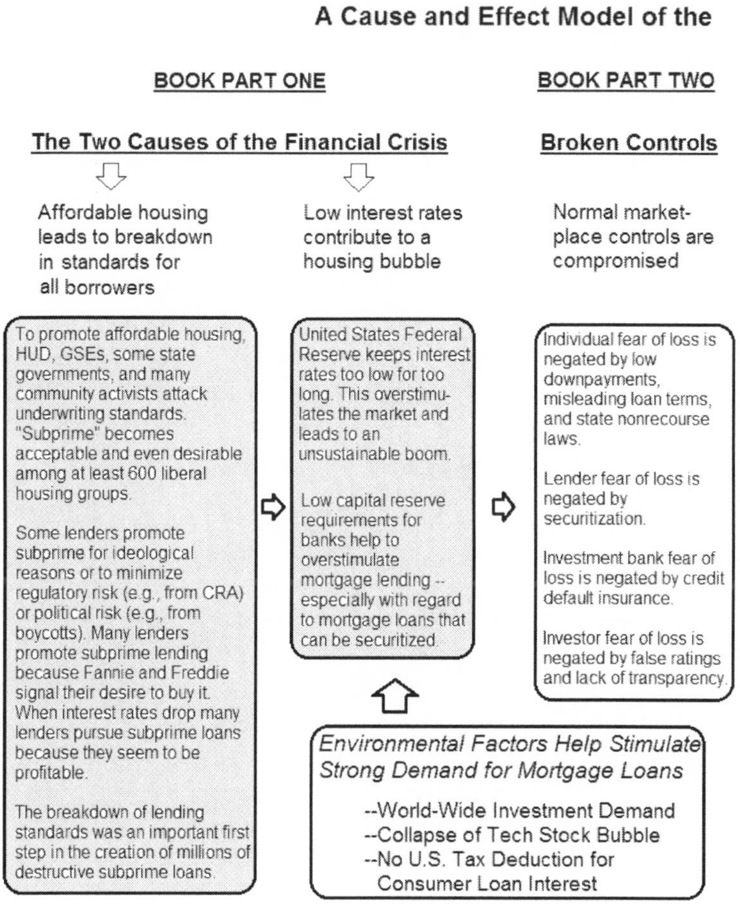

A Cause and Effect Model of the

BOOK PART ONE		BOOK PART TWO

The Two Causes of the Financial Crisis		Broken Controls

Affordable housing leads to breakdown in standards for all borrowers	Low interest rates contribute to a housing bubble	Normal marketplace controls are compromised

| To promote affordable housing, HUD, GSEs, some state governments, and many community activists attack underwriting standards. "Subprime" becomes acceptable and even desirable among at least 600 liberal housing groups.

Some lenders promote subprime for ideological reasons or to minimize regulatory risk (e.g., from CRA) or political risk (e.g., from boycotts). Many lenders promote subprime lending because Fannie and Freddie signal their desire to buy it. When interest rates drop many lenders pursue subprime loans because they seem to be profitable.

The breakdown of lending standards was an important first step in the creation of millions of destructive subprime loans. | United States Federal Reserve keeps interest rates too low for too long. This overstimulates the market and leads to an unsustainable boom.

Low capital reserve requirements for banks help to overstimulate mortgage lending -- especially with regard to mortgage loans that can be securitized. | Individual fear of loss is negated by low downpayments, misleading loan terms, and state nonrecourse laws.

Lender fear of loss is negated by securitization.

Investment bank fear of loss is negated by credit default insurance.

Investor fear of loss is negated by false ratings and lack of transparency. |

Environmental Factors Help Stimulate Strong Demand for Mortgage Loans

--World-Wide Investment Demand
--Collapse of Tech Stock Bubble
--No U.S. Tax Deduction for Consumer Loan Interest

Subprime Mortgage Crisis of 2007-2008

BOOK PART THREE		BOOK PART FOUR
Sparks	**Boom**	**Aggravating Factors**

These are just triggers	Bear Stearns & ML are sold, Lehman goes broke, AIG is downgraded, and Feds take over Fannie and Freddie	These factors complicate the crisis aftermath but do not cause the crisis

Mark-to-market accounting

Naked short selling

Sudden downgrades by rating agencies

Financial Crisis

Banks & borrowers are hurt because of documentation defects.

Taxpayers are hurt because bank capital reserves are deficient.

Homeowners are hurt by nearby foreclosures, which are aggravated by nonrecourse lending rules.

CHAPTER 1: THE ROSETTA STONE OF THE SUBPRIME LENDING
CRISIS

> For hundreds of years, Egyptian hieroglyphics were
> a mystery, even to language experts. Finally someone
> discovered the key to decoding them — on the Rosetta stone.

> – Robert Berendt

In 1995, the Department of Housing and Urban Development (HUD) produced a comprehensive document that is critical to understanding the subprime loan crisis — but you won't find it on the HUD Web site or anywhere else on the Internet. A few print copies exist in libraries but I suspect that Sandy Berger will be visiting those libraries soon — wearing oversized britches. Fingerprints are being wiped clean ...

The document, called *The National Homeownership Strategy: Partners in the American Dream* ("Strategy"), was compiled in 1995 by Henry Cisneros, President Clinton's HUD Secretary. It represented the collective wisdom of HUD, Fannie Mae, Freddie Mac, leaders of the housing industry, various banks, numerous activist organizations such as ACORN and La Raza, and representatives from several state and local governments. Important: The *Strategy* did not pertain solely to the loans purchased by Fannie or Freddie, or to Community Reinvestment Act loans. This was a broad, governmental plan for the entire lending industry, comprising "100 proposed action items," ostensibly designed to "generate up to 8 million additional homeowners" in America.[1] In reality, however, it was a blueprint for the destruction of the United States mortgage loan system.

This may not jibe with the education you received from the mainstream media about the root causes of the financial meltdown. You probably heard that the meltdown began around 2004 or 2005 in a perfect storm created by greedy Wall Street investment bankers and insurers, and/or dumb accounting rules ("mark to market"), and/or insatiable Chinese investors, and/or inept rating companies, and/or years of deregulation, and/or a "bet that blew up Wall Street." Indeed, some of these were significant factors, and most of these issues are analyzed in this book. But, as economist Thomas Sowell put it, they were "things *downstream* from the fundamental source of risk, the lowering of standards for making mortgage loans and the resulting delinquencies, defaults and foreclosures" (emphasis added).[2]

The problems in the lending industry, so prevalent after year 2000, were downstream from the cockamamie 100-point *Strategy* devised in 1995 by Mr. Cisneros. That *Strategy* was itself downstream from the Housing and Community Development Act of 1992 — legislation that established an affordable housing requirement for Fannie and Freddie.[3] "Lenders did not spontaneously begin to lend to people who would not have qualified for loans under the traditional criteria that had evolved out of years of experience...."[4] That level of stupidity requires mentoring, careful guidance — and an act of Congress.

Initially, the 1992 legislation required that 30 percent or more of Fannie's and Freddie's loan purchases be related to affordable housing. However, that was just the starting requirement. HUD (the primary regulator of Fannie and Freddie) was given the power to set future requirements, and it did so with vigor. The 30 percent requirement was increased to 40 percent for 1996 and to 42 percent for 1997. Later, the goals would be set to as high as 56 percent. In the view of HUD, a special *Strategy* was needed to achieve these goals.

---

1   United States. Dept. of Housing and Urban Development., The National Homeownership Strategy : Partners in the American Dream (Washington, D.C.: U.S. Dept. of Housing and Urban Development, 1995), 1-1.

2   Thomas Sowell, The Housing Boom and Bust (New York: Basic Books, 2009), 126.

3   Specifically, the requirement was created by Title XIII of the Act, known as the Federal Housing Enterprises Financial Safety and Soundness Act (FHEFSSA).

4   Sowell, The Housing Boom and Bust, 146.

HUD's 1995 *Strategy* was a self-described "action document, not an academic exercise. It is a call to action and a resource for *thousands* of national, State, and local organizations in the private and public sectors" (emphasis added).[1] Cisneros was particularly proud that he was able to bring several private banks and mortgage companies into his grand scheme. He noted: "In August 1994 these planning sessions culminated in a historic meeting at which industry representatives agreed to ... help develop the *National Homeownership Strategy*."[2] Make a note: It was the government seducing private lenders to participate — not the other way around.

The inclusion of private enterprise in federal affordable housing plans was not incidental: It was planned and strategic. The motivation was clearly explained at a "National Symposium," held in July 1997 by the Office of the Comptroller of Currency:

> The traditional reliance on government programs as the major source for affordable housing funding is rapidly changing. Scarce public resources are being used more often to leverage bank funds, spurring joint public-private efforts.[3]

The origin of no-down payment loans

Here is what we can decipher from the hieroglyphics on the subprime Rosetta stone (the "*Strategy*"). HUD was already touting the virtues of the zero-down payment mortgage as early as 1995. In the *Strategy*, HUD cites the work of one of its partners, the New Jersey Housing and Mortgage Finance Agency, noting that "its no-down payment 100 Percent Mortgage Financing Program" encourages home ownership among lower income households. The no-down payment loans touted by HUD were being directed to "lower income households" – not middle class people who might actually make the monthly payments.[4] Of course, in the inverse universe of the government this is perfectly logical.

To Cisneros and his gang, down payments and closing costs were bad because, for many potential homebuyers (specifically, the unqualified ones), they were "the major impediment to purchasing a home." The

---

1   United States. Dept. of Housing and Urban Development., The National Homeownership Strategy : Partners in the American Dream, 1-1.
2   Ibid., 1-3.
3   Janice A. Booker, "The Single Family Affordable Housing Market: Trends and Innovations" (paper presented at the A National Symposium, July 1997).
4   United States. Dept. of Housing and Urban Development., The National Homeownership Strategy : Partners in the American Dream, 4-7.

solution? Reduce or eliminate all mortgage-related costs. Extending this "logic," we would have a lot more medical doctors if we would just stop requiring medical degrees, and we would have more engineers if they did not have to go to college, etc. It all makes sense if you get yourself into a liberal-governmental frame of mind.

> Low down payment single family mortgages are the lifeblood of the affordable housing market....
>
> – Joint statement by The Enterprise Foundation and Local Initiatives Support Corporation[1]

If lenders couldn't be cajoled into giving no-down-payment and no-cost loans, HUD had another solution: It would give the potential buyer a second, unsecured, interest-free loan to cover the down payment and other costs.[2] That way, a person could own a home while maintaining the mentality of a free-spirited tenant. He wouldn't have to wait a few years to save for a down payment, and wouldn't have to feel he was risking anything, should he decide to skip out. In fact, he'd have less risk than a renter because a tenant breaking a lease can be held accountable, whereas a zero-down homebuyer can walk away (in many states) with impunity.

HUD's preoccupation with reducing or eliminating down payment requirements is evident from the pressure it put on its partners: "State agencies should be encouraged to ensure that sufficient funding is set aside from their overall budget resources for low-income homeownership down payment and mortgage subsidies." (Unfortunately, many states heeded this advice, as we see in Chapter 4.) Lending partners in the private sector were told they needed to be more "flexible about other forms of down payment assistance such as public subsidies or unsecured loans." They were also encouraged to accept down payment funding from alternative sources, which might include "foundations, private sector donations, religious organizations, employers, and others."[3]

> A no-down-payment policy reflects a belief that poor families should qualify for home ownership because they are poor, in contrast to the reality that some poor families are prepared to make the sacrifices necessary to own property,

---

1   LISC and The Enterprise Foundation, "Letter to Office of General Counsel of the OFHEO," (Washington, DC: March 2, 2000).

2   United States. Dept. of Housing and Urban Development., The National Homeownership Strategy : Partners in the American Dream, 4-14, 4-17.

3   Ibid., 4-8.

and some are not. Keeping their distance from those unable
to save money is a crucial means by which upwardly mobile,
self-sacrificing people establish and maintain the value of the
homes they buy.

– Howard Husock, Scholar with the Manhattan Institute[1]

If all else failed and the buyer was stuck making his own down payment, the HUD *Strategy* had one more creative idea: The buyer could
use her IRA or 401(K) funds to fund the down payment. To this end the
Strategy states: "The partnership should support legislation that removes
negative tax consequences for early withdrawal of money from tax-de-
ferred individual retirement accounts when the money is used for down
payment assistance...."[2] To anyone who has recently faced a home foreclosure, the brainstorm of using retirement funds as the down payment
probably doesn't seem so brainy. No wonder this government *Strategy* is
unavailable on the Internet.

Lender, Thou Shalt be flexible

Beyond the issue of down payments, the HUD consortium pushed
the general idea of underwriting flexibility. First, it gave a big pat on the
back to its wards, Fannie and Freddie (F&F), for setting standards that
would eventually lead the mortgage industry to doom:

> In recent years many mortgagees have increased underwriting flexibility.
> This increased flexibility is due, at least in part to ... liberalized affordable
> housing underwriting criteria established by secondary market investors
> such as Fannie Mae and Freddie Mac.[3]

You've probably heard that private lenders lowered underwriting
standards on their own initiative but the *Strategy*'s statement (above)
proves that is a lie. Consider the words again: "...Many mortgagees [pri-
vate lenders] have increased underwriting flexibility ... due, at least in
part to ... liberalized affordable housing underwriting criteria established
by ... Fannie Mae and Freddie Mac." Do you think Fannie and Freddie
still want the credit for getting private lenders to relax their standards?[4]

---

1   Howard Husock, "The Trillion-Dollar Bank Shakedown That Bodes Ill for
    Cities," City Journal   (2000), http://www.city-journal.org/html/10_1_the_
    trillion_dollar.html.
2   United States. Dept. of Housing and Urban Development., The National
    Homeownership Strategy : Partners in the American Dream, 4-8.
3   Ibid., 4-13.
4   Title XIII of the Housing and Community Development Act of 1992, which
    was known as The Federal Housing Enterprises Financial Safety and
    Soundness Act of 1992 (FHEFSSA), established for Fannie and Freddie

Fannie described its new "flexibility hotline,"[1][2] and Freddie once bragged of a special outreach program where lenders and community groups (e.g., ACORN and NACA) were brought together to discuss ways to "more flexibly interpret" underwriting requirements.[3] Freddie warned private lenders to not use a "cookie cutter" approach that might "unintentionally exclude good borrowers...."[4]

As an illustration of creative lending, the *Strategy* cites a Connecticut program that "allows for *nontraditional* employment histories, employment histories with gaps, short-term employment, and frequent job changes (emphasis added)."[5] Was this the genesis of the no-wage-statement loans (a.k.a. "stated loans") that became so prevalent a few years later?

The *Strategy* commends the Federal Housing Administration (FHA, which is a part of HUD) for its "significant improvements in its mortgage underwriting criteria," including ignoring any buyer debt that is due in less than 10 months, ignoring child care debt, allowing use of "cash saved at home," and "increasing flexibility in qualifying ratios and compensating factors."[6] If I understand this correctly, a lender would be encouraged to ignore a deadbeat dad's $10,000 trip to Las Vegas, provided he charged the trip on a short-term credit card.

"The government was screaming" for subprime

It is important to realize that HUD's efforts were not limited to FHA loans for modestly-priced homes, and F&F's efforts were not limited to the loans they bought, or were legally able to buy. This is a point routinely ignored by many journalists and academics. As we see in Chapter

---

HUD-imposed housing goals for financing of affordable housing. "Now they were mandated by FHEFSSA to make loans that were unsound under the guise of 'affordable housing.'" (Staff Writer, Originator Times, October 22, 2008, http://originatortimes.com)

1. United States. Dept. of Housing and Urban Development., The National Homeownership Strategy : Partners in the American Dream, 4-14.
2. Fannie Mae and Freddie Mac are government sponsored enterprises (GSEs). They were created by Acts of Congress, and they have the implicit backing of the United States government. However, their stock is privately traded.
3. ACORN stands for the Association of Community Organizations for Reform Now; NACA stands for the Neighborhood Assistance Corporation of America.
4. United States. Dept. of Housing and Urban Development., The National Homeownership Strategy : Partners in the American Dream, 4-13.
5. Ibid., 4-14.
6. Ibid., 4-15.

4, HUD and its friends were pushing borrower-friendly lending standards on hundreds of state and local governments and on "thousands of national, state, and local organizations in the private and public sector," including bankers, mortgage lenders, brokers, and nonprofit entities.[1] These persuasive efforts were not limited to jawboning: Billions of dollars were spent in an effort to chip away at prudent underwriting standards. HUD sought a massive "collaboration" that would add 8 million new homeowners and completely alter the business of mortgage lending. Unfortunately, HUD succeeded.

Consider the words of people who worked in the lending industry at the grassroots level — people who lived and breathed subprime every day. When did they start making subprime loans? Did they feel pressured by the government? As part of her work requirement for obtaining a PhD in Criminal Justice, Cynthia Koller interviewed 15 such individuals, including "1 appraiser, 1 realtor, 3 brokers, 8 lenders, and 2 account executives." Koller's goals included an examination of the growth of subprime lending and related fraud in the United States, and an assessment of how industry practitioners "perceived, utilized, and reinvented the subprime innovation for legitimate and fraudulent use...." Although the sample size was not large enough to justify statistical inferences, the responses obtained by Koller are enlightening:

> The interviewees were unanimous in their contention that subprime lending originated during the mid-1990s when the economy was strong, residential property was plentiful, housing values were increasing, lending guidelines were relaxed, and *government pressure* was such that the GSEs [Fannie and Freddie] were required to open up their portfolios to facilitate lending to individuals who were not traditionally qualified to purchase homes (emphasis added).[2]

An interviewed appraiser put it this way:

> I'll go back to the Clinton era where the policy was "homeownership is an American right. Everyone should be able to own a home. You banks and mortgage companies out there, make it easier for homeownership." And they did.[3]

A lender had this recollection:

> For the most part, that [subprime lending] originated with the Clinton administration. I remember seeing this in the paper all the time, when the

---

1   Ibid., 1-1.
2   Cynthia Koller, "Diffusion of Innovation and Fraud in the Subprime Mortgage Market" (University of Cincinnati, 2010), 90.
3   Ibid., 89.

government was screaming "we want programs available to more people who can't get a conventional, fixed-rate loan because they don't have the down payment...."[1]

And, here is one more example. A lender named Steve had this perspective:

> Bill Clinton is the one who brought subprime into existence. George Bush catches the flak for it a lot because of the collapse and everything else happened under his watch, but Bill Clinton was the one who actually signed subprime mortgage into law and made them available. And yeah, there was big pressure from the government....[2]

The deadly role of Fannie and Freddie

Although HUD was the architect of the *Strategy*, other elements of the federal bureaucracy were also instrumental in destroying lending standards. For example, three years prior to the roll-out of the *Strategy*, the Boston Federal Reserve produced a study that supposedly showed bank discrimination against minority borrowers. This report, produced in 1992, was repeatedly discredited by other analysts; nevertheless, on the basis of the report, Team Clinton began a quest to solve the "problem" (see page 127).

In 1998, the Federal Reserve Bank of Dallas published a paper titled, "Credit is Overdue for Subprime Mortgage Lending." The article hailed subprime lending because of its contribution to affordable housing:

> People who previously had difficulty obtaining mortgage financing now have greater access to mortgage credit. Viewed in this way, subprime mortgage lending is a good example of how our competitive market economy works to improve overall living standards.[3]

This is our Federal Reserve talking. It's the part of government that is supposed to monitor and minimize systemic risk in the financial system. The Fed is supposed to make sure our banks stay healthy; instead, it was promoting loans to people with weak credit histories.

Even more instrumental to the torching of sound lending standards were those government sponsored enterprises (GSEs), known as Fannie Mae and Freddie Mac (F&F). Although F&F were just two of hundreds of *Strategy* partners, they had enormous resources, were the primary pur-

1   Ibid.
2   Ibid.
3   Robert F. Mahalik and Kenneth J. Robinson, "Credit Is Overdue for Subprime Mortgage Lending," ed. Federal Reserve Bank of Dallas (United States, 1998), 1.

chasers of loans in the secondary market, and were required — by law — to buy affordable housing loans. This made them far more influential than any other entities or factors. Unfortunately, their influence was not positive. In the opinion of Josh Rosner, the Managing Director of Graham Fisher & Co. (a financial research firm), Fannie and Freddie had a devastating influence on the entire mortgage loan market:[1]

> By 1995, we saw home prices start to rise and home ownership levels also start to rise. How did we do that? There was no private label [mortgage] market at that point. We were really dealing in a world of enterprise [i.e., Fannie and Freddie] paper. We saw most of the features [of CDOs and structure assets] that we are now looking at as having been atrocious or irresponsible or poor risk management having started in the enterprise [Fannie and Freddie] markets. We saw changes in the LTV [ratio of loans to home values], changes from manual underwriting to automated underwriting. The approval models used were easy to game. We saw reductions in documentation requirements. We saw changes for mortgage insurance requirements. We saw the perversion of the appraisal process and a move to automated appraisals. All of these features which we now look at and point our fingers at the subprime originators and say "you bad boys," all started in the enterprise [Fannie and Freddie] market.[2]

Alarms were ringing years before the crisis

A cynic might say that Rosner is simply a Monday morning quarterback, blaming Fannie and Freddie, after the crisis. However, his company, Graham Fisher, was sounding alarms about F&F, and HUD's *National Homeownership Strategy*, years before the crisis occurred. In a report published in June 2001, the company outlined several serious concerns: "While the underlying initiatives of the [*Strategy*] were broad in content, the main theme ... was the relaxation of credit standards."[3] The manifestation of these relaxed standards, as identified by Graham Fisher, is itemized below:

- "The requirement that homebuyers make significant down payments was eliminated in the 1990s. The [Strategy] urged

---

1   Graham Fisher & Co. is an independent research firm for institutional investors.

2   Josh Rosner as cited by R. Christopher Whalen, "The Subprime Crisis: Cause, Effect and Consequences," (Social Science Electronic Publishing, Inc., 2008), http://papers.ssrn.com/sol3/papers.cfm?abstract_id=1113888&rec=1&srcabs=15108.

3   "Housing in the New Millennium: A Home without Equity Is Just a Rental with Debt," (New York: Graham Fisher, June 29, 2001), 6, http://ssrn.com/abstract=1162456.

and approved increasingly larger reductions in requirements. ... Down payment requirements have dropped to record low levels."[1]

- "Over the past decade Fannie Mae and Freddie Mac have reduced required down payments on loans that they purchase in the secondary market. Those requirements have declined from 10% to 5% to 3% and in the past few months Fannie Mae announced that it would follow Freddie Mac's recent move into the 0% down payment mortgage market."[2]
- "Private mortgage insurance requirements were relaxed."[3]
- New, automated underwriting software, developed by Fannie and Freddie, allows reduced loan documentation and "higher debt to income levels than does traditional underwriting." The underwriting systems were approved "even though they were stress-tested using only a limited number and breadth of economic scenarios."[4]
- The house appraisal process "is being compromised. We have spoken with real estate appraisers, fraud appraisers and national appraisal organizations and have been told, almost unanimously, that the changes in the appraisal process, over the past decade, have jeopardized the soundness of the process and skewed real estate prices."[5]

The report concluded that "the risk of credit relaxation and leverage can't be ignored."[6] Remember, these comments and warnings were published years before there was a financial crisis to blame on anyone or any political party. Graham Fisher's portrait of quickly-deteriorating standards can be traced directly to the (Rosetta Stone) *Strategy* and to the actions of Fannie and Freddie. Ultimately, these crumbling standards led us to financial catastrophe.

---

1   Ibid., 7.
2   Ibid., 8.
3   Ibid.
4   Ibid., 9.
5   Ibid., 10-11.
6   Ibid., 2.

CHAPTER 2: GARBAGE IN, GARBAGE OUT

> The first lender Mr. Evans approached turned him down
> for a conventional mortgage to finance a modest $80,000
> ranch house. His down payment, the lender said, was
> insufficient to consider him for anything but government-
> insured mortgage. Then, Mr. Evans found a small local
> lender that uses [Freddie Mac's] automated underwriting.
> Within three weeks of loan application, the 27-year-old was
> pocketing the keys to his first home.
>
> – Freddie Mac[1]

Nineteen hundred and ninety five was a very bad year. Not only was HUD launching jihad against common sense lending practices (Chapter 1); the HUD wards, Fannie and Freddie (F&F), were rolling out computerized "automated underwriting" (AU) programs that would dramatically alter, in a negative way, the manner in which the entire home loan industry would approve or reject mortgage loan applications. AU systems would accelerate the growth of thousands of sleazy mortgage brokers by enabling them to conduct business directly with F&F or directly with subprime mortgage aggregators, such as Countrywide Financial. The growth of these brokers and aggregators, at the expense of solid community banks, led to a surge in subprime and predatory lending.

To use one of these AU systems a lender would enter selected borrower application information into its computer and transmit the infor-

---

1   "Automatic Underwriting: Making Mortgage Lending Simpler and Fairer
     for America's Families," (Washington, DC: Freddie Mac, September 1996),
     Chapter 5.

mation to Freddie or Fannie, who would add credit information such as FICO scores.[1] Using general historical loan repayment data, the AU system would compute the statistical odds of the borrower's repayment. If satisfactory, the loan would be accepted "before the borrower [could] finish a cup of coffee" (Freddie Mac).[2]

In addition to saving processing costs, F&F had two major reasons for introducing their AU systems. First and foremost, F&F wanted to gain a competitive advantage over traditional banks. As reported by the Wall Street Journal in 2001:

> Industry veterans say automated underwriting has had another effect: By aiding brokers and diminishing the market muscle of banks, Fannie and Freddie have strengthened their own relative positions. This strengthening comes at the expense of traditional lenders that have resisted selling mortgage loans to Fannie and Freddie. In some cases, banks prefer to keep some of the loans they make, meaning that Fannie and Freddie don't get them.
>
> If brokers armed with automated-underwriting software were allowed to sell loans directly to Fannie and Freddie — cutting banks out of the loan-making business — that will make it easier for the two companies to feed their huge appetites for loans. If that happened, the technology could lead to ... *a radical reshaping of the mortgage market* (emphasis added).[3]

Of course, this is almost exactly what happened. Although brokers did not, for the most part, sell their loans directly to F&F (subprime loan aggregators such as Countrywide were used), the role of banks, using traditional underwriting, was undercut.

Instead of taking a month to approve a loan, the process could be completed in just a few days, and sometimes, as Freddie boasted, "before the borrower [could] finish a cup of coffee." We now know just how expensive that cup of coffee would be. Brokers were responsible for the overwhelming majority of subprime loans, and those loans were up to 20 times more likely to default than were conventional bank loans. As de-

---

1   The FICO corporation was founded in 1956 as Fair, Isaac and Company. It is a publicly-traded corporation that provides credit-scoring information. This information is often used by lenders and lessors to assist in evaluating the credit-worthiness of borrowers and lessees.
2   "Automatic Underwriting: Making Mortgage Lending Simpler and Fairer for America's Families," Ch. 2.
3   Patrick Barta, "Why Big Lenders Are So Afraid of Fannie Mae and Freddie Mac," Wall Street Journal, April 5 2001.

tailed in Chapter 6, the majority of those subprime loans were purchased by Fannie, Freddie, and FHA.[1]

The second motive for promoting AU had to do with affordable housing and diversity. F&F wanted to "level the playing field" with regard to ethnicity and race by expanding the housing market to "families who do not fit the traditional borrower profile."[2] To this end, the AU systems of Fannie and Freddie were designed to place relatively less importance on three requirements of traditional underwriting that were perceived to be potential obstacles to the disadvantaged and minority communities:

- having income
- having a down payment
- having documentation

Instead of these factors, the F&F AU systems relied "most heavily on the borrower's credit information" (e.g., credit ratings such as FICO scores).[3] A credit rating could be the "compensating factor," in the event there was a deficiency with regard to the traditional underwriting requirements (sort of like the extra credit assignment a student might prepare to compensate for a test he bombed).[4] By using this approach it would be possible to "identify many new families who represent acceptable mortgage credit risks."[5]

In a telling statement, Freddie implied that it is relatively easy to establish a good credit history:

> Fortunately, consumers are able to go from no credit history to an acceptable one relatively quickly, in perhaps one or two years. To do this, they need to open and use several credit accounts, and make timely payments without running up a large balance.[6]

---

1   Those who contradict this claim invariably use a specious definition of "subprime." Most frequently, they confuse subprime with high-interest-rate loans. On the other hand, Fannie and Freddie would classify loans as "subprime" only if the selling bank classified it as such. (And, the bank often did not, since it was financially better – for all parties – to treat it as being "prime.") A subprime loan is one given to someone who is not a good credit risk, given the size and repayment terms of the loan.

2   "Automatic Underwriting: Making Mortgage Lending Simpler and Fairer for America's Families," Executive Summary.

3   Lakhbir Hayre, Salomon Smith Barney Guide to Mortgage-Backed and Asset-Backed Securities, Wiley Finance Series. (New York: John Wiley, 2001), 215.

4   "Automatic Underwriting: Making Mortgage Lending Simpler and Fairer for America's Families," Ch. 3.

5   Ibid., Ch. 6.

6   Ibid.

In other words, you can "go from no credit history to an acceptable one" by opening up a few credit cards and shuffling money between them. And, this brand new credit history can be the "compensating factor" if you are kind of shaky with regard to old-fashioned things like down payments or wage earnings.

Like most liberal goals, fair and affordable housing is admirable, but this F&F strategy — building underwriting flexibility into their automated systems — had unanticipated consequences. Indeed, the AU systems of F&F played a key role in destroying prudent lending standards.

In retrospect it is easy to see the several major mistakes made by Fannie and Freddie in the testing and promotion of automated underwriting:

1.   Instead of using the systems to confirm the results of traditional underwriting techniques, they used them in lieu of traditional techniques. Immediately, income, down payment, and documentation requirements were reduced.

2.   Fannie and Freddie were in competition with each other to promote their respective systems to thousands of lenders. This led to a quick and widespread adoption of these untested, easy-approval software systems. As noted, many of the lenders targeted by F&F were mom and pop brokers, without the experience or, in some cases, the ethics required to use such systems.

3.   F&F aggressively targeted all loan areas, including subprime, Alt-A (low documentation loans) and jumbo loans. This was very risky because nonconventional loans require more hand-holding, and are not amenable to extreme levels of automation and/or reliance on credit scoring.

4.   When acceptance rates soared for AU underwriting, relative to traditional underwriting, Fannie and Freddie wrongly assumed the differences reflected the elimination or reduction of discrimination inherent in traditional underwriting. They continued to modify their systems to increase acceptance rates even more, despite the warnings of experts.

A discussion of each mistake follows.

Say "goodbye" to sensible underwriting standards

> Louise Beyler ... might seem to be an unlikely candidate for a mortgage to buy a $105,000 home. Self-employed and earning $19,000 a year, Ms. Beyler would have to spend nearly 45 percent of her income to cover the mortgage payments. Given her circumstances, many lenders might deny Ms. Beyler a mortgage. Thanks to automated underwriting, however, Ms. Beyler's application was approved — in just three days.

– Freddie Mac[1]

Loan Prospector had only been in service about a year when Freddie crowed about its special benefits:

> Freddie Mac is able to offer traditionally high-risk products ... with confidence that the borrowers will be successful homeowners.[2] In many instances, time-consuming *verifications of income and employment* as well as borrower letters to explain *employment gaps and derogatory credit incidents* are no longer needed. ... Given the company's confidence in Loan Prospector, fewer loan documents are required (emphasis added).[3]

These comments, made way back in 1996, go a long way toward explaining the liberal underwriting philosophy that seemed to spontaneously materialize in the private sector a decade later. To achieve their special mandates ("level the playing field" and expand housing to nontraditional owners) F&F actively promoted the relaxation of traditional underwriting standards pertaining to income, deposits, and related documentation: "The borrower's capacity [i.e., income level] is not given as much weight in the underwriting decision as previously."[4]

The GSEs (Fannie and Freddie) claimed that it was possible to safely relax the traditional standards and give loans to nontraditional borrowers because of the incredible "accuracy" of their new automated systems. As stated by Freddie:

> Automated underwriting is opening the doors of homeownership to new groups of borrowers. By increasing the accuracy with which mortgage applications are underwritten, systems such as Freddie Mac's Loan Prospector enable lenders to approve more first-time homebuyers....[5]

As early as 2001, Freddie's new computer system was being used heavily for "*higher-risk* mortgages, such as *zero-money-down* loans, Alt-A loans, which tend to have 'nontraditional documentation,' and A-minus loans, which pose a *significantly higher risk of default*" (emphasis added).[6]

1   Ibid., Ch. 1.

2   Ibid., Executive Summary.

3   Ibid., Ch. 2.

4   Hayre, Salomon Smith Barney Guide to Mortgage-Backed and Asset-Backed Securities, 215.

5   "Automatic Underwriting: Making Mortgage Lending Simpler and Fairer for America's Families," Ch.5, p.1.

6   Peter Zorn and Susan Gates and Vanessa Gail Perry, "Automated Underwriting and Lending Outcomes: The Effect of Improved Mortgage Risk Assessment on under-Served Populations," in Program on Housing and Urban Policy (Berkeley: University of California, August 2001), 18.

In that same year (2001), Freddie's share of lower down payment mortgage loans (36%) was greater than the share of such loans in the general primary market (33%). In 2003 Freddie continued to use Loan Prospector to push loans that would be substandard by any traditional measurement. In fact, it bragged about it:

> Loan Prospector can assess mortgages with very low (or no) down payments, A-minus mortgages and alternative-A (which generally have non-traditional documentation). Since introducing Loan Prospector in 1995, Freddie Mac has doubled the share of our purchases of mortgages with loan-to-value (LTV) ratios of 95 percent or above. By reducing down payment, Loan Prospector helps more families achieve homeownership.[1]

There were no regulatory constraints on F&F with regard to their automated systems. Indeed, the Office of Federal Housing Enterprise Oversight (OFHEO), a regulator of F&F, promoted a supposed benefit of using automated underwriting: the ability of the lender to "exempt" from documentation requirements "borrowers with high credit or mortgage scores ..."[2] Thus, the regulator was acting like a cheerleader, ignoring systemic risk, and giving Fannie and Freddie a pat-on-the-back for starting us on the path to liar loans.

Fannie and Freddie used automated underwriting as a vehicle for the curtailment of traditional underwriting standards, and they did this with increasing recklessness until 2005 or 2006. Worse, the decline in standards, caused by their AU systems, was not limited to the loans directly purchased by F&F: The entire industry was affected. As noted by Scholar Peter Wallison, writing for the American Enterprise Institute:

> Fannie and Freddie modified their automated underwriting systems to accept loans with characteristics that they had previously rejected. This opened the way for the acquisition of large numbers of nontraditional and subprime mortgages. These did not necessarily come from traditional banks, lending under the CRA [Community Reinvestment Act] but from lenders like Countrywide Financial, the nation's largest subprime and nontraditional mortgage lender....[3]

---

1   "Annual Housing Activities Report for 2002," (Washington, DC: Freddie Mac, March 17, 2003), 50.

2   Forrest Pafenberg, "The Single-Family Mortgage Industry in the Internet Era: Technology Developments and Market Structure," ed. Office of Federal Housing Enterprise Oversight (United States, January 2004), 25.

3   Peter J. Wallison, "Cause and Effect: Government Policies and the Financial Crisis," (Washington, DC: American Enterprise Institute, November 2008), 5, www.aei.org.

F&F pushed the new automated systems with gusto

> Automated underwriting will identify more qualified borrowers, not fewer. It won't just level the playing field — it will expand it.
>
> – Freddie Mac[1]

Fannie and Freddie (F&F) pushed their new AU systems with evangelistic zeal, and most United States conventional lenders were ultimately forced to use one of the systems, or both. Lenders (mostly small brokers) were told, in hundreds of "training sessions," of the enormous profits they could accrue if they expanded the market by using the flexible AU systems. In its 1996 Loan Prospector report, Freddie noted:

> To reinforce the message of underwriting flexibility, Freddie Mac has conducted hundreds of training sessions and created and distributed an underwriting guidebook, *Discover Gold Through Expanding Markets.* This booklet features more than 100 case studies illustration the flexibility available to lenders when evaluating more difficult loans.

The "gold" referred to in the title was a metaphor for the profits these lenders could acquire by giving loans to nontraditional borrowers. Think about it: By 1996 this government-backed entity (Freddie) was telling private-sector lenders of the fantastic profits they could have if only they would adopt more "underwriting flexibility." I suspect that some of the 100 case studies must have been hilarious, but we will never know for sure. Apparently, Sandy Berger has been wearing his pleated pants again.[2]

F&F are the largest sources of home mortgage funds in the nation, and they were able, eventually, to use more coercive methods to spread their easy-approval software. In a paper written in January 2004, OFHEO described the arm-twisting process:

> Once Fannie Mae and Freddie Mac began to use scoring and automated underwriting in their internal business operations, it was not long before each Enterprise *required* the single-family lenders with which it does business to use such tools. The Enterprises did so by including the use of those technologies in the conforming guidelines for their seller/servicers (emphasis added).[3]

---

1   Subcommittee on Capital Markets, Securities, and Government-Sponsored Enterprises, Oversight of the Federal National Mortgage Association (Fannie Mae) and the Federal Home Loan Mortgage Corporation (Freddie Mac), April 17, June 12, July 24 and 31, August 1, 1996, 334.

2   All efforts to find the booklet, from Freddie Mac, libraries, and lenders, were unsuccessful.

3   Pafenberg, "The Single-Family Mortgage Industry in the Internet Era: Technology Developments and Market Structure," 24.

Consider this again. F&F designed automated systems that dramatically weakened traditional underwriting standards and then, according to OFHEO (one of their regulators), they *"required"* private lenders to use those systems. This is one of the keys to the degradation of lending standards and the ensuing financial crisis.

Although F&F were not the only entities with AU systems, their systems quickly became dominant, capturing over 71 percent of the AU market by 1997.[1] In addition, the F&F AU systems were potentially the most destructive. Whereas some private AU systems merely automated the normal, relatively-high standards applied in manual underwriting, Desktop Underwriter and Loan Prospector substituted credit scoring for requirements found in traditional standards. In other words, their AU systems undermined traditional underwriting standards while automating them.

Of course, F&F didn't see it that way. They mistakenly thought the competing private systems were less accurate because they adhered to the traditional "rules." This is implied in a comment made by Freddie:

> Some chose approaches that simply converted existing underwriting standards to an electronic format. While the "rules-based" systems speed up the underwriting process, they do not improve the accuracy of lending decisions.[2]

Fannie and Freddie were relentless in their quests to dominate the AU market. In 1999, "Freddie Mac made an Internet version of Loan Prospector commercially available, putting the automated system in the hands of more than 11,000 mortgage brokers and 300 mortgage wholesalers."[3] To generate excitement, Freddie "pledged to give 10 free trips to Hawaii for brokers who use automated underwriting...."[4] Thousands more brokers were hooked up to Fannie's Desktop Underwriter. Remember, many of these mortgage brokers were fly-by-night enterprises who were at mortgage meltdown's ground zero. These guys never held the loans — they were, essentially, salesmen arranging deals between borrowers and lenders.

---

1   "Who's Top Provider of Automated Underwriting?," ABA Banking Journal 89 (1997).

2   "Automatic Underwriting: Making Mortgage Lending Simpler and Fairer for America's Families," Chapter 1, p.2.

3   Zorn and Susan Gates and Vanessa Gail Perry, "Automated Underwriting and Lending Outcomes: The Effect of Improved Mortgage Risk Assessment on under-Served Populations," 3.

4   Rick Grant, "GSE Looks to Reclassify 20% of Subprime as 'a'," National Mortgage News, May 25 1998.

Automation and subprime don't mix

Unfortunately, F&F did not restrict their new underwriting systems to prime loans (the only kind that they were legally able to buy). Rather, they targeted all types of loans, including subprime. Consider this early statement by Freddie:

> We initiated a pilot program in October 1995 to make automated under-writing available to the *subprime* mortgage market. Although the mort-gages originated under the pilot will not be sold to Freddie Mac, *other investors* stand ready to purchase these loans (emphasis added).[1]

It was not long before "pilot" became policy. In a 1996 publication Freddie predicted that automated underwriting would "put nearly three-quarters of a million of today's renters into their first homes, 80 percent of whom will be low-income or minority families."[2] In 1998 a Freddie spokesperson stated: "The subprime market disproportionately serves the low-income borrowers we're interest in. ... Subprime mortgage lenders may help to increase the rate of home ownership for low-income families" (emphasis added).[3]

Later, in 2000, Freddie was still pushing its product for use with sub-prime mortgages, as evident from this statement by a Freddie VP, who was delighted that an Internet marketer, LoanTrader, was giving a boost to Freddie's Loan Prospector:

> LoanTrader's decision to provide access to Loan Prospector on the Inter-net will enable lenders and brokers to offer the loan product that is right for the homebuyer, *whether conventional or subprime* (emphasis added).[4]

In a 2002 report prepared by the Urban Institute for HUD it was noted that Fannie and Freddie were "increasing their presence in the *subprime* market by rolling-out new *subprime* mortgage products through updated versions of their automated underwriting systems" (emphasis added).[5]

---

1   "Automatic Underwriting: Making Mortgage Lending Simpler and Fairer for America's Families," Ch. 5.
2   Ibid., Executive Summary.
3   Mahalik and Kenneth J. Robinson, "Credit Is Overdue for Subprime Mortgage Lending," 4.
4   "Loantrader.Com Marketplace Connects with Freddie Mac's Loan Prospector on the Internet," Business Wire (September 15, 2000).
5   Kenneth Temkin and Jennifer Johnson and Diane Levy, "Subprime Markets, the Role of GSEs and Risk-Based Pricing," (Washington, DC: Urban Institute, March 2002), 21.

There is no doubt that F&F promoted their AU systems to subprime lenders — something the government and its enterprises should never do. Subprime lending increases the systemic risk that the government is supposed to monitor and control. However, if we must promote this sort of risky lending, the very worst way to do it is with one of these Nintendo-like systems.

A 1997 study conducted by the Mortgage Information Corporation revealed that, although smaller subprime lenders were using Loan Prospector or Desktop Underwriter, the larger subprime lenders initially rejected them, as inadequate. In other words, large private-sector, subprime lenders initially rejected the low underwriting standards pushed by liberal-minded, government-supported F&F:

> Large wholesale lenders, as of 1997, did not use automated systems. These lenders believed that subprime mortgage underwriting involves making 'story loans,' in which underwriters must take into account factors beyond those that can be quantified.[1]

The next year (1998), the Federal Reserve Bank of Dallas issued a report describing the perils of AU usage for the subprime market:

> Many experts feel that even if automated underwriting is successful in the conventional market, it will not be as easily adapted to the subprime market because each borrower's financial situation is different and must be addressed on a case-by-case basis.[2]

Similar comments were elicited by the center-left Urban Institute, which interviewed various lenders and mortgage experts with regard to the possibility that F&F would use their automated systems for subprime lending:

> Representatives of subprime lenders said that they are skeptical that Fannie Mae and Freddie Mac can enter the subprime market without exposing themselves to a high level of risk. These lenders pointed out that the subprime industry is not highly automated; applicants receive specialize attention from underwriters who are not penalized if they deviate from written formal guidelines. It will be difficult, according to these interviewees, for the GSEs [Fannie and Freddie] to develop automated systems that can accurately assess the risks associated with lending to subprime borrowers.[3]

---

1   Ibid., 28.
2   Mahalik and Kenneth J. Robinson, "Credit Is Overdue for Subprime Mortgage Lending," 4.
3   Temkin and Jennifer Johnson and Diane Levy, "Subprime Markets, the Role of GSEs and Risk-Based Pricing," ix.

The biggest problem, according to the Urban Institute respondents, was the heavy emphasis on FICO scores, or similar credit scoring, in F&F's automated systems:

> [F&F] place too much weight on a borrower's FICO score (which may not be a good indicator for subprime borrowers' creditworthiness), and too little emphasis on the borrower's equity in the property [i.e., the down payment].[1]

This viewpoint was reiterated in Finsights, a publication of Infosys Technologies:

> Since approximately 50% of the score is based on past payment and credit history, FICO score is even less reliable for a sub-prime customer since the credit history is unreliable or in some cases does not exist.[2]

There was additional reason for caution. According to a report published by the Federal Reserve Bank of Dallas, AU systems were accelerating the growth of subprime loans by making it easier to securitize them:

> ...funding has become easier for most subprime lenders as technological advancements, such as automated underwriting, have resulted in the ability to securitize subprime mortgage loans. ... Subprime mortgage security production more than tripled over the past two years, increasing from $18 billion in 1995 to $66 billion in 1997. The percentage of subprime mortgages being financed by securitzation is rising: approximately 53 percent of all subprime mortgage loans originated in 1997 were sold in the securities market, compared with 28 percent in 1995.[3]

However, accelerating the growth of subprime was precisely what F&F wanted. Freddie planned from the beginning to use its AU system to aid in the securitization of jumbo and subprime loans. As early as October 1995, Freddie created pilot programs under which "companies that purchase and securitized jumbo and sub-prime loans have agreed to purchase these loans from our customers based on the credit assessment assigned by Loan Prospector."[4] Freddie wasn't supposed to buy such loans, but that didn't stop it from using Loan Prospector to promote the reckless securitization of such loans.

---

1   Ibid., 25.

2   T. Murali and S. Muralikrishnan and B. Yellavalli, "Sub-Prime Crisis and Credit Risk Measurement: Lessons Learnt," (July 8, 2009), http://www.infosys.com/FINsights/about/default.asp.

3   Mahalik and Kenneth J. Robinson, "Credit Is Overdue for Subprime Mortgage Lending," 3.

4   Oversight of the Federal National Mortgage Association (Fannie Mae) and the Federal Home Loan Mortgage Corporation (Freddie Mac), 335.

Push enough subprime and some will slip through

Fannie and Freddie (F&F) promoted this dangerous cocktail of automated underwriting and subprime loans even though they knew of the risks. This is evident from an internal Freddie Mac email from April 2004:

> The reasons against [using] LP [to source subprime loans] were LP weakness, if you throw nothing but subprime loans against LP, it will miss some, maybe even a lot.[1]

An email from a different Freddie Mac official (April 2004) describes another potential problem associated with the use of FICO-based AU systems for subprime loans:

> [T]he reason FICO predicts as well as it does for mortgages might have something to do with all the other processes traditionally required in mortgages [e.g., documentation, down payments, income streams]. Without these processes, the relationship between FICO and mortgage performance could change.[2]

In other words, the predictive quality of FICO could diminish or disappear unless documentation, down payments, income streams, etc., were required.

Despite these concerns, F&F forged ahead with their AU systems. Indeed, it is the belief of a Fannie Mae ex-officer that F&F liked the automated underwriting systems precisely because they could be used to snatch subprime loans from the private market. In testimony before Henry Waxman's House Committee on Oversight and Government Reform Edward J. Pinto, former Fannie Mae Chief Credit Officer (1987-89), stated:

> Fannie and Freddie used their automated underwriting systems to divert subprime and Alt-A loans from the private label securitizers, driving up the value of these loans and making mortgage brokers even more eager to find borrowers, no matter what their credit standing.[3]

It worked like this: Ostensibly, AU systems would only accept loans from "prime" borrowers. If, however, massive numbers of profitable subprime loans slipped through the AU system cracks, then — oh, well — the subprime time-bombs would be held by F&F and labeled as "prime." The vast subprime acquisitions of F&F are analyzed in Chapter 6. There were lots of concerns and warnings, but to no avail. Fannie and Freddie

---

1   Committee on Oversight and Government Reform, Statement of Edward Pinto, December 9, 2008, 4.

2   Ibid.

3   Ibid., 12.

wanted to promote subprime lending — even if they could not, officially, buy the loans.

Loans that had been, by all traditional measures, "subprime," suddenly became prime, simply because Loan Prospector and Desktop Underwriter were programmed to call them that. Freddie estimated that "10 to 30 percent of borrowers who obtained mortgages in the subprime market could have qualified for a conventional loan *through Loan Prospector*" (emphasis added).[1] How? Loan Prospector would reclassify these loans to prime by substituting credit scoring, such as FICO scores, for traditional standards such as income, down payment, and related documentation.

As this process took place, subprime lenders were squeezed into even riskier products. Their subprime became hardcore because the "quality" subprime was being gobbled up by Fannie and Freddie. There is no doubt that automated underwriting, as designed and promoted by F&F, was a huge factor in the growth of lending, generally, and in the growth of the subprime loan market, specifically. The AU reclassification of subprime loans into "prime" led to a harder and riskier definition of "subprime."

F&F also used their AU systems to promote jumbo loans. This was noted in a 2001 Berkeley conference on automated underwriting:

> The jumbo mortgage market also has been transformed by the rise of automated underwriting. Freddie Mac's Loan Prospector will assess the risk of loans that exceed the conforming loan limit and are thus ineligible for purchase by the secondary market company.[2]

It is highly significant that Fannie and Freddie exerted influence over the broader market, including the subprime and jumbo loan markets. Many apologists for F&F have claimed that F&F were not responsible for the subprime mortgage meltdown because they (supposedly) maintained relatively high standards for the loans they purchased. However, these easy-approval, push-button AU systems had an impact on virtually every lender, whether conventional, subprime or jumbo. This is because, according to an OFHEO research paper, "mortgage originators, whether or not they intended to sell their loans to the Enterprises, adopted the

---

1   Henry Cassidy and Robert Englestad, "Credit Scoring and the Secondary Market: Perceptions, Policies, Practices," in Community Developments, ed. Federal Reserve Bank of San Francisco, Community Development (United States, Summer 1998), http://www.frbsf.org/publications/community/investments/cra98-3/page2.html.

2   Zorn and Susan Gates and Vanessa Gail Perry, "Automated Underwriting and Lending Outcomes: The Effect of Improved Mortgage Risk Assessment on under-Served Populations," 4.

business practice of structuring their loan programs to conform to Freddie Mac and Fannie Mae underwriting guidelines."[1]

Further, the idea of replacing traditional underwriting standards with credit scoring, whether or not incorporated into an AU system, also came from Fannie and Freddie. According to OFHEO, "It was not until first Freddie Mac and then Fannie Mae introduced their AU [systems] in 1995 that lenders began to take scoring seriously."[2] Who says government bureaucrats can't produce innovations?

Risky, risk-based pricing

F&F deliberately blurred the line between subprime and prime, without considering the risk created for the health of the financial industry. They even promoted something called "risk-based pricing," which basically means that any loan, no matter how shaky, might be acceptable at the right price. In the words of Leland Brendsel, who was Freddie's CEO:

> The key message is that [there] is going to be one mortgage market in the future, with the distinction between prime and subprime only being a matter of grading [i.e., pricing].[3]

Fannie seemed to share this philosophy. It implemented a special "Expanded Approval" program that basically allowed substandard loans to be approved — for an extra fee.[4]

The fatal flaw here, of course, is that no amount of extra pricing for risky subprime loans does any good if the entire market collapses due to the infusion of vast numbers of unqualified buyers. Before promoting risk-based pricing the government and its surrogates should have considered the systemic risk to the U.S. financial system. They did not.

Fannie and Freddie misconstrued the warning signs

Almost immediately, acceptance rates were much greater with AU systems than with manual underwriting. However, this was not cause for concern: It was reason for celebration! After all, the differential in acceptance rates merely proved that a sophisticated computerized system was much more "accurate" and less bigoted than some middle-aged white

---

1   Pafenberg, "The Single-Family Mortgage Industry in the Internet Era: Technology Developments and Market Structure," 23.

2   Ibid., 22.

3   Mahalik and Kenneth J. Robinson, "Credit Is Overdue for Subprime Mortgage Lending," 3.

4   Temkin and Jennifer Johnson and Diane Levy, "Subprime Markets, the Role of GSEs and Risk-Based Pricing," 21.

guy with a pencil. Indeed, over the next several years Fannie and Freddie tweaked their systems to squeeze out any remaining drops of inaccuracy, bias, and discrimination. These changes led to higher and higher acceptance rates, particularly for minority borrowers.[1] See Figure 2.

Figure 2 – Loan Prospector Acceptance Rates for Minority Applicants

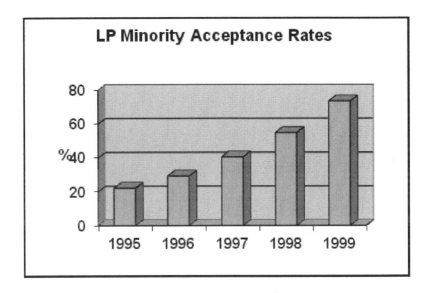

The Urban Institute described the automated underwriting changes made by Fannie and Freddie as an attempt to "serve more *marginal* borrowers" (emphasis added).[2] In the same report it was noted that, because of the ever-improving AU systems, some lenders were able to "increase volumes" and "focus underwriting resources on *borderline* applications" (emphasis added).[3]

By 2001, the cumulative impact of the AU modifications was dramatic and disturbing, as evident from some interesting research described in a conference at UC Berkeley. This research involved nearly 1,000 loans, originated in 1993 and 1994, and purchased by Freddie to promote affordable housing:

---

1   Zorn and Susan Gates and Vanessa Gail Perry, "Automated Underwriting and Lending Outcomes: The Effect of Improved Mortgage Risk Assessment on under-Served Populations," 17.

2   Temkin and Jennifer Johnson and Diane Levy, "Subprime Markets, the Role of GSEs and Risk-Based Pricing," 38.

3   Ibid., 41.

> [T]he loans were manually re-underwritten after Freddie Mac's purchase and categorized similarly to Loan Prospector's accept/caution designations. ... Next the loans were underwritten using the Loan Prospector system and today's [i.e., 2001's] underwriting standards. ... Manual underwriters rated 52 percent of the loans as accept, compared to the 85 percent rated accept by Loan Prospector. Borrowers are far more likely to obtain a mortgage under automated underwriting than under traditional methods.[1]

This is worth repeating: With manual underwriting the acceptance rate was only about 52 percent, whereas with Loan Prospector – applied to the very same loans — the acceptance rate was about 85 percent. These rates are depicted in Figure 3, below, which more aptly should be labeled, "Exhibit A for the prosecution."

Expressed as a percentage, the automated system was a stunning 65 percent more likely to find an application to be acceptable than was the manual system (85.2/51.7 = 1.65).

Figure 3 – Freddie's Manual vs. Automated Underwriting Acceptance Rates –For the same loans!

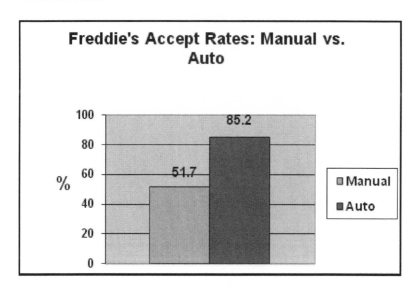

Conclusion

Ladies and Gentlemen of the jury: I submit to you that the underwriting systems of Fannie and Freddie, foisted upon the entire home-loan market (whether prime, subprime, or jumbo), poisoned that market

---

1   Zorn and Susan Gates and Vanessa Gail Perry, "Automated Underwriting and Lending Outcomes: The Effect of Improved Mortgage Risk Assessment on under-Served Populations," 13-14.

and contributed to its demise. These AU systems swiftly led to the end of traditional underwriting standards. Not only were acceptance rates tremendously higher using the AU systems, these higher rates were achieved by lending to "marginal" borrowers in risky subprime and jumbo loan markets. Many of the loans were not directly purchased by F&F; nevertheless, the damage was done, and Fannie and Freddie are directly responsible

Ladies and Gentlemen, I recommend that they be sentenced to ... a bailout of no less than $300 billion!

CHAPTER 3: APPRAISE A HOUSE WITHOUT LEAVING YOUR SEAT

> I do not remember the form saying "windshield," but
> that was the standard term in the industry for a quick and
> economical appraisal. For those with a limited imagination
> and whose appraisal experience has occurred more recently,
> that would mean that the appraiser drove past the home,
> eyeballed it through the windshield and drove on.
>
> – Charlie Elliott, MAI, SRA[1]

By the end of 1995 the automated underwriting systems of Fannie and
Freddie, described in Chapter 2, were each equipped with an auxiliary
feature: a collateral assessment program known as an "automated valuation model," or "AVM." This automated appraisal feature allowed many
borrowers to forgo the traditional house appraisal, opting instead for an
"exterior only" (or "windshield)" appraisal. A couple of years later, these
drive-by appraisals were used for up to 40 percent of Freddie's loan purchases, and appraisers were worried. The ABA Banking Journal reported
that Fannie and Freddie were "pushing the industry" to automate appraisals and to provide "instant collateral assessment" without relying
on a human appraiser.[2]

---

1   Charlie Elliott, "Why Not a Windshield Appraisal?," (October 2005), http://
    hubpages.com/hub/whynotawindshieldappraisal.
2   "The GSE Report," in Fannie Mae and Freddie Mac (Canfield & Associates,
    April 2, 1999), 15.

By 2001, Fannie told RealtyTimes.com that its automated system could "approve 70 to 75 percent of purchase-money mortgage applications without a traditional, full appraisal...."[1]

In a move called "ridiculous," "dangerous," radical," and "worrisome" by prominent members of the appraisal profession,[2] Fannie quietly implemented (in 2001) the complete elimination of traditional appraisals — even the quickie, drive-by kind — for certain AVM loans in an "appraisal waiver" pilot program. By 2004, Fannie and Freddie both offered no-appraisal AVMs on a regular basis for qualified loans. In Fannie's case qualified loans were single home purchase loans and refinance loans with limited "cash out,"[3] with fixed interest rates and loan to value ratios (LTVs) of no more than 90 percent. Freddie waived inspections for loans with LTVs of 80 percent in 2004. By 2005, however, Freddie relaxed its rules to include most loans with 90 percent LTVs.

Lending on the basis of Zillow estimates

In the words of Mark Zandi, author of *Financial Shock*, "An AVM is automated because it doesn't require an *actual human being* to look at the property; instead it uses statistics and computing power to estimate a home's value (emphasis added)...."[4] The information fed into the AVM might include the sales price of comparable homes and price trends. Fannie and Freddie pitched AVMs as devices that could dramatically lower closing costs and, in so doing, increase home ownership among low income and other disadvantaged people. Instead of paying $300 to $350 to an appraiser, the borrower would pay a fee of only, say $50. The fee wasn't paid to an appraiser: It was paid to, guess who? Fannie or Freddie.

The cost savings of these systems are beyond dispute. And, as a double check of the work of appraisers, they could be a very useful tool for the lender. After all, some appraisers are sloppy, improperly trained, or too cozy with realtors to give an accurate and independent assessment. But, as used by Fannie and Freddie — to curtail or completely eliminate

---

1   Ken Harney, "Fannie Mae Tries Appraisal Waivers, Seeks Reduced Consumer Costs," Realtytimes.com (December 17, 2001), http://realtytimes.com/rtpages/20011217_appraise.htm.

2   ———, "Fannie Mae Permits Some Lenders to Waive Appraisals," (January 6, 2002), http://articles.latimes.com/2002/jan/06/realestate/re-harney6.

3   In a "cash out" refinance transaction the borrower refinances his loan (usually at a lower interest rate) and walks away with some cash in his pocket.

4   Mark M. Zandi, Financial Shock : A 360* Look at the Subprime Mortgage Implosion, and How to Avoid the Next Financial Crisis (Upper Saddle River, N.J.: FT Press, 2009), 108.

real, physical appraisals, AVMs were a disaster.[1] This departure from traditional valuation methods was implemented without an adequate test period, and it was fraught with hazards. To get an idea of how dumb this idea was, imagine that lenders relied on Zillow estimates to assess the value of loan collateral.[2]

The many problems of the Automated Valuation Models

One deficiency of AVMs is their failure to consider all relevant valuation details. This point is illustrated by this real life story posted on a Web site frequented by certified appraisers. In 2002, a 21-year veteran appraiser did an appraisal of a home valued by an AVM at $2.2 million. The property had a high AVM value because it was located in a neighborhood of beautiful, contemporary $2-million-plus homes. "Turns out the subject property was actually built in 1949 and had an addition of 2,000 square feet which included a 650 sq. ft. garage and a 750 sq. ft. enclosed patio. Furthermore, the subject backed directly to a railroad spur which abuts a major interstate freeway." Real value? $750,000, of which 75 percent was for the land.[3]

Another AVM problem is described by Mark Zandi in his book, *Financial Shock*. He notes that, when conditions are changing rapidly, AVMs can "fall significantly behind market conditions...." He adds that, "for months after housing prices began to bust, automated valuation models were still showing values that reflected a much stronger market." Unfortunately, "lenders were much too comfortable with the [AVM] results and had come to totally rely on them."[4]

A third problem of automated valuation models (AVMs) is the old "garbage in, garbage out" phenomenon. Many times the input data comes from suspect databases with misleading or inaccurate sources. To illustrate this point, a certified appraiser described an automated valuation based, ostensibly, on 6 recent sales. In reality, however, only 3 of the sales were really comparable, and each of the 3 comparable sales was listed at

1   Fannie and Freddie still use automated appraisal systems, although they are used in more circumscribed situations.
2   Zillow.com is an online database of home values, created in 2005. According to an analysis prepared by the Wall Street Journal (James Hagerty, "How Good Are Zillow's Estimates?" February 14, 2007), Zillow's estimates "are often very good" but "when Zillow is bad, it can be terrible...."
3   Anonymous, "A Story to Tell (Letter to Editor)," The Big AVM Lie (October 2004), http://appraisercentral.com/AVMS1.htm.
4   Zandi, Financial Shock : A 360* Look at the Subprime Mortgage Implosion, and How to Avoid the Next Financial Crisis, 108-9.

the wrong price: "reporting sales prices in the $190s whereas the actual MLS sales prices were in the $160s–180s."[1] Another appraiser described his experience with an AVM that came in $30 to $40 thousand higher than his estimate of value for a two-family property. Why? The AVM was based on 17 comparables, 15 of which were condominiums. And, even the two pertinent comparables (2-family rental units) were dissimilar in many other respects.[2]

A big AVM problem concerns the down payment assistance plans that became so popular with affordable housing activists in California and other high-priced housing states. In most of these areas, homes had become unaffordable for low-income people, mainly because of decades of building restrictions related to wildlife, water conservation, visual esthetics, the need to keep lots of flammable brush and other kindling close to homes (important habitat for endangered bugs, you know). Instead of easing up on the onerous building restrictions, activists (with the implicit backing of HUD) encouraged home sellers to, effectively, reimbursed the buyer for any down payment he might have to pay. Of course, there is no free lunch in life, so sellers simply marked up the sales prices of their homes by the amount of the reimbursement.[3] This process, which encouraged higher selling and appraisal prices, was described by a program administrator for the Colorado Board of Real Estate Appraisers:

> In some neighborhoods in Denver and surrounding counties, we're seeing over half the sales involving these seller-funded down payments. In the majority of those sales, the buyer is paying the full asking price, plus an amount equal to the servicing fee charged by the DPA [down payment assistance] provider. After closing, the property records often don't indicate that DPA was used, so the full-value-plus-servicing-fee price appears without a note about seller concessions and is used as a comparable for the next sale.[4]

---

1   Anonymous, "A Rebuttal (Letter to Editor)," in The Big AVM Lie (Appraiser Central, March 2002), http://appraisercentral.com/AVMS1.htm.

2   Jerry Kedziora, "Two-Family Rental (Letter to Editor)," in The Big AVM Lie (Appraiser Central, July 2006), http://appraisercentral.com/AVMS1.htm.

3   In a HUD report dated March 1, 2005 (prepared by the Concentrance Consulting Group under contract No. C-OPC-22550/M0001) it was noted that "over 50% of the respondents in each subject group including appraisers, mortgage lenders, underwriters, seller-funded down payment assistance providers and real estate agents, indicated that seller-funded down payment assistance programs inflated the property sales price and appraised value."

4   Dona DeZube, "The Gift Business," Mortgage Banking (August 1, 2003), http://www.thefreelibrary.com/The+gift+business.+(New+Products).-a0106142697.

The process is described in detail in Chapter 4. The point for now, however, is that these bogus, marked-up prices were fed into the Fannie/ Freddie AVMs, which treated them as real prices.

If you think about it, we had 3 "progressive" ideas converging in a perfect storm: (1) Land and building restrictions drove up housing values. (2) This caused housing activists to induce sellers to pay down payment costs on behalf of buyers. To compensate, sellers simply inflated their sales prices. (3) The inflated sales prices were fed into AVMs, which were designed by Fannie and Freddie with the liberal notion of lowering closing costs for low-income buyers. The inflated prices were then used by realtors and appraisers to justify higher prices for subsequent sales — thus contributing to a housing bubble. Whew!

Concerns about the property appraisal process were particularly acute with regard to subprime lending. By the end of 2001 Fannie and Freddie were already buying "about 14 percent of subprime loans originated," and they were expected to eventually "purchase as much as 50 percent of the overall subprime mortgage volume."[1] The use of an automated property appraisal system seemed problematic. A study performed in 1999 by the Urban Institute noted that "the lack of suitable comparable sales data on inner-city neighborhoods may make it difficult to conduct appraisals of homes purchased by many lower-income and minority borrowers."[2] In 2002, the Urban Institute warned HUD, a primary regulator of Fannie and Freddie, of the inadequacy of their automated systems — particularly with regard to subprime purchases.

In a paper requested by and prepared for HUD, an interviewed lender complained that Fannie and Freddie did not subject their appraisals "to a thorough review as is needed in the subprime market (sic)." Other interviewees maintained:

> Appraisal fraud is rampant in the subprime market. Without intensive quality control over appraisals, [Fannie and Freddie] could be purchasing loans collateralized by properties that may be overvalued, and thus the true loan-to-value ratio may exceed any loan-to-value ratio acceptable to the prime lender or [Fannie and Freddie]. As a result, any foreclosure

---

1   Temkin and Jennifer Johnson and Diane Levy, "Subprime Markets, the Role of GSEs and Risk-Based Pricing," vii.

2   Kenneth Temkin and George Galster and Roberto Quercia and Sheila O'Leary, "A Study of the GSE's Single-Family Underwriting Guidelines," (Washington, DC: Urban Institute, April 1, 1999).

on that property forces the holder of the mortgage to recover even less of their loss.[1]

Needed for appraisals: A Full Monty

Perhaps the most serious problem caused by AVMs was the impact they had on certified appraisers. Potentially, there had always been the problem of the appraiser who would inflate a valuation estimate, due to pressure exerted by a realtor; however, the rapid adoption of AVMs greatly aggravated this problem. Suddenly, many appraisers could find little work, and realtors knew it. For the surviving appraisers the pressure to come up with the "right" value became enormous. Graham Fisher, the independent housing research firm, described the sad state of the appraisal business, based on its research conducted in 2001:

> We have spoken with real estate-appraisers and national appraisal organizations and have been told, almost unanimously, that the changes in the appraisal process over the past decade [i.e., the 1990s] have jeopardized the soundness of the process and skewed real estate prices.[2]

Graham Fisher added that appraisers were being "hand picked" by realtors and that "almost all of the appraisers with whom we spoke stated that they have felt pressure to 'hit the bid'" Although the research firm did not directly tie the appraiser independence problems to the introduction of AVMs, it stated that lax appraisal standards were an indirect outgrowth of the *Strategy* concocted by HUD and the gang in 1995 (Chapter 1): "The overall tone of that *Strategy* [*The National Homeownership Strategy*] helped to facilitate the relaxation of standards."[3] And Graham Fisher noted that some experts questioned the wisdom of using AVMs: "While the automated appraisal process may be efficient, is it effective or prudent? Wouldn't it be more prudent and in the long term less costly to strengthen the independence of appraisers?"

In 2004 Fitch Ratings Ltd., one of the big investment rating firms, declared that anything less than the "full Monty — an on-site, exterior and interior professional appraisal — is likely to overstate the true worth of the property if it's located in any of dozens of slowly appreciation mar-

---

1   Temkin and Jennifer Johnson and Diane Levy, "Subprime Markets, the Role of GSEs and Risk-Based Pricing," 25.
2   "Housing in the New Millennium: A Home without Equity Is Just a Rental with Debt," 11.
3   Ibid., 7.

kets around the country."[1] For valuations lacking the "full Monty," Fitch began to impose a 10 to 15 percent "haircut." That meant it would slice 10 to 15 percent off the property value as estimated by Fannie or Freddie. This is another example of the private sector acting with greater prudence than Fannie or Freddie.

There were some other efforts made to strengthen the integrity of the appraisal process, albeit too little and too late. For example, in 2003 the FHA (Federal Housing Administration) began a controversial electronic monitoring program called, "Appraiser Watch." It employed statistical reviews of defaulting loans in an attempt to spot appraisers who may be overvaluing collateral estimates.[2] In August 2004 RealtyTimes.com reported that the Bush Administration would "now penalize lenders who knew — or should have known — that the appraiser they hired submitted an intentionally inaccurate valuation on a home." The lenders were subject to "fines and other administrative actions from FHA."[3] There was also a bipartisan effort to "require a physical appraisal of the property for certain loans by a certified or license appraiser...."[4] Unfortunately, the "Responsible Lending Act," sponsored by Republican Bob Ney and Democrat Paul Kanjorski, died in a House committee.

For a lender, collateral is a firewall that is supposed to save him from loss when all else fails. But, years before the subprime mortgage loan crisis became apparent, the firewall for many lenders was completely broken. To a large extent, appraised property values were undermined by Mickey Mouse drivel, spit out by the Zillow-like AVM systems of Fannie and Freddie. These $50-a-pop pseudo appraisals spread like wildfire, making real appraisers — the kind that actually visit the house — desperate to the point of losing all independence. Yes, many appraisers probably compromised their standards, but did this bother Fannie and Freddie? Some critics think it did not. In mid-2001, an independent research firm suggested that Fannie and Freddie had no problem whatever with a weakened appraisal system:

1 Ken Harney, "Mandate for Full Appraisal Could Mean Higher Costs, Longer Waits for Buyers," Nation's Housing 2004.

2 ———, "FHA Begins Controversial Electronic Monitoring System Despite Appraisers' Protests," Realtytimes.com (November 3, 2003), http://realtytimes.com/rtpages/20031103_appwatch.htm.

3 ———, "New Federal Policy Extends Liability for Inflated Appraisals to Mortgage Lenders," Realtytimes.com (August 9, 2004), http://realtytimes.com/rtpages/20040809_inflatedapps.htm.

4 Shawn McGowan, "Lender Pressure and Appraiser Independence - Gimme Shelter," Mortgage Banking (January 1, 2006).

> Weakening the appraisal process allows [Fannie and Freddie] to claim
> that, by automating it, they are benefiting the system. Critics of Fannie
> and Freddie argue that ... [they] are trying to "creep" into as many new
> businesses as possible while reducing underwriting standards. By reduc-
> ing underwriting standards it becomes difficult to distinguish between
> those who cannot afford homeownership and those who have been de-
> terred [by discrimination] from homeownership.[1]

This viewpoint is a little too conspiratorial for me but, whether intentional or not, Fannie and Freddie greatly damaged the traditional appraisal system with their fast roll-out of an untested, unreliable alternative system.

Epilogue

After the financial crisis gripped the United States in 2007/08, Fannie
and Freddie cut back on use of automated valuations. The Government
Accountability Office (GAO) stated, in a report to Congress required by
the 2010 Dodd–Frank legislation, that the two GSEs (Fannie and Freddie) required some sort of real human being appraisal for 94 percent of
their 2009 mortgage purchases. However, that rate slipped back down
to 85 percent in 2010, and is likely to slide much further as a result of a
new program of the Obama Administration.

In October 2011, the Federal Housing Finance Agency (FHFA) announced the requirements of its latest version of HARP (Home Affordable Refinance Program) for the loans of Fannie and Freddie. Because of
disappointing participation in previous HARP versions (introduced in
2009 and thereafter) the government removed the traditional appraisal
requirement. Now, only automated appraisals are needed to qualify for
HARP.

In case you feel the government is being reckless by promoting (once
again) the automated valuation model (AVM), let me put your mind at
ease — at least with regard to HARP. In addition to eliminating the traditional appraisal, the HARP program eliminated loan-to-value requirements. Here are examples of the HARP program in action: Let's say you
have a house worth $100,000 but the loan you need to refinance is for
$300,000. No problem: You qualify to refinance with HARP. Could you
refinance a $400,000 loan for a house worth just $75,000? Hmmm ... let
me see. Yes! You still qualify!

---

1   "Housing in the New Millennium: A Home without Equity Is Just a Rental
with Debt," 12-13.

By getting rid of the loan-to-value requirement, the HARP program made property values completely irrelevant. That means the automated valuation models are extremely well-suited to the HARP program. They can provide all of the information that is required ... which is nothing!

CHAPTER 4: A LIBERAL PINCER CREATES A THOUSAND POINTS OF
BLIGHT

> [T]he biggest concentrations of foreclosures can be
> found in well-to-do areas like Boca Raton, Riverside County
> near San Diego, and of course Las Vegas. Does anyone really
> believe that there was an explosion of lending in Vegas
> because banks were attempting to meet some sort of quota
> of lending to poor folks?
>
> – Blogger Mike Volpe[1]

Perhaps you have heard an argument similar to the one made by blogger Volpe. The reasoning goes like this: The meltdown could not have
been created by affordable housing programs because Community Reinvestment Act (CRA) loans and FHA loans were only a tiny fraction of
the loans originated in recent years. Besides, many of the neighborhoods
with the worst foreclosure rates had homes with price tags too high to
be associated with affordable housing programs. These arguments sound
reasonable but are highly misleading. The assault on prudent lending
practices comprised multiple parts, some of which affected both the affluent and the poor, and nearly every neighborhood in America.

Let's study the illustration in Figure 4. At the top is HUD, a federal
agency committed to the expansion of home ownership to millions of
disadvantaged renters (8 million, to be specific). The illustration depicts

---

1   Mike Volpe, "Where Were Foreclosures Most Concentrated: Countering
     CRA as the Cause of the Mortgage Meltdown," The Provocateur, September
     17, 2008, http://theeprovocateur.blogspot.com/2008/09/where-were-foreclo-
     sures-most.html.

3 major arms, or pincers, extending from HUD. The policies generally acknowledged to have contributed to the growth of subprime lending are depicted by the pincer arm on the right side of Figure 4. Most people know that our government made a concerted effort to expand lending in low and moderate-income areas in Cleveland, Detroit, Oakland, etc. It did this by having the FHA (Federal Housing Administration) insure bank loans to moderate and low-income borrowers, and it did it by using the Community Reinvestment Act (CRA) to pressure private banks to lend to borrowers with moderate or low incomes.[1]

Figure 4 – The assault on lending standards comprised three parts – not just one

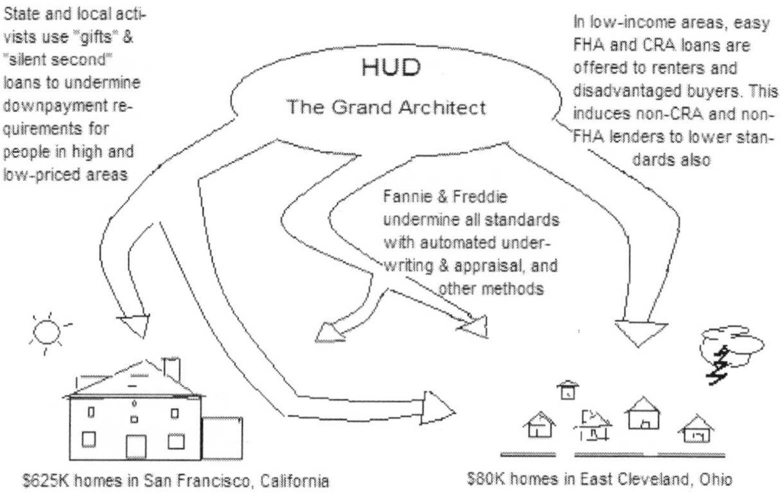

State and local activists use "gifts" & "silent second" loans to undermine downpayment requirements for people in high and low-priced areas

HUD
The Grand Architect

In low-income areas, easy FHA and CRA loans are offered to renters and disadvantaged buyers. This induces non-CRA and non-FHA lenders to lower standards also

Fannie & Freddie undermine all standards with automated underwriting & appraisal, and other methods

$625K homes in San Francisco, California $80K homes in East Cleveland, Ohio

Although CRA requirements applied only to banks and thrifts (savings and loans), the threat of similar legislation for mortgage corporations (nonbanks) affected their methods of business. In his book, *Architects of Ruin*, Peter Schweizer describes some of the CRA-type pressure applied to nonbanks by Clinton's HUD Secretary, Henry Cisneros:

> Cisneros was tasked with signing seventy-five voluntary agreements from private lenders to comply with federal fair lending laws. However, "voluntary" was not quite how many in the industry saw it. As the *ABA Banking*

---

1   To be more precise, CRA-qualified bank loans generally go to people with family incomes below 80 percent of the median family income level for the relevant metropolitan statistical area, or people with higher incomes provided they live in a neighborhood where the median family income is below 80 percent of the median family income for the relevant metropolitan statistical area.

Journal noted, "Bank lenders involved in the negotiations complained that HUD representative were trying to ram the 'voluntary' agreements down their throats."[1]

In short order, the largest subprime lender, Countrywide Financial, signed one of the voluntary agreements, called a "Declaration of Fair Lending Principles and Practices."[2]

Nonbanks were also affected by the competitive pressures generated by FHA and CRA lending. As banks loosened their underwriting standards in an effort to target marginal, low-income borrowers, mortgage brokers, who generally acquired customers on the basis of underwriting flexibility rather than low interest rates, strived to maintain their advantage by loosening their own underwriting standards. For this reason, FHA and CRA had far more impact on subprime lending than many people understand. Nevertheless, these programs, by themselves, cannot be blamed for creating most subprime lending. (FHA, CRA, and other programs aimed at low-income neighborhoods are the subject of Chapter 8.)

The second part of the subprime lending crusade is depicted in the middle of Figure 4. Starting in 1995, there was a major relaxation of underwriting standards through the widespread and almost evangelistic promotion of automated underwriting (Chapter 2). Another means was the curtailment and outright elimination, in many cases, of traditional house appraisals (Chapter 3). Fannie and Freddie promoted affordable housing in other ways, including the designing of reckless products offered by lenders and the encouragement of private subprime lending by entities such as Countrywide Financial (Chapter 7), and the purchase of subprime loans and related securities (Chapter 6).[3]

The present chapter, however, is devoted to the subprime lending activities depicted by the pincer arm on the left side of Figure 4. Here, we focus on the "thousand points of blight" (sorry, President George H.W.) created by state and local private and public affordable housing activists, who used special "gifts" and "silent second" loans to undermine the

---

1   Peter Schweizer, Architects of Ruin (New York: HarperCollins, 2009), 62.

2   The Declaration of Fair Lending Principles and Practices was patterned after the model "Best-Practices" agreement signed in 1994 by HUD and the Mortgage Brokers Association of America.

3   The typical analysis limits the culpability of Fannie and Freddie to their direct subprime loan and security purchases (not their advocacy). It then understates the amount of their purchases, and further understates the delinquency rates experienced by Fannie and Freddie. In Chapters 5 and 6, reasonable estimates of GSE delinquency rates and subprime purchase amounts are presented.

down payment system that had been a mainstay of traditional lending for decades. These activities produced loans that were given to subprime borrowers in expensive neighborhoods as well as in low-income neighborhoods, and it is likely that these programs triggered the beginning of the housing boom, which started in 1998. (See page 159 for research supporting this contention.) Yet, this phenomenon has been almost totally ignored by analysts.[1]

The sound of silence

> Yolanda's income is only $944 with social security and disability, yet as of this April she owns a large three-bedroom, two bath home with a nice yard.... Yolanda has a house note of $986 per month in which Section 8 pays a whopping $877 and she only has to pay $14 per month and she is the owner. She only had to put 1% down on a sales price of $172,000, which amounted to $1,720.... She also has two *silent* 30-year 2nd and 3rd loans in order to help her qualify (emphasis added).[2]

In Figure 4, above, you may have noticed that the large home, shown on the left side, is associated with a $625,000 price tag. Is that your idea of low-income housing? No? Well, San Francisco thought it was. In fact, the city of San Francisco had a special "silent second" loan program, designed to put low-income, first time yuppie buyers in homes costing up to $625,500.[3] A "silent second" was a supplementary loan to the homebuyer that was intended to cover all or part of his down payment and closing costs. It was called "silent" because it "was not disclosed to the first mortgage lender at the time of origination."[4] The bank thought that

---

1   A borrower can be subprime for 3 basic reasons: lack of steady and sufficient net income, lack of sufficient cash reserves, or poor credit history. These 3 factors have to be measured in relation to the price of the home and the size of the loan. For example, a woman may be a prime borrower with regard to an $80,000 loan on a $100,000 home, but would probably be subprime with respect to an $800,000 loan on a million-dollar home. By definition, anyone who needs government assistance to pay the down payment and closing costs on a loan would be subprime.

2   Jo-An Turman, "Los Angeles NHS Turns Section 8 Renter into a Homeowner," (Neighborhood Reinvestment Corporation), http://www.nw.org/network/newsroom/articles/071603.asp.

3   House value limit as of January 2009, per San Francisco Mayor's Office of Housing Web site (retrieved on September 24, 2009).

4   Adam Ashcraft and Til Schuermann, "Understanding the Securitization of Subprime Mortgage Credit," (Federal Reserve Bank of New York, March 2008), 16.

---

the buyer had a significant amount of his/her own money at risk. But, thousands of sophisticated folks in San Francisco and other parts of California knew better.

The homebuyer was expected to repay the silent second loan only when and if he re-sold the house. If house values fell the buyer could simply walk away from his "silent" loans, and in many states, his primary loans as well. The silent second loan completely undermined the concept of the down payment by eliminating the financial risk of the buyer.

How did this loony notion get started? You will recall from Chapter 1 that, in 1995, HUD started the affordable housing jihad that is outlined in its *National Homeownership Strategy*. At that time HUD decided to leverage its impact by working with "thousands" of partners in "national, State, and local organizations" and in "private and public sectors."[1] In that same *Strategy*, HUD illustrated how down payment requirements could be negated with secondary loans from the government. The response of many of HUD's state and local governmental partners was to create "silent second" loan programs, designed to reduce or eliminate down payments.

Silent second loans spread quickly through the numerous HUD affiliates. Just two years after HUD laid out its *Strategy*, the State of California published (in June 1997) a document identifying silent second loan programs in dozens of its counties and cities.[2]

It has been noted by economists with the New York Federal Reserve that, in many cases, private lenders were totally in the dark regarding the secondary loans.[3] This fact is also evident from a publicity sheet put out by the Neighborhood Reinvestment Corporation (NRC), a national nonprofit corporation, created and funded by the U.S. Congress. In its promotional material, NRC describes how its affiliates in Long Island and Nashville issued silent second loans that were to be paid using the borrowers' Section 8 vouchers. But, no one was to know of this, including the "local conventional lender":

> [The NRC affiliates] hold the second mortgages. Instead of going to the family, the monthly voucher is paid to [the NRC affiliates]. In this way

---

1   United States. Dept. of Housing and Urban Development., The National Homeownership Strategy : Partners in the American Dream, 1-1.

2   "First Time Homebuyer Directory," ed. Department of Housing and Community Development (State of California, 1997).

3   Ashcraft and Til Schuermann, "Understanding the Securitization of Subprime Mortgage Credit," 7.

the voucher is "invisible" to the traditional lender and the family (emphasis added).[1]

Concealing a down payment loan from the primary lender is mortgage fraud, so these government-financed idiots were probably breaking the law and, by example, encouraging a whole industry to do the same. Will the U.S. Justice Department investigate this case? That would be like Claude Raines investigating gambling in Rick's Café.

The Neighborhood Reinvestment Corporation is tiny compared to HUD: Think of it as HUD's Mini-Me. However, by conventional standards it is massive. Doing business as Neighbor-Works America, this government-authorized nonprofit organization had about 240 affiliates promoting silent second loans or other types of down payment assistance in 4,400 communities across America.

Neighbor-Works had several commercial "partners," including some that are no longer with us because of their reckless subprime lending activities. Some of these subprime partners, which were given a touching "salute" by Neighbor-Works in its 2006 Annual Report, are (or were) Ameriquest, Countrywide Financial, GMAC Mortgage Corporation, New Century, Option One, and Washington Mutual. At one time or another, *each and every one* of these lenders was on someone's "top ten" list of subprime loan scoundrels. Thus, Neighbor-Works was in bed with more unsavory characters than Madonna and Lady Gaga put together (on a single night, anyway). Its contribution to these "partners" was to greatly increase the risk of their already risky loans by ensuring that the borrowers had to pony-up little or nothing for the down payments and closing costs.

Although San Francisco is the example used, its program was similar to the reckless "down payment assistance" programs located in scores of cities and towns throughout California and other states. Here, for example, is a case from the San Diego area, as reported by local TV News in 2006:

> Owning a home is something Craig Hyde and his wife, Britta, thought would never happen. ... Britta is a stay-at-home mom while Craig works as a substitute teacher, DJ and soccer coach.[2]

---

1   "Neighborworks Organizations Use Section 8 Vouchers for Home Ownership: Fact Sheet," (Neighborhood Reinvestment Corporation, September 3, 2004), 2, http://www.nw.org/network/comstrat/section8/documents/VoucherFactSheet.pdf.

2   "Silent Loans Help First-Time Homebuyers Get into Market," (10news.com), http://www.10news.com/money/7264580/detail.html.

Although the couple's total income was less than $55,000 per year, they were able to purchase a home for $425,000. How did they do it?

> The San Diego Housing Commission gave them 25 percent, $106,000, as a *silent second* loan.... They also received a $15,000 grant [gift] for their down payment" (emphasis added).[1]

Do you think San Diego will ever get its money back? Do you think that house is still worth $425,000? Do you think the City of San Diego, through its actions, demonstrated to banks the importance of maintaining responsible and prudent lending standards?[2]

The following is a list of California cities that had down payment assistance programs (usually in the form of a silent second loan) as of April 1, 2009, according to a HUD Web site.[3] There were many more programs in earlier years, before the you-know-what hit the fan:

- Alameda
- Aliso Viejo
- Anaheim
- Bakerfield
- Belmont
- Brea
- Calexico
- Carlsbad
- Chowchilla
- Chula Vista
- Clovis
- Corcoran
- El Cajon
- El Centro
- Encinitas
- Escondido
- Fairfield
- Fresno
- Hanford

---

1   Ibid.
2   Don't feel too sorry for San Diego. After using millions of dollars from HUD to destroy housing, it is now getting millions from HUD "to prevent blight in communities suffering the highest foreclosure rates" (per San Diego Housing Commission Website). The same thing is happening in other irresponsible cities. Hold your wallets! Liberal programs are going to rescue us again.
3   "Homebuyer Programs Sorted by City," United States Department of Housing and Urban Development, April 1, 2009, http://www.hud.gov/local/ ca/homeownership/prgmscity.cfm.

- La Mesa
- Menlo Park
- Modesto
- National City
- Oceanside
- Pittsburg
- Porterville
- Redding
- Richmond
- Riverside
- Rohnert Park
- Santee
- San Diego
- San Jose
- San Pablo
- Shasta Lake
- Sonora
- South Lake Tahoe
- Sunnyvale
- Tulare
- Turlock
- Vallejo
- Vista
- Yorba Linda

The down payment assistance programs of these cities were financed by federal pass-through funds and hundreds of millions of dollars from the taxpayers of the State of California (the state with 9 of the top 10 subprime lenders).[1] Ultimately, billions of dollars of mortgage loans were corrupted because a single dollar of down payment can relate to $20 or more of loan. Perhaps I am being too conservative: Neighborworks claims that some "loan programs provide leverage as high as 50 to 1."[2]

Thus, these down payment programs in California (and other states such as Florida, Arizona, and Nevada) created billions in subprime loans — loans that were likely to default as soon as housing prices declined.

---

1   California had 9 of the top 10 subprime lenders according to John Dunbar, "Economy: Want to Know Who's Responsible for the Economic Meltdown?" (The Center for Public Integrity, May 6, 2009).

2   "Neighborworks America Annual Report," (Neighborhood Reinvestment Corporation, 2005), 29.

What Katrina teaches us about the mortgage crisis:

Many of the lessons of Hurricane Katrina, and the government's related response, have been discussed ad nauseam. My Katrina lesson, however, is one that you probably have not heard. It is that every unnecessary death that took place in New Orleans was the result of a failure by local officials — not federal — to timely execute the evacuation plan for which they were responsible. As noted in the Washington Times:

The city of New Orleans followed virtually no aspect of its own emergency management plan in the disaster caused by Hurricane Katrina. New Orleans officially also failed to implement most federal guidelines.[1]

The city of New Orleans — not the federal government — was supposed to evacuate the city's residents. Had New Orleans done this thoroughly and in a timely manner there would have been no one in the city to drown, and there would have been no rapes, looting, and general chaos. End of story.

Despite this clear and irrefutable truth, most people focused far more on subsequent federal-level Katrina failures than on state and local failures. No doubt, part of this was due to Bush hatred, but I believe it is also human nature to give short shrift to the good and bad things done at "lower" levels. This can lead to faulty analysis.

When it comes to the subprime mortgage crisis, we have a similar situation. A lot of light has been shone on the big federal players — President Bush, the SEC, the Federal Reserve, Fannie and Freddie — but hardly any attention has been given to the state and city players and the hundreds of activist housing organizations, all of which played a huge role in the subprime debacle. That is why we have this chapter.

Table 1 – "Affordable housing" price caps for select California counties as of February 27, 2007

County	General limit	Limit for targeted areas*
Alameda	$652,257	$797,203
Contra Costa	613,146	797,203
Los Angeles	571,278	698,229
Monterey	655,836	801,577

1   Audrey Hudson and James Lakely of the Washington Times as cited by Douglas Brinkley, The Great Deluge (New York: Harper Collins, 2007), 19.

Orange	571,278	698,229
San Diego	548,657	670,580
San Francisco	652,257	797,203
San Luis Obispo	546,871	668,398
Santa Barbara	707,988	865,319
Santa Clara	673,953	823,720
Stanislaus	429,619	525,090
Ventura	605,487	740,040

*A targeted area would be some sort of blighted neighborhood where, apparently, homes cost a fortune..

One can only imagine how much federal and state money, pissed away by California cities on silent second loans, will never be repaid. But, of course, the Golden State doesn't need the money (ha, ha) and it was spent on a good cause: helping needy people, many of whom were having trouble making their Beemer payments. Besides, every American needs to live in a home costing $500,000 or more. Right?

Table 1, above, shows the 2007 house sales price limits that applied to the so-called "affordable housing" programs of cities in a few California counties.[1] Although these were the price caps based on federal guidelines, and cities could opt to use lower price limits (and many did), it seems extraordinary that our government would even consider spending tax dollars to put people in houses costing this much. I've got a better idea for the people of California: If you can't afford to live there, move out! There are places in America with much more affordable housing and better employment opportunities (and fewer fires and mudslides). You don't need a green card to move to another state.

Were silent second loans prevalent enough to contribute to the demise of Wall Street? They were a *huge* factor. Research cited on page 160 suggests they had a major role in creating the housing bubble. According to a Federal Reserve Bank analysis of loans within mortgage-backed securities (MBS), silent second liens were associated with 27.5 percent of all subprime loans and 38.9 percent of all Alt-A (low documentation) loans originated in 2006.[2] Those were just the silent seconds with liens. We can only speculate on the higher total amount of silent second loans because, by design, many of them did not have liens (to avoid detection).

1   "Updated Sales Price Limits," Homeownership Program Bulletin (California Housing Finance Agency, March 2007).

2   Ashcraft and Til Schuermann, "Understanding the Securitization of Subprime Mortgage Credit," 16.

The existence of these undisclosed second loans made these subprime and low documentation loans even shakier than the lenders and investment banks probably realized. And, we have yet to discuss two other big torpedoes hitting the traditional down payment: "piggybacks" and down payment "gifts."

The sound of ... pigs?

Before long, many lenders became aware of the silent second loans, and acclimated to the competitive advantage of their use. Indeed, it was not long before private lenders jumped with both feet into the same dirty business: They provided their own down payment loans, which were called "piggybacks" rather than "silent seconds."[1]

According to one estimate, by 2004, about 42 percent of all U.S. mortgage loans were accompanied by piggyback loans.[2] In the high appreciation neighborhoods — the ones that ultimately were hit hardest by the subprime mortgage crisis — the percentage was much higher. Research performed by financial services giant, Credit Suisse indicates that "[m]ore than 60% of homes purchased in 2006 had piggyback loans attached to them in hotbeds such as Los Angeles, the Inland Empire [Riverside and San Bernardino counties in California], Las Vegas, and Sacramento."[3] Incredibly, these piggyback loans were usually not factored into housing stats. According to Credit Suisse:

> [T]he widespread popularity of second mortgages (piggybacks) in recent years, which are not included in traditional loan-to-value calculations, has made these LTV data points particularly misleading and almost irrelevant.... Even we were surprised by just how little money recent homebuyers have put down.[4]

These words should be carefully considered by those who are quick to assume "Wall Street" knew the loan securities it bought and sold were junk. If Credit Suisse, a giant financial services entity heavily vested in the research of housing issues, was misled regarding down payment statistics, it is entirely believable — even probable — that many on Wall Street were also mislead.

---

1   A piggyback is a loan issued by the lender originating the primary loan. A "silent second" loan is an undisclosed loan, usually funded with government funds.

2   Heide Malhotra, "Popularity and Pitfalls of Piggyback Loans," The Epoch Times, August 8-14 2005, A5.

3   Ivy Zelman and Dennis McGill and Justin Speer and Alan Ratner, "Mortgage Liquidity Du Jour: Underestimated No More," in Equity Research (USA: Credit Suisse, March 12, 2007), 6.

4   Ibid., 30.

The nutty piggyback/silent loan concept, initiated by housing activists and government do-gooders in California, spread through the governmental and private financial sectors like one of those California brush fires (the kind caused by not clearing brush because it might be home to endangered critters). In the end, nearly half of all U.S. mortgages were compromised — not by high interest rates or adjustable rate provisions — but by the reduction or elimination of down payments. To this very day, our government approves of many down payment assistance programs, and does not even classify them as "subprime" unless accompanied by high interest rates.

It gets worse: Down payments are "gifted"

> We didn't even have $100 in the bank.... Our real estate agent told us about the AmeriDream Down payment gift program and two months later we bought our first home.

– Beverly Queen, Fort Washington, MD.[1]

Silent second and piggyback loans were sometimes fraudulent — and always stupid. They were stupid because a person does not value something unless he has to work and scrimp and save for it, and put his own hard-earned funds at risk. If the buyer is spared the cost of a down payment and closing costs, he still thinks and acts like a tenant. And, when the going gets tough he will take a hike.

Down payment *gifting* programs (as opposed to down payment *lending* programs) were even worse. They had all of the negatives of the down payment loan programs plus an additional problem: If the seller paid (directly or indirectly) for the buyer's down payment, he would invariably charge for this kindness by jacking up the selling price of the property. That would result in larger primary loan payments for the buyer. In addition, the artificially-high sales price would lead appraisers and future home buyers to overvalue other homes in the neighborhood.

The gift racket worked like this. Let's say someone wanted to buy a $100,000 house but didn't have the required down payment and closing costs, which we will say totaled $6,000. A nonprofit "affordable housing" organization would provide the required $6000 to the homebuyer as a "gift" and, simultaneously, collect the same amount — plus a tidy fee (usually 1% or a flat fee) — from the seller. The amount collected from the seller was called a "donation" but, in reality, it was simply money

---

1   "To Have a Home Business You Have to Have a Home!," http://work-at-home.business-opportunities.biz/2005/09/29/to-have-a-home-business-you-have-to-have-a-home/.

laundering, conducted by pious organizations that talked about the poor and needy while raking in millions in revenues.

The origins of down payment assistance programs, and their meteoric growth, were described in a Mortgage Banking article written in 2003:

> Conceived in California in 1997 *as a way to raise homeownership levels among the state's low-income population*, today down-payment assistance (DPA) programs have blossomed into a booming business. The programs provided funding for a quarter of a million mortgage transactions last year, according to data collected by the Homeownership Alliance of Non-profit Down payment Providers (HAND), Bethesda, Maryland (emphasis added).[1]

Note the liberal purpose that inspired the creation of the gifting program. Is anyone surprised that California gave birth to this Rosemary's baby of the mortgage world? It is important for us to understand who steered us onto the dangerous road that took us over the subprime loan cliff. Although gifting programs were used in connection with mortgage loans from private lenders, this lunacy was created by affordable housing activists in California nonprofit housing organizations, determined to help low-income homebuyers by getting rid of that horrible and arcane financial requirement known as the down payment. And, once the idea was introduced, down payment assistance plans could not be limited to low-income borrowers because, if eliminating down payments was safe for the poor, it was surely a safe practice for everyone else. So, most gifting organizations used the gimmick for borrowers at all income levels and in all types of neighborhoods and in all sizes of home.

In the years preceding the mortgage meltdown there were hundreds of "nonprofit" gift programs undermining the down payment requirements associated with billions of dollars of mortgage loans. One of the oldest and largest organizations that promoted this form of down payment assistance is the Nehemiah Corporation, which was "founded by a young African-American preacher [and real estate attorney] with a $5,000 loan form a Baptist church in Sacramento, California."[2] Before the end of 2001, Nehemiah had used its gift sham to corrupt over $9 billion in loans to families in "5,257 cities across the country." In that year, Nehemiah's $800-per-gift fee was raking in "charitable contributions" (from

---

1   DeZube, "The Gift Business."
2   "The Nehemiah Story," Nehemiah Corporation of America, 2009, http://www.nehemiahcorp.org/about.cfm.

sellers) of over $150 million per year.[1] By the end of 2005, Nehemiah had hurt or destroyed prudent lending standards for loans totaling about $35 billion, while pocketing well over a $1 billion in revenue.[2]

Other big players included AmeriDream (corrupted around $20 billion in loans), Buyer's Fund (corrupted about $17 billion in loans), Genesis Foundation (corrupted about $7 billion in loans), and Housing Action Resource Trust (corrupted about $6 billion in loans). I reviewed public information filings for about 28 down payment "gift" organizations, and found that these 28 affordable housing enterprises had eliminated part or all of the down payments associated with an estimated $130 billion in loans, many of which were made in the years 2000 through 2005.[3] Undoubtedly, a complete analysis of all gifting programs would produce a much larger number. This is not "peanuts," folks. It is such a large number that it had to be one of the major factors leading up to the subprime crisis — yet, has it even been reported?

Why did these programs become popular so quickly? Here is the reason given by www.downpaymentsolutions.com, a Web site that maintains resource information on "over 1,000 down payment assistance programs":

> Frankly, it's a Terrific Way to buy a home! There are absolutely no income restrictions, no housing price caps and no restrictions on prior home ownership. It can be done just as easily with a million dollar home purchase as it can with a fifty thousand dollar home purchase.... We jokingly refer to it as "Legalized Money Laundering."[4]

Funny joke, eh? Those of you who are squeamish about the "money laundering" terminology may prefer the description of columnist Elizabeth Weintraub. She described gift programs as "money falling from the sky for homebuyers."[5]

---

1   David Broder, "The Finer Points of Faith-Based Assistance," Washington Post, October 2, 2001.

2   Based on author's analysis of Nehemiah tax return filings (Forms 990) for 2001 through 2006.

3   Nonprofit organizations are required to make available their annual federal information returns (Form 990, "Return of Organization Exempt from Income Tax). For larger organizations these are usually published on the Internet.

4   "Charity Not-for-Profit Home Buyer Assistance," Downpayment Solutions, http://www.downpaymentsolutions.com/about.shtml.

5   Elizabeth Weintraub, "The Nehemiah Program and FHA Loans," http://homebuying.about.com/od/financingadvice/a/061708_Nehemiah.htm.

Ironically, many or most of the loans with the gifted down payments were not even classified as "subprime" by "experts" such as economist Paul Krugman. This was the case even though each and every loan was subprime by virtue of the fact that the borrower could not or would not produce the required down payment. As explained on page 87, in today's politically correct world, loans are not categorized as subprime based on attributes of the borrowers (as they should be); rather they are called subprime if the interest rates are high. This nonsensical methodology leads to many stupid conclusions, but it serves the purpose of those individuals who seek to beatify Fannie and Freddie (more on that later).

What did HUD think about this? It reviewed the matter carefully ... then gave its blessing. These wretched gifting programs would have been stillborn were it not for HUD's express willingness to guarantee the related FHA loans. As reported in the Wall Street Journal, HUD blessed the gifting scams in 1998, even though it knew of the enormous risks:

> FHA [which is part of HUD] worried about the default risk and also the possibility that sellers who gave down-payment money might boost their prices to recover it. If they did, this could mean the homes were selling at inflated prices, so that the FHA couldn't recoup the full loan amount in the event of a foreclosure. [Nevertheless, FHA] agreed in 1998 to guarantee the mortgages.[1]

In 2000, HUD's Inspector General urged that seller-funded gift programs be banned. In 2002, the Inspector General noted that default rates on the down payment-gifted loans it studied quadrupled, from 4.64% in October 1999 to 19.39% in February 2002. Ultimately, HUD decided it would not guarantee loans with seller-funded down payments. However, there was one minor exception: The HUD prohibition did not apply to "affordable housing" programs. Since each and every one of the hundreds of programs claimed to be for the purposes of promoting affordable housing, there was, in reality, no HUD prohibition—zip, nada, nothing.

In 2008, well after the financial sector went into full meltdown, HUD acknowledged the error of its ways. If you are trying to figure out who was responsible for the horrific financial crisis of 2007 and 2008, remember the following words from a HUD document. They constitute a virtual confession:

> HUD's current policies in connection with down payment assistance have given rise to a practice known informally as seller-funded down payment

---

1   Patrick Barta and Queena Sook Kim, "Home Buyers' Down Payments Are Now Paid by Some Builders," The Wall Street Journal, December 10 2002.

assistance that has resulted in disproportionately high borrower default and claim rates....[1]

Seller-funded down payments were finally banned by an act of Congress in late 2008 (after the economy was in ruins). For the ten years prior to that time, we might characterize HUD's official policy for such programs as it is depicted in Figure 5:

Figure 5 – HUD's official policy for seller-paid down payment "gifts"

Essentially, HUD ignored the problem because the agenda of HUD is, first and foremost, to promote affordable housing. Other considerations, such as credit risk and the systemic risk of financial institutions, are secondary.

What did F&F think of down-payment ~~corruption~~ assistance?

They loved it! In fact, they had their own down payment and closing cost programs. In its 2005 Annual Housing Activities Report, Fannie said: "Fannie Mae and its lender partners developed a suite of down payment mortgages under the Flexible mortgage product line. These products permit the borrower to obtain funds for a down payment and closing costs from ... 1) a gift from a relative, domestic partner, fiancée or fiancé; 2) a grant from an employer, public agency, or nonprofit organization; 3) an unsecured loan from a relative, domestic partner, fiancée or fiancé, employer or nonprofit organization; and 4) secured borrowed funds and Community Seconds" (Fannie's term for silent second loans).

---

1   "Standards for Mortgagor's Investment in Mortgaged Property: Additional Public Comment Period," ed. Department of Housing and Urban Development (United States of America, 2008), 2, http://portal.hud.gov/fha/investment/5087-N-04_DPA_Pub_6-11-08.pdf.

Later, Fannie further liberalized the requirements by allowing the use of "cash-on-hand" in lieu of the down payment.[1]

Freddie had its own version of silent second loans, called "Affordable Seconds." In a document created in 2004, Freddie noted that the use of Affordable Seconds in lieu of down payment costs did not require its prior approval.[2] In addition, Freddie was a "Charter Member" of The Homeownership Alliance,[3] a group that actively pushed the concept of using Section 8 rental vouchers to fund down payment requirements.[4]

Fannie and Freddie did not allow the seller to be the *direct* source of the down payment (the seller's money had to be laundered by a nonprofit entity), but that is a distinction without a difference. Read on ...

This focus on the seller is a red herring. Objective evidence shows that down payment gifts, *whatever the funding source*, are financially risky:

> With regard to down payments, the smaller the down payment, the higher the risk. In addition, the down payment must be the *borrower's* money (emphasis added).
>
> – Joseph Birbaum, VP, Affordable Housing, Mortgage Guaranty Insurance Corporation[5]

An analysis of more than 4 million FHA mortgages opened between 1998 and 2001 showed that default rates were sky-high for loans involving down payment gifts, *whether the gifts were funded by sellers or by relatives*. The analysis, prepared by a business consulting firm in 2003, showed an astonishing default rate of 20.6 percent for FHA mortgage loans with *seller-funded* down payments, versus an almost-as-astonishing default rate of 18.5 percent for FHA mortgage loans with *relative-funded* down

---

1   "Annual Housing Activities Report for 2005," (Washington, DC: Fannie Mae, March 16, 2006), 9-10.

2   "Opening Doors to Home Ownership," (Washington, DC: Freddie Mac, 2004), 9.

3   The Homeownership Alliance promoted affordable housing in America and comprised a coalition of almost 20 members including, Habitat for Humanity, La Raza, the Urban League, and various organizations of lenders and realtors.

4   Section 8 vouchers were historically used to assist low-income households with their rental payments. However, legislation enacted during the Clinton Administration and expanded during the Bush Administration gave HUD authority to use the vouchers for home purchases (in many cases).

5   Joseph L. Birbaum, "The Single Family Affordable Housing Market: Trends and Innovations," in A National Symposium (Office of the Comptroller of the Currency, July 1997), 17.

payments.[1] Despite this, gifted down payments are just fine with the U.S. government, even after the financial crisis of 2007/08, provided the funds for the down payment do not come from the seller. What's worse, the Congressional Black Caucus, Congressional Hispanic Caucus, and several Democrats in the House have even advocated legislation to eliminate the ban on seller-funded down payments. Some people never learn.

The real reason we lack affordable homes

As noted, lending shenanigans like piggyback loans were more often found in neighborhoods that lacked affordable housing. These loan gimmicks were the political activists' answer to high housing prices. But, why did these neighborhoods lack affordable housing while others had plenty of reasonably-priced housing? Why, for example, were so many of the high-priced homes in California?

In *The Housing Boom and Bust*, Economist Thomas Sowell persuasively argues that unaffordable housing is usually the product of excessively restrictive building standards. With regard to California, Sowell notes that property values did not become unreasonably high until the 1970s, when a political change took place:

> The decade of the 1970s saw a rapid spread of laws and policies in California severely restricting the use of land. Often these laws and policies forbade the building of anything on vast areas of land, in the name of preserving "open space," "saving farmland," "protecting the environment," "historical preservation" and other politically attractive slogans.[2]

Sowell notes that the routine transfer of land from one usage to another was often prevented, so that, for example, "a farmer who quit farming was not allowed to sell the land to someone who might build houses on the site." Instead, the land would effectively become "open space." It is ironic, Sowell notes, that "supposedly sophisticated people apparently believe that there is an actual physical shortage of land" in places such as California.

Although the United States has, in general, very affordable housing compared to most other nations, the nation's economy was ultimately devastated by a subprime mortgage meltdown triggered by a housing bubble in a few localities. Consider the conclusions of The Independent Institute, which analyzed California housing prices in 2006. It noted that,

---

1   "Report: Most Non-Performing FHA Loans Start with Downpayment Gift from Relatives," in Business Wire (Washington: Gale Group, October 7, 2003).
2   Sowell, The Housing Boom and Bust.

due to urban planning and related land-use restrictions, "Californian suffers from having the least affordable housing in the nation." It added:

> California's land-use planning system forces homebuyers to pay penalties ranging from $70,000 per median-value home in Bakersfield to $850,000 per home in the San Francisco metropolitan area. Indeed, Californians must pay fully half the total cost that planning imposes on homebuyers in the US.[1]

Prophetically, the Independent Institute also noted (in 2006) that the United States economy was threatened by prices that "have careened wildly up and down and are poised for another gigantic fall."[2] But the problem was never national. In the words of Holman Jenkins of the Wall Street Journal, it is a "striking fact that much of the subprime crisis stemmed from just a handful of fast-growing counties in four states where housing prices zoomed then plummeted."[3] Those 4 states, California, Florida, Nevada, and Arizona, had 62 percent of the nation's foreclosures in 2008, and an estimated 87 percent of the nation's housing losses.[4] Most of those losses come from just 2 of the 4 states: California and Florida — states with gigantic state down payment assistance programs. Too bad we have 50 states. If we had just 46 there wouldn't have been much of a crisis. Thus, as with Katrina, we must not overlook the extremely detrimental role of the state and local players.

Summary

We have seen that numerous state and local governments and non-profit organizations ran "affordable housing" programs that issued "silent second" loans designed to reduce or eliminate down payment and/or closing costs. These programs, which started in the mid-1990s, were funded with state money, HUD money, or a combination of the two. In the early 2000s private lenders started issuing their own second loans, know as piggybacks. By 2004, over 40 percent of homebuyers were financing their down payments with silent seconds or piggybacks.

---

1   Randal O'toole, "The Planning Penalty: How Smart Growth Makes Housing Unaffordable," (June 12, 2006), http://www.independent.org/publications/article.asp?id=1746.

2   Ibid.

3   Holman Jenkins Jr., "How Democracy Ruined the Bailout," The Wall Street Journal (2009), http://online.wsj.com/article/SB123491508784704057.html.

4   William H. Lucy and Jeff Herlitz, "Foreclosures in States and Metropolitan Areas," (University of Virginia: Department of Urban and Environmental Planning, February, 2009), 1,13.

In the mid-1990s, nonprofit organizations began special "gifting" programs for the purpose of promoting affordable housing. Although it was repeatedly warned of the risks, HUD never shut down these gifting programs. Indeed, it specifically approved of them, provided they were related to "affordable housing" programs. After reviewing tax information filings for 30 large gifting nonprofit organizations, I estimate that those 30 entities detrimentally impacted at least $130 billion in loans. This is in addition to the even larger amount of loans affected by piggyback and silent second loans.

Seller-funded gift programs were finally banned by an act of Congress in late 2008; however, other types of down payment gift and loan programs are still allowed, and even promoted, by the government. Research suggests that any form of down payment assistance can lead to high default rates.

The root cause of these special down payment assistance programs may be the very high housing costs found in certain regions of the country. Some economists, such as Thomas Sowell, believe that excessively restrictive building standards is the primary cause of these unusually high housing costs. It has been noted that much of the mortgage crisis can be traced to the collapse of a housing bubble in just a few states.

Chapter 5: Fannie and Freddie fudge their delinquency stats

> [I]f Freddie Mac renegotiates the terms of the loan with someone who is delinquent, then, voila, that person is no longer delinquent. It seems to me that since about June of 2006, Freddie Mac is struggling to keep this Ponzi scheme afloat.
>
> – Mike (Mish) Shedlock, Investment Advisor and Economic Blogger[1]

When the subprime mortgage crisis erupted in 2007, many individuals in academia, the media, and government rushed to the defense of affordable housing programs. With religious zeal, they argued that affordable housing had nothing to do with the crisis. The reasoning? Only a small percentage of loans were issued under the Community Reinvestment Act (CRA), so the CRA could not have been the problem. And, although Fannie and Freddie bought massive numbers of loans, those loans were rock-solid compared to those made and resold by Wall Street investment banks. As evidence they cited the (supposedly) low delinquency rates of Fannie and Freddie (F&F) loans. The conclusion: This crisis was mostly or entirely caused by "Wall Street," and by the government's lack of regulation thereof.

---

1   Mike Shedlock, "The Truth About Us Mortgage Default Rates," MoneyWeek (February 7, 2007), http://www.moneyweek.com/news-and-charts/economics/the-truth-about-us-mortgage-default-rates.

The Community Reinvestment Act is examined in Chapter 8. This chapter focuses on the (supposedly) rock-solid performance of Fannie's and Freddie's loans and related investments.

Once a crook, always a crook

Imagine that Enron, famous for its creative and self-serving accounting manipulations, survived its bankruptcy in 2001. A few years later Enron became involved in a controversy related to the integrity of its financial records. Would academics, Congressmen, journalists, and "Nobel Laureates" regurgitate the claims of Enron — a proven dissembler — without scrutiny? I don't think so. Yet, in the case of Fannie and Freddie, each of which had an established record of "cooking the books," there was almost no skepticism regarding their claims about loan delinquency rates. Instead, the assertions were almost universally accepted at face value, and cited as evidence of their superior performance. In this chapter we examine those claims and we estimate F&F's real delinquency rates — right after we review the sordid record of their earlier accounting transgressions.

"Steady Freddie" was run by crooks

In December 2003 the Office of Federal Housing Enterprise Oversight (OFHEO), a regulator of Fannie and Freddie, issued a blistering report describing the accounting manipulations of Freddie Mac:

> Freddie Mac cast aside accounting rules, internal controls, disclosure standards, and the public trust in the pursuit of steady growth. The conduct and intentions of the Enterprise were hidden and were revealed only by a chain of events that began when Freddie Mac changed auditors in 2002.[1]

More specifically, Freddie,

- "created and maintained reserve accounts that did not comply with GAAP [Generally Accepted Accounting Principles] and entered into transactions with little or no economic substance...."[2]
- "created an essentially fictional transaction with a securities firm to move approximately $30 billion of mortgage assets

---

1   "Report of the Special Examination of Freddie Mac," ed. Office of Federal Housing Enterprise Oversight (U.S. government, December 2003), i, http://www.fhfa.gov/webfiles/749/specialreport122003.pdf.
2   Ibid.

from a trading account to an available-for-sale account [and thereby manipulate earnings]."[1]

- "adopted, and then quickly reversed, a dubious change in its methodology for valuing swaptions [options to buy swaps]. That change had the effect of reducing the value of the derivatives portfolio of the Enterprise by $730 million."[2]
- "entered into [a transaction] for the purpose of disguising the effective notional amount of the Freddie Mac derivatives portfolio and thereby allay the concerns of an investor."[3]
- "changed key assumptions in the calculation of [a non-GAAP reserve] when necessary to achieve a desired earnings result."[4]

Due to these and other manipulations, designed to give investors the false impression that Freddie had steady earnings, Freddie was ultimately required to make a $5 billion restatement of its financial statements, and to pay a penalty of $125 million.

Fannie was more crooked

After regulators looked at Freddie's books, they started to examine the financial records of Fannie. In September 2004 and May 2006, OFHEO issued its findings for Fannie:

- "By deliberated and intentionally manipulating accounting to hit earnings targets, senior management maximized the bonuses and other executive compensation they received, at the expense of shareholders."[5]
- "Fannie Mae reported extremely smooth profit growth.... Those achievements were illusions deliberately and systematically created by the Enterprise's senior management with the aid of inappropriate accounting and improper earnings management."[6]
- "Fannie Mae management expected to write the rules that applied to the Enterprise and to impede efforts at effective safety

---

1 Ibid., iii.
2 Ibid.
3 Ibid.
4 Ibid.
5 "Report of the Special Examination of Fannie Mae," ed. Office of Federal Housing Enterprise Oversight (U.S. government, May 2006), Summary, http://www.fanniemae.com/media/pdf/newsreleases/FNMSPECIALEXAM.pdf.
6 Ibid.

and soundness regulations. Those rules included managerial latitude in deciding when to comply with Generally Accepted Accounting Principles (GAAP) and engaging in and concealing improper earnings management...."[1]

- "...the picture of the Enterprise as a 'best-in-class' financial institution was a 'facade.' To maintain that facade, senior executives worked strenuously to hide Fannie Mae's operational deficiencies and significant risk exposures from outside observers...."[2]

- "A large number of Fannie Mae's accounting policies and practices did not comply with Generally Accepted Accounting Principles (GAAP). The Enterprise also had serious problems of internal control, financial reporting, and corporate governance."[3]

As a result of these errors and irregularities, Fannie Mae subsequently announced a $6.3 billion restatement of its earnings — the largest in United States history.

The management of Fannie was more dishonest than Ken Lay and colleagues at Enron, some of whom went to prison. In the case of Enron it could be argued that management unsuccessfully tried to protect workers and investors by using complex accounting gimmicks to conceal a period of poor profits, failed deals, and excessive debt. The effort was misguided, illegal, and completely unsuccessful, but it is not clear that the motivations were all bad. In the case of profitable Fannie and Freddie, however, it appears that management was motivated entirely by personal greed. This is especially true of Fannie, whose then-CEO, Francis Raines, acted like a bandit — stealing from the company. Raines and other officers of Fannie manipulated earnings levels even though profits were already quite good. They used accounting manipulations, not to keep a leaky ship from sinking, but rather, to add millions to their own pay bonuses. OFHEO reported that $52 million of Raines' $90 million in compensation (1998-2003) was in the form of bonuses tied to the company's earnings per share (EPS). OFHEO also noted that, "by deliberated and intentionally manipulating accounting to hit earnings [EPS] targets, senior management maximized the bonuses and other executive compensation they received, at the expense of shareholders."[4] My only

---

1   Ibid., 1.
2   Ibid., 2.
3   Ibid.
4   Ibid., Summary.

question is, why didn't Raines et al. go to jail? (Answer: They had lots of friends in Congress.)

Like Sinatra, they did it their way

> At the end of 2006, only 0.53 percent of Freddie Mac-owned single-family loans were 90-days or more delinquent or in foreclosure, down from 0.69 percent at the end of 2005. ... Nationally, severe prime conventional loan delinquencies ended 2006 at 0.86 percent, according to data from the Mortgage Bankers Association.
>
> – Freddie Mac (Press Release)[1]

It's amazing! In 2005 and 2006, delinquency rates across America were beginning to rise but Freddie's delinquency rates, according to Freddie, started dropping. The trends are depicted in Figure 6, below.[2]

Figure 6 – Freddie's serious delinquency rates vs. that of conventional loans (single family loans)

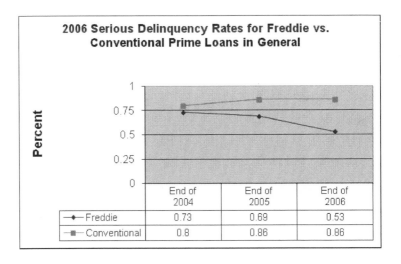

As you can see, Freddie's serious delinquency rate was falling while the rate for conventional prime loans, as a whole, was climbing.

We have a known obfuscator — Freddie Mac — reporting numbers that don't make sense in the context of the overall lending industry. Does

---

1   "2006 Drop in Delinquencies Show Shifting Reasons Behind Single Family Late Payments," (Freddie Mac, April 25, 2007), www.freddiemac.com/news/archives/servicing/2007/20070425_singlefamily.html.

2   Sources are the 4th Quarter 2009 National Delinquency Survey of the Mortgage Bankers Association and the Monthly Volume Summaries of Freddie Mac (available on the Freddie Mac Investor Relations Web site).

this inconsistency produce intellectual skepticism within our esteemed academic community? No, it produces accolades. For example, in a piece titled, *Beleaguered Fannie Mae and Freddie Mac: Beacons of Stability*, finance professor Anthony Sanders of the W.P. Carey School of Business regurgitated F&F-produced delinquency stats, noting how moderate those rates were in comparison to market-wide rates. The professor concluded: "It is clear that Fannie and Freddie are the remaining source of stability and prudent underwriting practices among financial intermediaries."[1]

What about the regulators of Fannie and Freddie? Did they apply professional skepticism to the information put forth by the disgraced duo? Unfortunately, it appears that their primary regulator (currently), the Federal Housing Finance Agency (FHFA), did not scrutinize F&F's delinquency information. Otherwise, it would not have relayed this misleading information to Congress, and the rest of the nation. In its 2008 "Report to Congress" FHFA reported that the serious delinquency rate for prime conventional loans was 3.7 percent, while it was only 2.4 percent for Fannie, and a mere 1.7 percent for Freddie. Where did FHFA get those figures? From Fannie and Freddie, the entities FHFA was supposed to be regulating.

What's wrong with the F&F delinquency stats?

Let's revisit the information provided in Figure 6, above. Freddie reported a delinquency rate that dropped from .73 at the start of 2005 to .53 at the end of 2006. That is quite impressive compared to average conventional loan delinquency rates; however, Freddie got this favorable trend by quietly making a major change to its accounting method for delinquencies. Evidence of the accounting change can be found in Freddie's loan activity reports — provided you have good vision and a powerful magnifying glass. From a solitary footnote attached to one of the reports, we can deduce that, beginning sometime in 2005, Freddie began removing from the serious delinquency category any loan less than 90 days delinquent under *"modified* contractual terms" — even if the loan was seriously delinquent under the *original* terms.[2]

---

1   "Beleaguered Fannie Mae and Freddie Mac: Beacons of Stability," ed. WP Carey School of Business (Arizona State University, July 22, 2008), http://knowledge.wpcarey.asu.edu/article.cfm?articleid=1644#.

2   Starting with footnote 13 to its unaudited Monthly Volume Summary for December 2005, Freddie added this phrase: "Excludes mortgage loans whose original contractual terms have been modified under an agreement with the

Here's how it worked. Let's say that Freddie had a loan that was six months past due. At Freddie's urging, its loan servicers called borrowers and offered new payment plans that required monthly payments to resume in, say, 4 months. Of course, the borrower was glad to accept the easier terms (since they still didn't have to comply with them). Even though there would be no payments for a span of at least 10 months (6 past and 4 future), the loan was not counted in Freddie's delinquency stats because it was no longer 90 days delinquent under the new terms. Give credit to blogger and investment advisor, Mike (Mish) Shedlock (http://glcbaleconomicanalysis.blogspot.com/), for spotting this deceptive practice.

Apples vs. Oranges

Freddie did not have a valid reason to change its method of reporting delinquencies, and it did not make the change in a transparent manner. Investors look at delinquency rates to assess the quality of loan underwriting and the level of credit risk faced by the loan holder. Those investors can only be confused when thousands of delinquent loans are reclassified on the basis of tenuous loan modifications and forbearance arrangements. In all likelihood, Freddie changed its methodology to give the false illusion of a positive delinquency trend line.

In addition, Freddie was misleading the public by comparing apples to oranges. Consider again the words from Freddie's April 2007 press release, quoted on page 71 and repeated below:

> At the end of 2006, only 0.53 percent of Freddie Mac-owned single-family loans were 90-days or more delinquent or in foreclosure, down from 0.69 percent at the end of 2000.... Nationally, severe prime conventional loan delinquencies ended 2006 at 0.86 percent, according to data from the Mortgage Bankers Association.

Freddie publicly compared its delinquency rate to the conventional loan delinquency rate (.86 percent), as published by the Mortgage Bankers Association (MBA). However, the MBA specifically includes, as delinquent, loans that are subject to modified payment plans. Freddie had to know this because the MBA clearly explains its methodology in its publication:

> Loans subject to forbearance agreements are reported as delinquent, even if a restructured loan payment plan has been agreed to by both parties. The length of the delinquency is determined by the number of missed pay-

borrower as long as the borrower complies with the modified contractual terms." That phrase was not used prior to December 2005.

ments. The loan remains delinquent *until it is current in accordance with the original loan contract* (emphasis added).[1]

Is there anything ambiguous about the MBA's method of calculating the number of delinquent loans? Why would Freddie compare its dramatically-reduced delinquency rate to the unreduced rate published by the MBA? There is a one-word answer: dishonesty. This needs to be investigated and people within Freddie need to be held accountable.

What were the real delinquency rates?

Retained and guaranteed loans only

By using information pulled from different Freddie Mac documents, it is possible to *roughly* estimate what Freddie's delinquencies might have been had it not removed modified loans from other delinquent loans. See Table 2, below.[2]

Table 2 – Freddie Mac: Estimation of serious delinquency rates for 2004 vs. 2006 (single family loans)

Year →	2004		2006	
Amount →	Number	%	Number*	%
Delinquency amounts are reported	74604	.73	60547	.54
Add modified loans (removed by Freddie)			59100	
Adjusted delinquency amounts	74604	.73	119647	1.07

*59,100 is the number of modified loans at the end of 2006, as reported by Freddie. I am assuming that this number of loans was deducted from delinquency statistics, although Freddie's exact methodology is not a matter of public record.

If my estimate is correct, we have a very different, much more alarming delinquency trend line. Freddie's reported delinquency amounts and rates and my estimates of its delinquency amounts and rates are shown in Figure 7, below.

Notice the dramatic change in the trend line, from a strong decrease to a strong increase in delinquencies. Now things make sense. If its delinquency rates were really getting better, it is unlikely that United States

---

1   "National Delinquency Survey: Facts," (May 2008), http://www.mbaa.org/files/Research/Flyers/NDSFAQ.pdf.

2   Sources for delinquencies: Freddie Mac 2005 Annual Report Table 6.3, Freddie Mac 2007 Annual Report Table 5.6. Source for modifications: Federal Home Loan Mortgage Corporation Annual Housing Activities Report for 2006, published March 16, 2007 (page 35).

taxpayers would now be bailing out Freddie to the tune of more than $300 billion.[1]

Figure 7 – Freddie's reported serious delinquency rates versus estimated rates (single family loans)

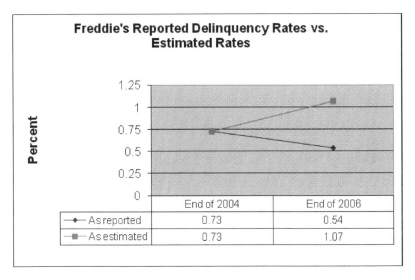

As noted, Fannie was a bigger crook than Freddie, so it should not surprise anyone that it also fudged its delinquency statistics. However, this is something that had to be deduced and then confirmed through personal correspondence, since Fannie made no explicit disclosure regarding the calculation of its delinquency rates — not even a tiny footnote in 10-pitch font. Prior to 2006, Fannie's monthly delinquency reports had this simple footnote to explain the calculation of the serious delinquency rate:

> Includes conventional loans three or more months delinquent or in foreclosure process as a percent of the number of loans.[2]

After 2006, the footnote changed significantly. Fannie now explained its delinquency rate calculation in this manner:

---

1   Bailout payments to Fannie and Freddie totaled about $169 billion as of August 2011; however, that was the White House estimate. The Congressional Budget Office estimated, in June 2011, that the complete bailout was about $317 billion. It calculated that amount by adding the fair value deficit of the GSEs to $130 billion, which was the total of bailout payments at the time. The fair value deficit reflects the amount of GSE debt and debt guarantees after subtracting the value of their assets.

2   Fannie Mae's Monthly Summary for December 31, 2005, footnote 2.

> We classify single-family loans as seriously delinquent when a borrower has missed three or more consecutive monthly payments, *and the loan has not been brought current or extinguished through foreclosure, payoff, or other resolution* (emphasis added).[1]

From this post-2006 footnote we know that Fannie had begun reducing its population of delinquent loans by those loans "brought current or extinguished through foreclosure, payoff, or other resolution." Did "other resolution" include loans modified to give more liberal payment terms? I asked Fannie Mae's department of "investor relations," and this is the answer I received:

> Fannie Mae derives the data about delinquency for its periodic reports and monthly summaries from its servicers. At the time that a formal modification of a loan is effected, the servicer reports the loan as current if the borrower is in compliance with the terms of the executed modification (emphasis added).[2]

Thus, Fannie changed its definition of "delinquency" in much the same way that Freddie changed its definition — at around the same time, no less. But, Fannie was more secretive about it than was Freddie.

I wasn't able to ascertain exactly when Fannie started lowering its delinquency rate by foreclosures and modifications, but it appears that it happened sometime in 2006. This can be surmised by reviewing its delinquency rate trend, as depicted in Figure 8, below.[3]

Do you notice that, between the end of 2005 and the end of 2006, there is a decline in Fannie's delinquency rate, as compared to the rest of the industry? This decline does not appear genuine, given the state of the loan industry in 2006. The graph depicted in Figure 9, below, shows Fannie's reported delinquency rate versus my rough estimate of its delinquency rate.

By the way, both Fannie and Freddie have boasted many times of their aggressive outreach programs, designed to encourage borrowers to seek loan modifications and forbearance plans. It is good public policy and, given their new accounting methods, any loan modification make their delinquency stats look so very low.

---

1   Fannie Mae's Monthly Summary for December 31, 2007, definition of "Serious Delinquency Rates" in Glossary.

2   Associate Investor Relations Manager Nikki Spears, Fannie Mae, e-mail, June 2, 2009.

3   Sources are the 4th Quarter 2009 National Delinquency Survey of the Mortgage Bankers Association and the Monthly Summaries of Fannie Mae (available on the Fannie Mae Investor Relations Web site).

Figure 8 – Fannie's serious delinquency rates vs. that of conventional loans (single family loans)

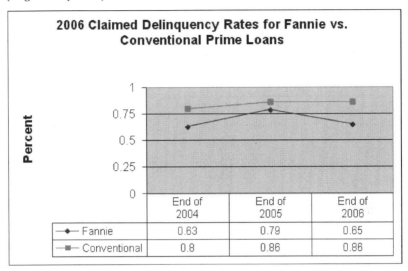

Figure 9 – Fannie's reported serious delinquency rates versus estimated rates (single family loans)

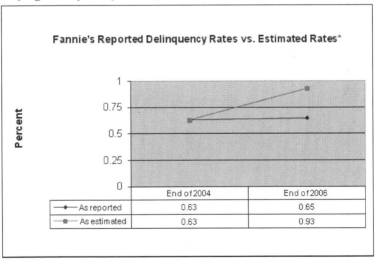

*Estimated by adding the percentage of "loan workouts" per Table 36 in Fannie's 2006 Annual Report to the unadjusted delinquency percentage as of the end of 2006

As early as 2001, F&F were already pushing lenders to modify loans, "as opposed to the traditional collection and foreclosure practices." In a report released in 2001, Graham Fisher, an independent research company, noted that F&F were paying lenders 'incentives' to "modify or recast loans." One lender told Graham Fisher that he was required, by Fannie and Freddie, to report modified loans as "current." He added: "The real issue it seems to me is whether or not Fannie and Freddie report these loans as current or troubled/modified in their SEC filings."[1] We can now answer his question: The loans were treated as current — even in SEC filings.

In 2008, Fannie revised its policy with regard to loan modifications. Under the new approach, the company's loan servicers (independent companies throughout the nation) are required to tell borrowers that, if they are fairly certain that changes in their income could cause them to miss a loan payment, they can qualify for an advance loan modification. This new policy should help to maintain the appearance of a nice, low delinquency rate.

The real delinquency rates are much higher

Someone like Paul Krugman, who writes for the New York Times, might argue that, even if we factor in the loan modifications, the de-linquency rates on the loans held or guaranteed by Fannie and Freddie (F&F) would still be far lower than the rates for subprime loans. That would be true but misleading, for two important reasons. First, many toxic loans of Fannie and Freddie were not held directly — they were held as investments in high-risk private mortgage-backed securities (MBS). As noted in Chapter 6, F&F invested heavily in these toxic secu-rities in the years 2004 through 2006. Generally, they bought the upper tranches (layers), and those purchases enabled many other investors to buy the lower tranches. Some economists (e.g., Wallison and Calomiris) believe that, without F&F's involvement, many or most MBSs would have been unmarketable. The delinquency stats discussed heretofore (and everywhere else in this chapter) pertain only to the loans deemed good enough to be held directly by Fannie or Freddie in their portfolios or trusts.

There is a second reason the low delinquency rates of F& F are mis-leading. As any good economist knows, delinquency rates must be evalu-ated by product — not just for the company as a whole. This is a critical point, so please consider this clarifying analogy. Let's assume that hy-pothetical Fannie's Pharmaceuticals is a drug distributor that has one product — aspirin. Its sales of this aspirin are huge — let's say $10 bil-lion per year. Now assume that Fannie starts distributing a controversial

---

1   Joshua Rosner, "Housing in the New Millennium: A Home without Equity Is Just a Rental with Debt," Graham Fisher & Co., June 29, 2001, http://papers. ssrn.com/sol3/papers.cfm?abstract_id=1162456.

new leukemia medicine, and sales for this new drug are relatively small — say one-half billion dollars. We are interested in evaluating the safety and efficacy of the new leukemia drug. Would we do this by averaging in the safety and efficacy stats for Fannie's aspirin sales? The answer is no. To do so would completely obscure the results of the controversial new drug, and it would also make meaningless comparisons with competitors (who might produce nothing but leukemia drugs). Instead, we would evaluate Fannie's new leukemia treatment on its own, and in the context of alternative treatments for leukemia.

Now, let's return to Fannie and Freddie. For years they operated with relative prudence and insisted on sound underwriting standards for any loan they purchased. I don't know of anyone who has complained about the lax underwriting standards of Fannie and Freddie prior to, say, 1990. However, something happened after that. Fannie and Freddie continued to buy and sell prudent loans (their "aspirin") but they also bought risky new loan products in an attempt to comply with the affordable housing mandates established by law and regulated by HUD. In many cases, F&F designed the loan products used by lenders; then, F&F purchased the loans from those same lenders. They were subprime loans, such as these:

- Low and no-down payment loans.
- Loans for people with low FICO credit scores.
- Loans for people with undocumented income.

Our focus must be on the dollar-amount, safety, and efficacy of these new products — on their own and in relation to alternative products (from the private sector).

Table 3, below, shows the serious delinquency rates (i.e., delinquencies lasting for "3 monthly payments or more") for some of Freddie Mac's loan purchases as of December 31, 2010 (source: 2010 Form 10-K). Note how much those rates have to be increased when the calculation is prepared in accordance with the standards of the Mortgage Bankers Association (MBA). As of December 31, 2010, the overall serious delinquency rate of Freddie's single-family credit guarantee portfolio was just 3.84. However, the high-risk loans of Freddie had far higher delinquency rates, and this was especially true after they had been calculated in the same manner as the private lender loans reported by the MBA.

It must be acknowledged that the fourth quarter 2010 serious delinquency rate for subprime loans, overall, was 27.46 percent (per MBA), which is an amount higher than for any single high-risk characteristic. One reason for this could be that the rates shown in Table 3 are for each separate factor. In many cases, a single loan will have multiple factors, which contribute to even higher rates. For example, a loan to a borrower with a low FICO rate might also have an LTV of over 90 percent. Such a loan could have a sky-high delinquency rate.

Table 3 – Freddie Mac 2010 serious delinquency rates by characteristic, and with adjustment for modifications (source, 2010 Form 10-K, Table 44)

High-risk characteristic	Delinquency rate reported by Freddie	Loan modifications	Adjusted delinquency rate
Alt-A	12.2	5.8	18.0
Interest-only loans	18.4	.5	18.9
Option ARM loans	21.2	3.1	24.3
Original LTV › 90%	7.8	5.3	13.1
FICO less than 620	13.9	10.4	24.3

It also should be conceded, however, that it is entirely possible that Fannie and Freddie did have somewhat lower delinquency rates — even for their high-risk loans. Due to their size and government backing they could probably "cherry pick" the best of the junk, if they wished.

More creative accounting

> Investors might want to take a closer look at Fannie Mae's latest earn-ings report. Lost in the unsurprising news of the mortgage lender's heavy losses was a critical change in the way the company discloses its bad loans — a move that could mask credit losses that are rising above levels that the company predicted just three months ago.

> – Peter Eavis, Fortune Senior writer, November 15, 2007[1]

You might think that Peter Eavis, quoted above, was talking about the same issue presented earlier in this chapter — the self-serving change in the way Fannie (and Freddie) calculated delinquency rates. But, you'd be wrong. Eavis was pointing out yet another way Fannie bamboozled investors, and everyone else.

Investors assess the financial health of a lender by evaluating its "credit loss ratio," which is the ratio of bad loan losses divided by total

1   Peter Eavis, "More Doubts About Fannie Mae's Disclosures," CNNMoney.com, November 16, 2007, http://money.cnn.com/2007/11/16/news/companies/fannie_follow.fortune/.

loans. In the middle of 2007, Fannie quietly changed the way it calculates its credit loss ratio. After that, losses on repurchased loans, known as "SOP 03-3 fair value losses" (named after the governing accounting standard), would not be included in the credit loss ratio calculation. As SOP 03-3 losses skyrocketed, Fannie had an epiphany: Stop reporting those darn losses!

Peter Eavis illustrates how SOP 03-3 losses are normally computed:

> If a homeowner falls significantly behind on his payments, Fannie Mae has to buy back the loan from the bondholder. If the mortgage has an outstanding amount of, say, $100,000 and unpaid interest of $5,000, Fannie Mae would have to pay $105,000 — its full value — to make the bondholders whole.

> However, the $105,000 loan may actually be worth less on the market. It is Fannie Mae's job to estimate the market value, or fair market value, of the loan and to record that price on its books. So if the fair market value is $80,000, Fannie Mae takes a loss of $25,000 (the difference between $105,000 and $80,000). That loss is considered an SOP 03-3 loss....[1]

What impact did the change in accounting method have? As can be seen In Figure 10, below, the new method ostensibly led to a dramatic reduction in Fannie's loss ratio. Without the accounting change, the ratio would have been 85 percent higher.

Figure 10 – Suddenly, Fannie needed to modify its accounting method for credit losses[2]

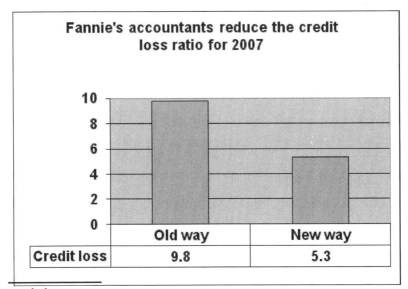

Fannie's accountants reduce the credit loss ratio for 2007		
	Old way	New way
Credit loss	9.8	5.3

---

1   Ibid.
2   Per pages 79 and 80 of Fannie's 2007 Form 10-K.

By excluding SOP 03-3 losses, Fannie minimized its losses. That encouraged investors to keep buying Fannie's stock and it encouraged the many Fannie-loving pundits to maintain their support. Life was good. Too bad it all blew up a year later.

As an accountant I'd like to say a word or two about accounting standards generally, and accounting changes, specifically. Contrary to popular perceptions, accounting involves more than arithmetical calculations: It involves numerous principles, judgments and estimates. There is some flexibility with regard to the selection of accounting principles, but once adopted, they should change infrequently, and only with good justification and clear disclosure. I read Fannie's SEC filings with regard to its calculation of credit loss ratios, and could find no indication that the method selected by Fannie in 2005 and 2006 became inappropriate in 2007. The only thing that changed in 2007 was that SOP 03-3 losses were exploding. Apparently, Fannie needed a way to confuse its investors with regard to those losses.

Armando Falcon, who led the investigation of Fannie and Freddie while he headed the Office of Federal Housing Enterprise Oversight, summed up the situation aptly:

> This just smacks too much of the accounting games the company was playing a couple years ago. They have very little room to play with here when it comes to trust and credibility.[1]

Smoke and mirrors

The accounting shenanigans we just reviewed took place in 2007. Fast forward to early 2008. Now the executives of Fannie and Freddie were starting to sweat because delinquencies were soaring on those subprime loans — the ones that Paul Krugman said didn't exist.

How could the GSEs (Fannie and Freddie) minimize losses on their delinquent loans? For many companies this would be a challenging problem, but for the heavily-experienced GSE executives it was really quite simple. Charles Duhigg of the New York Times explained how the problem was solved.

> Both companies have ... recently changed their policies on delinquent loans, which they previously recorded as impaired when borrowers were 120 days late. Now, some overdue loans can go two years before the companies record a loss.

---

1   Associate Press, "Traders Wary of Fannie's Mortgage Math," MSMBC. com (November 16, 2007), http://www.msnbc.msn.com/id/21836728/ns/ business-real_estate/t/traders-wary-fannies-mortgage-math/.

There it is: a simple and elegant way to improve profits. All you have to do is deem the past-due loans to be good for an additional 20 months. I guess that's why these guys were paid the big bucks.

Epilogue

They won't be doing a perp walk, but the wheels of justice are starting to turn against 6 former executives of Fannie and Freddie. In December, 2011, the Securities and Exchange Commission (SEC) announced that Fannie's ex-CEO, Daniel Mudd, Freddie's ex-CEO, Richard Syron, and 4 other GSE executives were being charged with securities fraud. The allegations were that "they knew and approved of misleading statements claiming the companies had minimal holdings of higher-risk mortgage loans, including subprime loans." For this alleged fraud the executives face "financial penalties, disgorgement of ill-gotten gains with interest, permanent injunctive relief and officer and director bars...."[1]

Regarding the phony delinquency stats, I have discussed the matter with SEC investigators, and have sent them a copy of this chapter. They seemed very interested. When the case is over and the guilty are being punished I'll be reviewing court documents with great interest — looking for a sign that I may have helped to make life a bit harder for the 6 defendants. Then, I'll have a glass of fine Merlot.

---

1   "SEC Charges Former Fannie Mae and Freddie Mac Executives with Securities Fraud," Securities and Exchange Commission, December 16, 2011, http://www.sec.gov/news/press/2011/2011-267.htm.

CHAPTER 6: FANNIE AND FREDDIE'S JUNK LOAN ORGY

> [Fannie and Freddie] didn't do any subprime lending, because they can't; the definition of a subprime loan is precisely a loan that doesn't meet the requirement, imposed by law, that Fannie and Freddie buy only mortgages issued to borrowers who made substantial down payments and carefully documented their income.
>
> – Paul Krugman, New York Times, July 14, 2008

There have been millions of words written about the subprime mortgage debacle but none more insightful than those little pearls, above. Paul Krugman — economist, columnist, and Nobel Laureate — assures us that Fannie and Freddie did not buy subprime loans: They only bought the loans of borrowers who made "substantial down payments and carefully documented their income." How does Mr. Krugman know this? It's the law!

Paul's Principle, explained

Let's see if the simple and elegant logic of Paul's Principle (people can't do things if the law says they aren't allowed to) might be used in other situations involving controversy. Perhaps it could be used by:

- A murder defendant — "Judge Krugman, It is against the law to kill a man: That proves I am innocent." *The Court finds the defendant not guilty.*
- A woman accused of exceeding the speed limit — "Officer Krugman, I could not have been speeding because it is against

the law." *Sorry Ma'am, I should have known that. You can be on your way now.*

- A student accused of cheating — "Professor Krugman, It is not possible that I cheated: It is against the rules." *I forgot there were rules against that. Please don't give me a bad evaluation at the end of the semester.*

According to Paul's Principle, formulated in 2008, it was impossible for Fannie or Freddie to invest in subprime loans; however, they did not seem to realize this. In its 2004 Annual Report, Freddie stated: "We participate in the subprime market segment in two ways. First, our retained portfolio makes investments in ... securities that were originated in this market segment. ... Second, we guarantee securities backed by subprime mortgages." Fannie stated (in its 2004 SEC filing): "[W]e have been working with our lender customers to support a broad range of mortgage products, including subprime products...." Indeed, Freddie and Fannie reported billions of "subprime" investments in each of their annual reports and other filings for 2004, 2005, 2006, and 2007. It is too bad that Fannie and Freddie didn't know about Paul's Principle: They could have "fixed" their books to reflect this great law of economics! (They do know how to fix books.)

In reality, Fannie and Freddie were the primary forces pushing subprime lending on the entire home loan industry. Their junk loan investments, along with FHA junk loans, exceeded that of all private lenders — combined. This is not surprising. They were mandated to buy vast quantities of affordable housing loans. As their regulator, HUD, increased the required affordable housing percentages (to as high as 56 percent of all purchases), and as other parties competed for those very same loans, it became impossible for Fannie and Freddie to achieve the goals without degrading lending standards. Contrary to what the F&F defenders say, these companies were heavily involved in subprime junk — and this was *prior* to the big expansion of private-label junk loans and mortgage-backed securities that started in 2004. Fannie and Freddie led the way towards financial calamity.

We have already seen (in Chapters 2 and 3) how Fannie and Freddie promoted the wide-spread use of their automated underwriting and appraisal systems — systems that lowered standards for the entire industry. Now consider a more direct way that they promoted subprime: via massive purchases. F&F's subprime purchases were massive, and had a huge impact on the rest of the lending industry.

What are subprime loans?

Before reviewing estimates of F&F's subprime investments we must define the word, "subprime." Fannie Mae and Freddie Mac had a very arbitrary and restrictive definition. They reserved the term for loans purchased from lenders who mostly or entirely made subprime loans. This definition grossly understated their subprime purchases because there were plenty of lenders who did not "specialize" in subprime, but were perfectly willing to sell massive quantities of such loans to F&F. In those cases there was a "don't ask and don't tell" policy. (Fannie and Freddie didn't ask and the loan originators didn't tell.)

A meaningful definition of "subprime" must reflect other factors — ones that reflect the documented creditworthiness of the borrower with respect to the size of the loan and its repayment requirements.[1] Often, it is not possible to obtain information that directly describes borrower attributes, and analysts may, out of necessity, deduce this information by studying the terms of the loans. That is OK, provided the terms of the loans can be connected to the borrower attributes in a meaningful way.[2]

The relevant borrower attributes can be categorized in various ways, but they usually include a borrower's credit reputation (generally measured with a FICO score) and the size of his income and assets in proportion to the loan and any other financial burdens he has. Of course, the borrower should have documentation that supports all of the above. Specifically, the borrower should have:

- A good FICO credit score.
- Sufficient income to pay loan principal and interest, and other obligations, over a reasonable period (normally not more than 30 years).
- Enough assets to provide a solid down payment.
- Documentation that supports all of the above.

---

1   According to the June 2007 edition of Monetary Trends, an online publication of the Federal Reserve of St. Louis, "... the Board of Governors of the Federal Reserve System, the Office of the Comptroller of the Currency, the Federal Deposit Insurance Corporation, and the Office of Thrift Supervision – specify that 'subprime' refers to the credit characteristic of individual borrowers."

2   Many misguided researchers ignore the attributes of the borrower, and simply define subprime loans as those carrying an interest rate 3 points or more higher than the rates on conventional loans. This is a lazy, inaccurate, and biased definition that, essentially, equates subprime loans with predatory loans. While high-interest rate loans are often given to subprime borrowers, there are millions of subprime borrowers who get loans that do not have high-interest rates.

If any one of these 4 attributes is missing, the loan is risky and cannot be considered "prime" — even if the interest rate on the loan is moderate and even if the borrower has above-average income.

The junk loan orgy

F&F Subprime purchases — per Wallison & Calomiris

An early estimate of F&F's subprime purchases was prepared by Peter Wallison and Charles Calomiris (scholars at the American Enterprise Institute). They estimated that, as of August 31, 2008, F&F were holding at least a trillion dollars of high risk, subprime single-family mortgage loans and investments. In making their estimate, which was based on verifiable information, Wallison and Calomiris considered 5 high-risk factors, each of which can be used as a proxy for a specific borrower attribute:

1. Negative loan amortization. (Payments are less than interest, so the loan balance grows. This feature is used by borrowers with inadequate income.)

2. Interest-only loans (used by borrowers with inadequate income).

3. Borrower FICO scores under 620. (This indicates poor credit reputation.)

4. Loan-to-value ratios over 90%. (This indicates borrower has insufficient assets.)

5. Alt-A loans, which usually lack documentation. (See descriptive box on page 91.)

The calculations of the Wallison/Calomiris estimates are shown in Table 4, below. The estimates are simply aggregations of amounts within the published financial statements of F&F.[1]

Wallison and Calomiris found that, during the years 2005 through 2007 there was an increase in F&F's percentage of loans with subprime characteristics, suggesting the possibility that they ramped up their high-risk loan purchases in the years just after their accounting scandals and just before the big financial meltdown.[2]

---

1 Peter J. Wallison and Charles Calomiris, "The Last Trillion-Dollar Commitment: The Destruction of Fannie Mae and Freddie Mac," (Washington, DC: American Enterprise Institute, September 2008), 7-8, www.aei.org.

2 Ibid., 7.

Table 4 – Wallison & Calomiris: High risk (subprime) single family loan as-sets held by Fannie and Freddie as of June 30, 2008

Entity→ Type of asset held at June 30, 2008	Fannie	Freddie	Total
Subprime or Alt-A loans held or guaranteed (esti-mated by using the 5 high-risk factors)	553	258	811
Private label subprime loans and/or securities backed by subprime loans (as reported by Fannie or Freddie)	66	134	200
Total (billions)	$619	$392	$1011

Dwight M. Jaffee (Haas School of Business) also noted the increase in subprime purchases. After reviewing credit supplements issued by Fannie and Freddie in 2009, he observed:

> ...for both GSEs [Fannie and Freddie] and for almost all years [2004-2007] and high-risk characteristics, rising shares are evident through to 2007.[1]

The percentages of GSE loan purchases with various subprime characteristics are shown in Table 5, below.

Table 5 – Wallison & Calomiris: Percentages of 2005-2007 loan acquisitions with subprime characteristics

Subprime characteristic	Fannie	Freddie
Negative loan amortization	62	72
Interest-only loans	84	90
FICO score less than 620	58	61
Loan-to-value ratio over 90%	62	58
Alt-A loans	73	78

The surge in subprime spending, reported by Wallison and Calomiris and Jaffee, was also noted by James Lockhart, director of the Federal Housing Finance Agency (a regulator of Fannie and Freddie since late, 2008). As reported in the Washington Post, Lockhart said:

> Fannie Mae and Freddie Mac purchased and guaranteed "many more low-documentation, low-verification and non-standard" mortgages in 2006

---

1 Financial Crisis Inquiry Commission, Statement of Dwight M. Jaffe, February 27, 2010, 10.

and 2007 "than they had in the past." He said the companies increased their exposure to risks in 2006 and 2007 despite the regulator's warnings.[1]

Other financial analysts (Evans and Jain) describe the important role of Fannie and Freddie with respect to the growth in subprime lending:

> The GSEs [Fannie and Freddie] became involved in the subprime market by changing the standards for qualifying mortgages and then purchasing and securitizing subprime MBSs.... These purchases of subprime mortgages by the GSEs freed the capital of subprime mortgage originators and allowed the originators to make additional subprime loans.[2]

As noted, Wallison and Calomiris attribute this subprime urge to the GSE accounting scandals that were exposed in 2003 and 2004:

> The central problem was their [Fannie's and Freddie's] dependence on Congress for continued political support in the wake of their accounting scandals in 2003 and 2004. To curry favor with Congress, they sought substantial increases in their support of affordable housing, primarily by investing in risky and substandard mortgages between 2005 and 2007.[3]

Some argue that profits motivated F&F to buy the subprime — not affordable housing. That seems to be the position of Standard & Poors:

> Fannie and Freddie dominated the MBS market until 2004, when they saw their market share plummet to about 40% from 70% in 2003, reflecting increased competition from privately issued securitizations. Consequently, in 2005-2006, Fannie and Freddie engaged in aggressive growth strategies in an attempt to regain market share and boost shareholder returns by purchasing large volumes of PLMBS [private label mortgage-backed securities] backed by assets such as *Alt-A and subprime* mortgages with higher loan-to-value or debt-to-income ratios (emphasis added).[4]

In his "Dissent from the Majority Report of the Financial Crisis Inquiry Commission," Peter Wallison strongly refutes the notion that Fannie and Freddie promoted subprime lending because it was profitable. First, he points out that "Fannie and Freddie exceeded the AH [affordable housing] goals virtually each year [1996 through 2008], but not by

---

1   Zachary A. Goldfarb, "Affordable-Housing Goals Scaled Back," The Washington Post (September 24, 2008), http://www.washingtonpost.com/wp-dyn/content/article/2008/09/23/AR2008092301718.html.

2   Elizabeth A. Evans and Sushrut Jain, "Understanding the Financial Crisis: A Look Back," (The Analysis Group, June 2010), 20.

3   Wallison and Charles Calomiris, "The Last Trillion-Dollar Commitment: The Destruction of Fannie Mae and Freddie Mac," 1.

4   "The FHFA's Proposed Plan for Fannie and Freddie Could Shrink the Mortgage Market," Standardandpoors.com (March 12, 2012), http://www.standardandpoors.com/ratings/articles/en/us/?articleType=HTML&asset ID=1245330742771.

---

significant margins."[1] If profits had been the main goal we would expect to see F&F exceed the goals substantially.

Wallison also quotes an internal Fannie Mae document that describes the difficulties *and costs* of its affordable housing acquisitions.

> In 2002, Fannie Mae exceeded all our goals for the 9th straight year. But it was probably the most challenging environment we've ever face. Meeting the goals required heroic 4th quarter efforts on the part of many across the company. Vacations were cancelled. The midnight oil burned. Moreover, the challenge freaked out the business side of the house. Especially because the tenseness around meeting the goals meant that we considered not doing deals — not fulfilling our liquidity function — *and did deals at risks and prices we would not have otherwise done* (emphasis added).[2]

Other documents cited by Wallison show that Fannie officials had serious concerns about the impact of affordable housing loans on the company's profits. These documents strongly suggest that affordable housing goals, and related subprime loan acquisitions, were not pursued by F&F for profits. However, it almost does not matter. Whether Fannie and Freddie acted out of fear of HUD regulators, fear of Congressional wrath, altruistic concern for poor Americans, greed, or the movements of a Ouija board, affordable housing was (at the very least) the excuse that could be used to justify their reckless subprime investments. Without the imprimatur of affordable housing, Fannie and Freddie could not have justified their risk-taking to government regulators.

What are Alt-A loans?

Some sources indicate that the term "Alt-A" is short for "Alternative A-paper," a type of mortgage loan that falls short of the standards of prime, or "A-paper." Others believe the term stands for "Alternative-documentation" loans. A third group thinks that "Alt-A" means "Alternative to agency," and refers to loans that do not meet the normal, legal standards of federal agencies, such as Fannie Mae.

The important thing to know is that these are garbage loans. They have little or no documentation to support the financial credit claims of the borrower, or they have some other feature that does not meet traditional underwriting standards. For example, Alt-A loans might start with low, "teaser" rates, or have excessively high loan-to-value ratios (too much loan in proportion to the value of the house). They are also known as stated loans, "liar loans," and no-doc loans.

Fannie and Freddie liked to distinguish subprime loans from Alt-A loans, as if to imply Alt-A loans are better than subprime loans. In fact,

---

1   Peter J. Wallison, "Dissent from the Majority Report of the Financial Crisis Inquiry Commission," (Washington, DC: American Enterprise Institute, January 2011), 70, www.aei.org.

2   Ibid., 72.

Alt-A loans are often much worse! In 1991, the Wall Street Journal reported this statement made by Angelo Mozilo, Ex-Chairman of Countrywide Financial Corp:

> At one time, I was a prophet of low-doc [Alt-A]. The problem is that it went much too far. Human beings are basically rotten. If you give them an opportunity to screw up, they will.[1]

I would argue that it is not simply a matter of people screwing up. Many of the people getting Alt-A loans were simply scoundrels who got loans by using lies and deception.

At the end of 2011, the Securities and Exchange Commission charged 6 former executives of Fannie and Freddie with securities fraud for concealing the amount of their subprime loan purchases. It was alleged that many subprime loans were hidden by the two GSEs within the Alt-A classification.

F&F's subprime purchases — per Edward Pinto

In December 2008, Edward J. Pinto, Executive Vice President and Chief Credit Officer of Fannie Mae (1987-89), gave testimony before a U.S. House of Representatives Committee on Oversight and Government Reform. After introducing himself and thanking Chairman Henry Waxman for the opportunity to testify, Mr. Pinto gave extensive and detailed testimony that established clearly the leading role played by Fannie and Freddie in the subprime lending crisis:

> Fannie Mae and Freddie Mac played multiple roles in what has come to be known as the subprime lending crisis.

> Fannie and Freddie went from being the watchdogs of credit standards and thoughtful innovators ... to the leaders in default prone loans and poorly designed products. They introduced mortgages which encouraged and extended the housing bubble, trapped millions of people in loans that they knew were unsustainable, and destroyed the equity savings of tens of millions of Americans.[2]

According to Mr. Pinto, Fannie and Freddie "adopted accounting practices that masked their subprime and Alt-A lending." In fact, Fannie and Freddie engaged in an orgy of junk loan buying.

Pinto developed a list of 7 factors that he used to separate risky from less risky loans. His list of high-risk factors is the same as the list used by Wallison and Calomiris, with two additional factors: loans to borrowers with FICO scores between 620 and 660, and loans with combined LTV greater than 90 percent. The combined LTV reflects the ratio of primary and secondary loans (such as home equity loans) to the house value.

1   Statement of Edward Pinto, Attachment 4, page 4.
2   Ibid., 3.

The inclusion of loans to borrowers with FICO scores between 620 and 660 is somewhat controversial because, all other factors being equal, such loans perform better than loans to borrowers with FICO scores below 620. However, there is authoritative support for using 660 as the demarcation between prime and subprime. As noted by Pinto:

> In 2001 federal regulators issued "Expanded Guidance for Subprime Lending Programs," which set forth a number of credit characteristics for subprime borrowers including: "Relatively high default probability as evidenced by, for example, a credit bureau risk score (FICO) of 660 or below (depending on the product/collateral).[1]

The other extra factor used by Pinto — the inclusion of loans that, in combination with secondary loans, exceed 90 percent of house value — is important for an accurate estimation of subprime loan purchases, and this has been acknowledged by Fannie:

> Although only 10% of our conventional single-family mortgage credit book of business had an original average LTV ratio greater than 90% as of December 31, 2007, we estimate that 15% of our conventional single-family mortgage credit book of business had an original *combined* average LTV ratio greater than 90%. The combined LTV ratio takes into account the combined amount of both the primary and second lien financing on the property. Second lien financing on a property increases the level of credit risk... (emphasis added).[2]

Pinto's estimate of total high-risk (i.e., subprime) loans as of June 30, 2008, is presented in Table 6, below. After reviewing his sourcing, calculations, and assumptions, I find nothing inaccurate or unreasonable in Pinto's work.[3]

Table 6 – Edward Pinto: Estimate of high-risk (subprime) loans as of June 30, 2008

Unit used →	$ in billions		# in millions	
Entity →	Fannie	Freddie	Fannie	Freddie
Private subprime MBS	36	82	.235	.535
Private Alt-A MBS	30	41	.175	.233
Loans with high-risk characteristics	1011	635	6.616	4.155
Totals	1077	758	7.026	4.923
Grand totals	$1835		11.949	

1   Edward Pinto, "Government Housing Policies in the Lead-up to the Financial Crisis: A Forensic Study," (Washington, DC: American Enterprise Institute, October 11, 2010), Memorandum 3, p.1.
2   Ibid., Memorandum 2, p.6.
3   Ibid., Memorandum 2, p.4-9.

As we see in Table 6, Pinto estimated that Fannie and Freddie held nearly 12 million junk loans as of June 30, 2008, with a face value of $1.835 trillion. By number, this was nearly half of all subprime loans outstanding in the United States. If we factor in the subprime loans held by FHA, the U.S. federal government had its fingers in well over half of all nonprime loans, according to Ed Pinto.

Although the Pinto estimates are huge, they may not be high enough. In late 2011, the SEC offered its own estimates of subprime loans (numbers and dollar amounts). Its figures, which are even higher than the Pinto amounts, are presented at the end of this chapter.

F&F paid top dollar for subprime

The acquisitions of Fannie and Freddie (F&F), entities that had the government's "Good Housekeeping" seal of approval, created an enormous demand for junk loans, and stimulated the production of subprime loans in every nook and cranny of the loan industry. Lenders and investment banks could not help but notice that the two biggest buyers in town were looking for a subprime "high." In 2008, Howard Husock related: "One chief executive of a significant New York bank recently told me that Fannie Mae 'scooped up' all of the CRA [Community Reinvestment Act] loans he originated."[1] And, Wallison and Calomiris noted:

> ...in 2004, when Fannie and Freddie began to increase significantly their commitment to affordable housing loans, they found it easy to stimulate production in the private sector by letting it be known in the market that they would gladly accept loans that would otherwise be considered subprime.[2]

By 2004, the affordable housing goals established for Fannie and Freddie were heating up the housing market to such a degree that even realtors were concerned. When HUD proposed to increase the affordable housing goals for 2005 through 2008, the National Association of Realtors formally protested, saying that it was "vitally concerned" that the goals were "too optimistic," and that the "aggressive goals and subgoals may cause the GSEs [Fannie and Freddie] to take actions that will distort mortgage markets...." The organization noted that "Goals that are set too high can be just as damaging as goals that are set too low."[3] And, it stated:

---

1   Howard Husock, "The Financial Crisis and the CRA," City Journal (October 30, 2008), http://www.city-journal.org/2008/eon1030hh.html.

2   Wallison and Charles Calomiris, "The Last Trillion-Dollar Commitment: The Destruction of Fannie Mae and Freddie Mac."

3   "Proposed Housing Goals for Fannie Mae and Freddie Mac for 2005-2008," ed. Housing and Urban Development (U.S. Government, July 15, 2004).

Increases in housing prices have exceeded income growth in the past few years, interest rates are on the rise and rental markets are soft. The credit scores of renters have declined significantly over time, reducing the number of qualified buyers.[1]

Imagine. Realtors, not exactly known for fiscal prudence and definitely not known for turning away business, were trying to get the government to cool it with regard to affordable housings. Why? They were concerned that the affordable housing goals were unsustainable, and that the overheated market could collapse. Now, after the fan has been hit, the government and its supporters want to put all blame for the crisis on private enterprise. Remarkable!

Fannie and Freddie also signaled their interest in subprime by the high price they were willing to pay for it. In testimony before the Congressional Financial Crisis Inquiry Commission (April 7, 2010) Former Federal Reserve Chief Alan Greenspan made note of the crucial role played by Fannie and Freddie in the subprime mortgage crisis, and their willingness to pay premium amounts to buy massive quantities of subprime:

> Of far greater importance to the surge in demand, the major U.S. government sponsored enterprises (GSEs), Fannie Mae and Freddie Mac, pressed by the U.S. Department of Housing and Urban Development and the Congress to expand "affordable housing commitments," chose to meet them in a wholesale fashion by investing heavily in subprime mortgage-backed securities. The firms purchased an estimated 40% of all private-label subprime mortgage securities....

> To purchase these mortgage-backed securities, Fannie and Freddie paid *whatever price was necessary to reach their affordable housing goals.* The effect was to preempt 40% of the market up front, leaving the remaining 60% to fill other domestic and foreign investor demand. Mortgage yields fell ... exacerbating the house price rise ... (emphasis added).[2]

If government-backed entities are willing to buy millions of junk loans, and to pay top dollar for them, we should not be surprised when the private lending community supplies those loans. Given the reckless actions of Fannie and Freddie, we can only conclude, as Edward Pinto did, that "this was not a failure of the free market. It is a failure of Congress and the ill-conceived regulatory regime it implemented."[3]

---

1   Ibid.
2   Financial Crisis Inquiry Commission, Testimony of Alan Greenspan, April 7, 2010, 3-4.
3   Statement of Edward Pinto, 13.

Purchases of subprime were leveraged

Although most of their subprime investment was in the form of loans they bought to hold in portfolio or to securitize and sell, Fannie and Freddie also purchased subprime in the form of privately-created mortgage-backed securities (MBS). This was an activity that was officially sanctioned by the government starting in 1995. Although the amounts invested in private subprime MBS seem relatively small, the impact was huge, due to the concept of leverage.

If you want to maximize the impact of a charitable contribution, you might offer to match the contributions of others. That way, every dollar you donate would lead to two dollars of charity. In effect, you would be leveraging your contribution. Likewise, Fannie and Freddie leveraged their subprime investments by purchasing the upper tranches of subprime loan securitizations. A tranche is a portion of a security with a specific risk level. An upper-level tranche generally has less risk because it has a first lien on the underlying pool of assets. On the other hand, lower tranche levels have second liens or no liens at all and are, therefore, more risky. Figure 11 illustrates a pool of mortgage loans that happens to be divided into 8 equal-sized parts (tranches), each with a different investment rating to reflect the difference in risk. The upper-level tranche (AAA) is the least risky.

Figure 11 – Illustration of Tranches for a Pool of Mortgage Loans

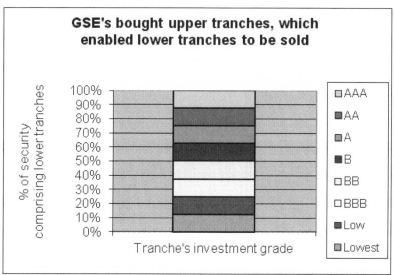

Generally, Fannie and Freddie bought massive amounts of the upper-level tranches of mortgage loan pools — more than anyone else. F&F supporters argue that their purchase of upper tranches, as opposed to lower tranches, is evidence of their investment prudence. But this was about as prudent — and safe — as buying the upper cuts of meat from a steer with mad cow disease. Ultimately, the whole cow dies and even the prime cuts are unsafe to eat. Further, by purchasing only part of each mortgage pool, Fannie and Freddie made matters worse because every one of the dollars they invested in an AAA tranche enabled securitizers to obtain several more dollars (from other investors) for the lower, cheaper, and riskier subprime tranches. This leveraging, done on a huge scale, made the whole securitization process work, and it led to a grand promotion of subprime. As noted by economists Peter Wallison and Charles Calomiris:

> Without their commitment to purchase the AAA tranches of these securitizations, it is unlikely that the pools could have been formed and marketed around the world.[1]

The Fannie and Freddie apologists and their logic errors

It should now be clear to everyone — even Nobel Laureates — that the balance sheets of Fannie and Freddie were loaded with subprime loans and investments — purchased for top-dollar prices. This is obvious because the federal government's F&F bailout costs have already exceeded $300 billion, by CBO estimates.[2] If F&F only bought "mortgages issued to borrowers who made substantial down payments and carefully documented their income," no bailout of these entities would be needed.[3]

Nevertheless, many on the political left and in the mainstream press cling to the belief that Fannie and Freddie had a marginal and belated role in the explosion of subprime lending that lead up to the mortgage crisis. Some, like Paul Krugman, state that Fannie and Freddie didn't buy

---

1   ———, "The Last Trillion-Dollar Commitment: The Destruction of Fannie Mae and Freddie Mac."

2   Bailout payments to Fannie and Freddie totaled about $169 billion as of August 2011; however, that was the White House estimate. The Congressional Budget Office estimated, in June 2011, that the complete bailout was about $317 billion. It calculated that amount by adding the fair value deficit of the GSEs to $130 billion, which was the total of bailout payments at the time. The fair value deficit reflects the amount of GSE debt and debt guarantees after subtracting the value of their assets.

3   Paul Krugman, "Fannie, Freddie and You," The New York Times (July 14, 2008), http://www.nytimes.com/2008/07/14/opinion/14krugman.html.

subprime because they weren't allowed to. This silly argument is particularly specious in view of the documented fact that Fannie and Freddie were quite capable of ignoring the law, accounting principles, and
prudent disclosure rules. They were proven to have done so in 2003 and
2004.

Other supporters of Fannie and Freddie were, undoubtedly, deceived
by the way they reported their subprime investments. Whoops! They accidentally put them in the "prime" category. As noted by ex-Fannie Chief
Credit Officer Edward Pinto:

> [Subprime loans were] "carried in databases as prime loans when they
> were purchased by Fannie and Freddie, which conveniently allowed them
> to deny that they were active in the subprime market."[1]

Some of their proponents acknowledge that Fannie and Freddie
bought subprime, but argue that this subprime was purchased belatedly,
and only when necessitated by competitive pressures from the private
sector. This misconception is understandable, given that Fannie and
Freddie were especially assiduous in concealing their early subprime
purchases. In 2002 and 2003 Fannie and Freddie acknowledged making
(combined) subprime purchases of $120 billion. However, according to
Dwight Jaffee of the University of California at Berkeley, in those two
years Fannie and Freddie really bought $761 billion of high-risk loans and
investments that were, essentially, subprime (i.e., had the characteristics
of subprime).[2] It wasn't until much later that Fannie finally started to
come clean. In his testimony to the Financial Crisis Inquiry Commission,
Alan Greenspan noted when it happened:

> The enormous size of purchases by the GSEs [Fannie and Freddie] in
> 2003-2004 was not revealed until Fannie Mae in September 2009 reclassi-
> fied a large part of its securities portfolio of prime mortgages as subprime.[3]

People have also been misled because, in the early years of the financial
crisis, F&F manipulated their loan delinquency rates. This made their
early loan investments appear to be of superior creditworthiness. (See
Chapter 5 for a detailed explanation of this delinquency rate deception.)

Based on a year-by-year analysis of subprime purchases, Ed Pinto noted that F&F were leaders — not followers — when it came to subprime:

> The above analysis makes it clear that the GSEs' subprime acquisitions
> exceeded subprime PMBS [private mortgage-backed security] issuanc-

1   Statement of Edward Pinto, 3.
2   Statement of Dwight M. Jaffe, 10, Table 2.
3   Testimony of Alan Greenspan.

es and that their dominance predates the dramatic rise of the subprime PMBS market in 2004.[1]

Another common error made by F&F supporters 81 the one discussed on page 78. (See the analogy involving "Fannie's Pharmaceuticals.") Some people erroneously believe F&F did not buy subprime loans, and as evidence they cite the overall delinquency rates of Fannie and Freddie, which were much lower than the rates of private entities that specialized in subprime. The logic error they make is to use the overall, company-wide delinquency rates. For decades, Fannie and Freddie have had a corner on prime, safe, fixed-rate mortgage loans. Due to their size and government support they dominated that market, and continue to do so. No one claimed that Fannie and Freddie converted all of their prime loans to subprime. That would be absurd. The complaint is that, starting in the mid-1990s, they ventured into new and risky product lines. Whatever their motivations, they used affordable housing as a justification for these dangerous new products, and those new products have high default rates. That is why taxpayers are being asked to give billions to Fannie and Freddie.

Last but not least, you will find F&F apologists who proudly point out that Fannie and Freddie bought only the upper (AAA) tranches of subprime securitizations. As noted, this is true, but no less damning. By purchasing only part of each tranche, the efforts of Fannie and Freddie were leveraged because every dollar they invested in an AAA tranche enabled the securitizers to obtain several more dollars (from other investors) for the lower tranches. F&F's purchases were essential to making the whole subprime securitization process work.

Ed Pinto: A man completely vindicated

Ed Pinto, former Chief Credit Officer for Fannie Mae (1987-89), has been a one-man wrecking crew — obliterating many of the fallacies put forth by defenders of Fannie, Freddie, CRA, and government lending programs in general. Mr. Pinto recognized that existing estimates of GSE subprime investing were understated. He created a truer estimate by identifying loans with features generally reserved for borrowers with impaired credit. As a veteran accountant and financial auditor, I find Pinto's thought process and analytical procedures to be entirely reason-

---

1   "The GSE Report," in Fannie Mae and Freddie Mac (Canfield & Associates, October 26, 2009).

able, and highly insightful. However, his methodology has received much criticism.

In early 2011, the left-leaning Center for American Progress published a lengthy analysis of Mr. Pinto's work, and it was not very kind. The study, called "Faulty Conclusions Based on Shoddy Foundations," seemed to rely on hyperbole and name dropping more than logical analysis. The Center's number one complaint can be summarized in a word montage:

> Mr. Pinto used a "radically revised" definition of subprime — "not consistent with how the terms subprime and Alt-A are used for data collection." His definitions are "not used by other scholars" and his opinions are "far afield of the conclusions of other analysts." The "misleading data peddled by Pinto" leads to "counterproductive solutions," and his "newly invented definitions are totally inconsistent with how the terms 'subprime' and 'Alt-A' are used in any research." His terms are "not used by any other analysts."[1]

As you can see, the basic complaint was that Pinto didn't use the same definition of "subprime" used by "other analysts." What is the proper definition of "subprime"? In its analysis, the Center defined it as "actual" subprime" — without further clarification. Pinto's definition of subprime should have been the *actual* one. Is that clear?

I doubt Pinto felt intellectually challenged by the Center's critique, or by their suggestion that his estimate of the subprime and Alt-A loans held by Fannie and Freddie was 5 *times too high*. If he did, however, Pinto could take solace in an event that occurred just a few months later. In December 2011 the SEC charged several Fannie and Freddie ex-officers with securities fraud for concealing their subprime and Alt-A loan purchases — presumably, the "actual" ones. How did the executives conceal the bad loans? They did it precisely as determined by Ed Pinto: by misclassifying subprime and Alt-A loans into other, more benign-sounding categories.

To be fair, the SEC's estimate of subprime was not the identical to Pinto's: It was even higher. Whereas Pinto had estimated that Fannie and Freddie held (at 6/30/08) about 12 million subprime and Alt-A loans with a face value of $1.8 trillion, the SEC estimated that the duo held over 13 million such loans with a value over $2 trillion.[2]

---

1 Quotations are from David Min, "Faulty Conclusions Based on Shoddy Foundations," Center for American Progress (February 2011), http://www.americanprogress.org/issues/2011/02/pdf/pinto.pdf.

2 Peter J. Wallison and Edward Pinto, "Why the Left Is Losing the Argument over the Financial Crisis," (Washington, DC: American

Perhaps the Center for American Progress will issue a critique of the "Faulty Conclusions" of the Securities and Exchange Commission. We're waiting.

Enterprise Institute, December 27, 2011), http://www.aei.org/article/why-the-left-is-losing-the-argument-over-the-financial-crisis/.

CHAPTER 7: MORE SUBPRIME PROMOTION BY FANNIE AND FREDDIE

> ...Congress does not simply expect the GSEs [Fannie and Freddie] to strive toward achievement of these purposes [the affordable housing mission] but rather to lead the mortgage finance industry ...
>
> – HUD in 2004 (as quoted and emphasized by Fed Chairman Bernanke on March 6, 2007)

With respect to subprime lending, Fannie and Freddie did what HUD demanded: They led the mortgage loan industry. They decimated underwriting standards with their automated systems, which they pushed on big and small lenders throughout the industry (Chapter 2). Fannie and Freddie created "drive-by" appraisals with their automated appraisal software programs (Chapter 3). Along with FHA, they purchased more than half (by number) of all subprime loans or investments backed by subprime loans. This dramatically drove up the price of subprime loans and stimulated enormous demand, industry-wide (Chapter 6).

In this chapter we outline seven other ways that subprime lending was advanced by Fannie and Freddie:

- Promoting the growth of thousands of fly-by-night mortgage brokers.
- Giving preferential treatment to subprime aggregators, such as Countrywide.
- Cheerleading, and signaling their desire to buy large amounts of subprime.

- Designing the reckless products offered by private lenders.
- Misleading the loan industry by concealing past subprime purchases.
- Expanding the definition of "conforming loan" to include subprime loans.
- Fighting against laws designed to curb predatory lending.

Each of these subprime actions is discussed below.

Fannie and Freddie promoted brokers over banks

> ...mortgage brokers are bottom feeding scum. Completely useless profession that did nothing positive this decade. And before someone calls me a jerk or something, answer me this question: "How come some guy from my high school who dropped out, has a cocaine problem, and sold cars before getting into mortgage was able to become a mortgage broker?"
>
> – Blogger with the handle "Bobarty"[1]

This is the single factor that may be most responsible for the subprime mortgage crisis. In the years preceding the financial crisis. Fannie and Freddie promoted small, thinly capitalized mom and pop mortgage brokers over regulated community banks. Some mainstream bankers alleged that F&F did this even though they knew, no later than 1999, that 65 percent of fraud cases related to loans produced by these third party brokers, and the majority of those fraud cases related to *defective loans*.[2] For reasons that possibly involved profit, diversity, and/or affordable housing, Fannie and Freddie made a conscious effort to promote the very entities that would ultimately be most associated with subprime and predatory lending.

If there was a love affair between F&F and the mortgage brokers, it probably started in the mid-1990s with the rollout of the automated underwriting systems. As noted in Chapter 2, "the online technology, provided for a modest fee ... quietly fragmented the lending business and shifted power to brokers by allowing them to perform some of the services once provided exclusively by banks." In 2001 the Wall Street Journal reported that the underwriting software was "made available to *thousands* of mortgage brokers" and made these "brokers and other small players a threat to larger banks" (emphasis added).[3]

---

1 Bobarty, Orange County Register, July 21, 2008, http://mortgage.ocregister.com/2008/07/21/wachovia-says-bye-bye-to-mortgage-brokers/1261/.
2 Statement of Edward Pinto, Attachment 10.
3 Barta, "Why Big Lenders Are So Afraid of Fannie Mae and Freddie Mac."

This excerpt from the October 19, 2001 "GSE Report" makes it clear that, by 2001, Fannie and Freddie ("the GSEs") had already made a multi-year effort to automate the small brokers:

> "...it is not surprising that both the GSEs would become more actively involved in broker originations," said Joseph Falk, the President of the National Association of Mortgage Brokers, noting that over the past few years, they have promoted their technology at mortgage broker conventions.[1]

Freddie's Loan Prospector automated system was already in the hands of "7,000 mortgage broker companies representing 20,000 total users...." That was no later than March of 2000, according to Leland Brendsel, Freddie's CEO.

In the opinion of some anonymous industry veterans, interviewed in 2001 by the Wall Street Journal, F&F were plotting to grab business from banks:

> According to this scenario, Fannie and Freddie would in effect become lenders themselves, relying on an army of brokers and small mortgage companies — some of them operating online — as field agents [of Fannie and Freddie].[2]

Holding loans in portfolio was particularly profitable for Fannie and Freddie, but many banks had resisted selling their mortgage loans to them. On the other hand, "brokers armed with automated-underwriting software" could sell loans directly to F&F, thereby "cutting banks out of the loan-making business." That would make it easier for F&F "to feed their huge appetites for loans."[3]

If that was the original business growth plan for F&F, it was ultimately changed to incorporate intermediaries that aggregated the broker loans and then sold them in bulk to Fannie and Freddie and the large investment banks. For the most part, those aggregators, such as Countrywide, Indy Mac, and Washington Mutual, were the ones who directly dealt with the sleazy brokers. Except for this added twist, the bankers interviewed by the Wall Street Journal may have been right. F&F promoted small brokers and made them a threat to larger banks, many of which were rock-solid community banks that didn't do subprime.

The motivation of Fannie and Freddie in these matters was not necessarily related entirely to profit: There were social and political factors as well. In early 2000, Leland Brendsel, Freddie's CEO at the time, ex-

---

1   "The GSE Report," in Fannie Mae and Freddie Mac (Canfield & Associates, October 19, 2001).
2   ———, "Why Big Lenders Are So Afraid of Fannie Mae and Freddie Mac."
3   Ibid.

plained why Freddie used automated underwriting to boost the small lender, relative to larger banks. This would "play to the strength of lenders who [were] already out there in the community." He noted that Freddie was experimenting with subprime products in order to give more people access to credit and to expand home ownership rates beyond the mainstream. "Home ownership rates for African Americans and Hispanics are significantly lower than those for whites," he said. "There are a lot of people who are not homeowners because they are not getting the kind of service or access to financial products that they need."[1] In short, it was thought that the little brokers might reach some of the disadvantaged people, missed by banks, "out there in the community."

Like Freddie, Fannie used small lenders to encourage lending diversity. For example, in 2002, Fannie gave its support to a small lender in an effort to encourage homeownership among the growing U.S. Muslim population (per Kelly Zito, San Francisco Chronicle):

> ...Fannie recently agreed to purchase $10 million worth of home loans from Lariba, a small lender in Southern California. Lariba lends money for homes and cars based on Islamic religious principles that prohibit the collection of interest.[2]

Now, there is a great business model! Give loans to people who don't believe in paying interest.[3]

For the purpose of diversity, the GSEs (Fannie and Freddie) also tried to recruit minority-owned businesses to serve as their loan originators. As early as 1996, a major effort was being made in this regard, according to James A Johnson, Fannie's CEO at the time:

> In the last two years, Fannie Mae has conducted a nationwide search to locate minority-owned mortgage lenders and make each of them a Fannie Mae seller-servicer, which means they can sell loans to Fannie Mae and will be authorized to service those loans. We have almost doubled the number of minority-owned seller-servicers. We are now talking or working with every minority-owned lender in the United States....[4]

---

1   James R. Peterson, "Leland Brendsel: "The Tide Is Turning toward the Small Lender"," AllBusiness.com (July 1, 2000), http://www.allbusiness.com/finance/475685-1.html#ixzz1YdTdk9Qq.

2   Kelly Zito, "Leland Brendsel: "The Tide Is Turning toward the Small Lender"," SFGate.com (December 15, 2002), http://articles.sfgate.com/2002-12-15/real-estate/17574263_1_home-loans-muslim-yahia-abdul-rahman.

3   This is not an attempt to blame Muslims for the subprime loan crisis. It is merely an example of the kind of goofy rationale Fannie used to justify support for the small lender vs. the larger bank.

4   James A. Johnson, Showing America a New Way Home (San Francisco: Josey-Bass Publishers, 1996), 109.

Of course, there were and are many reputable mortgage brokers, and I personally knew some of them — before they went out of business. But, after the introduction of F&F's easy automated underwriting systems (and, subsequently, the automated systems of private lenders), thousands of additional brokers seemed to materialize — almost overnight. At the peak of the housing boom there were as many as 75,000 small mortgage banks and brokers, across the United States.[1] As noted earlier in the chapter, many of these were inexperienced fly-by-night outfits, engaged in predatory lending. They preyed on friends, neighbors, and less sophisticated subprime borrowers. In addition, several studies show that "mortgage brokers originated the vast majority of subprime loans..." and other studies have found that delinquency rates for subprime loans could be "20 time higher than the rate for prime conventional loans."[2][3] Putting these facts together, it is clear that the small mortgage broker — the kind promoted by F&F and others — was at the epicenter of the subprime mortgage crisis.

Brokers were regulated by the individual states, but that was like no regulation at all, as noted by Paul Muolo and Mathew Padilla in their book, *Chain of Blame*:

> When Dan Perl and Bill Ashmore became brokers, they could get by with a Realtor's license. By 2006 all states required individual loan brokers (a flesh-and-blood loan officer) to be licensed or registered — but that didn't mean they were regulated. Unlike banks and S&Ls, which took federally insured deposits from the public and were regulated by the Federal Deposit Insurance Corporation, Federal Reserve, or another agency, mortgage brokers reported to no one. They had no regulator.[4]

More investigation is needed to determine the accuracy of the allegations about Fannie and Freddie (F&F), made by some bankers. Did F&F deliberately promote small brokerages to gain a competitive advantage over banks? Did they do it despite knowing of the credit default risks to themselves and, ultimately, to taxpayers?

---

1   Zandi, Financial Shock : A 360* Look at the Subprime Mortgage Implosion, and How to Avoid the Next Financial Crisis, 98.
2   Financial Crisis Inquiry Commission, Testimony of Julia Gordon, Center for Responsible Lending, January 13, 2010.
3   Joint Center for Housing Studies, "Credit, Capital and Communities: The Implications of the Changing Mortgage Banking Industry for Community Based Organizations," (Boston: Harvard University, March 9, 2004).
4   Paul Muolo and Mathew Padilla, Chain of Blame : How Wall Street Caused the Mortgage and Credit Crisis (Hoboken, N.J.: John Wiley & Sons, 2008), 67.

They got cozy with subprime aggregators

> It didn't take long for Jim Johnson [Fannie's CEO] to re-
> alize that Mozilo "was the guy," said one of Johnson's aides.
> "Jim knew that he had to do everything he could to make An-
> gelo think, 'I'm his best friend.'" If Jim was traveling to the
> West Coast he'd say, "We need to call Angelo and set up a
> golf game."[1]

As noted, Fannie and Freddie actively promoted thousands of small, lightly capitalized mortgage brokers by means of their automated under-writing and appraisal systems. When it came to purchasing the loans, however, Fannie and Freddie preferred to deal with larger companies that would fund and aggregate the many loans originated by the small brokers. Fannie dealt with many aggregators but the main one was Countrywide, a company reported to have financed 20 percent of all mortgages in the United States in 2006.

As early as 1984, Countrywide started funding the mortgage loans brought to it by freelance brokers. The brokers had no assets to guaran-tee these loans, and neither did Countrywide, so it used a line of credit to fund the loans. Nevertheless, Fannie Mae eagerly bought as many Coun-trywide loans as it could. When Jim Johnson became Fannie's new CEO, in 1991, he was pleased to see the high volume of profitable loans coming to Fannie by way of Countrywide, and he wanted to cement the relation-ship between the two companies by becoming the best friend of Angelo Mozilo, Countrywide's CEO. Johnson "wanted Countrywide to sell all, or at least most, of its billions in loan originations to Fannie Mae...."[2]

The cozy relationship between Fannie and the subprime king, Coun-trywide, is described in *Chain of Blame*, by Muolo and Padilla: "Over the next 15 years Countrywide and Fannie Mae — Mozilo and Johnson and then Mozilo and Franklin Raines, Johnson's successor — would be linked at the hip."[3] Fannie executives frequently flew on the Countrywide cor-porate jet, Mozilo attended retreats with Fannie's leadership, there was golfing and concerts together. It was a love affair that only grew stronger as Countrywide became the nation's leading subprime lender.

Depending on the year, up to 30 Percent of Fannie's loans came from Countrywide, and Fannie was so grateful that it rewarded Countrywide with sweetheart terms — better than those offered to real (solid and rep-utable) banks. According to Muolo and Padilla, Fannie normally charged

---

1   Ibid., 112.
2   Ibid.
3   Ibid., 113.

a loan guarantee fee of .23 percent to lenders from whom it bought loans. For Mozilo's company, however, that fee was reported to be as low as .13 percent.[1]

Of course, Freddie played the same game. According to Edward Pinto, the former Fannie Mae officer, "Fannie and Freddie offered its best pricing to its largest (and riskiest) customers (i.e.., Countrywide, Indy Mac) while offering much worse pricing to customers [such as] community banks, with proven track records of delivering high quality loans done the traditional way."[2] Indeed, Fannie and Freddie had close working relationships with a who's who list of subprime lenders, including Ameriquest, New Century Financial Corp., Option One mortgage Corp., Wachovia, Chase Home Finance, HSBC Finance Corp., and others. The bottom line is this: Many of the largest subprime lenders, who were generally aggregators of loans originated by small brokers, could not have expanded and prospered, or even existed, without tremendous support from Fannie and Freddie. Their willingness to buy subprime loans at favorable prices was crucial. Angelo Mozilo certainly thought so. He once commented that "If Fannie and Freddie catch a cold, I catch the fucking flu."[3]

They were cheerleaders for subprime

> The ripple effect of Fannie's plunge into riskier lending was profound. Fannie's stamp of approval made shunned borrowers and complex loans more acceptable to other lenders, particularly small and less sophisticated banks.
>
> – The New York Times[4]

Years before the subprime mortgage crisis erupted, F&F were promoting subprime lending — industry wide. In 1997, Matt Miller, a Director of Single-Family Affordable Lending at Freddie Mac, addressed private lenders at an Affordable Housing Symposium. He said that Freddie could usually find a way to buy and securitize their affordable housing loans "through the use of Loan Prospector research and *creative credit* enhancements ... (emphasis added)." Then, Mr. Miller added: "But what can

---

1   Ibid., 13.
2   Statement of Edward Pinto, 12.
3   Muolo and Padilla, Chain of Blame : How Wall Street Caused the Mortgage and Credit Crisis, 114.
4   Charles Duhigg, "Pressured to Take More Risk, Fannie Reached Tipping Point," The New York Times (October 5, 2008), http://www.nytimes.com/2008/10/05/business/05fannie.html?pagewanted=all.

you do if after all this analysis the product you are holding is not up to the standards of the conventional secondary market?"[1] [In other words, what if Freddie can't legally buy the loans — even after putting lipstick on them with Loan Prospector?]

Matt Miller had a solution: Freddie would work with "several firms" in an effort to find buyers for these extra-smelly loans. These flunky firms would, at the behest of Freddie, buy the garbage loans that were so bad they could not be called, "conforming."

In 1999, the New York Times reported this effort by Fannie to promote the subprime loan industry:

> In a move that could help increase home ownership rates among minorities and low-income consumers, the Fannie Mae Corporation is easing the credit requirements on loans that it will purchase from banks and other lenders.
>
> The action, which will begin as a pilot program involving 24 banks in 15 markets — including the New York metropolitan region — will encourage those banks to extend home mortgages to individuals whose *credit is generally not good enough to quality for conventional loans.* Fannie Mae official say they hope to make it a nationwide program by next spring (emphasis added).[2]

Question: If quasi governmental entities signal that they want to buy sub-standard loans, should we be surprised when private companies rush to supply those substandard loans? It is sort of like the "Cash for Clunkers" program. When the government signaled that it would pay people if they traded-in worthless automobiles, that is exactly what people did. If we eventually decide that Cash for Clunkers was a bad program that hurt the economy, should we blame the former clunker-owners — or the government that pushed the program?

The New York Times's prophecy

> While reporting in 1999 about the new Fannie Mae program for credit-impaired borrowers, New York Times columnist, Steven A. Holmes, made this prophetic prediction: "In moving, even tentatively, into this new area of lending, Fannie Mae is taking on significantly more risk, which may not pose any difficulties during flush economic times. But the government-subsidized corporation may run into trouble

---

1   Matt Miller, "A National Symposium," in The Single-Family Affordable Housing Market: Trends and Innovations (Washington, DC: Office of the Comptroller of the Currency, July 23, 1997).

2   Steven A. Holmes, "Fannie, Freddie Mae Eases Credit to Aid Mortgage Lending," The New York Times (September 30, 1999), http://www.nytimes.com/1999/09/30/business/fannie-mae-eases-credit-to-aid-mortgage-lending.html.

in an economic downturn, prompting a government rescue similar to that of the savings and loan industry in the 1980s."[1]

In a speech given at a mortgage bankers convention in late 2004, Fannie's CEO, Franklin Raines advised the lenders that they "need to learn the best from the subprime market and bring the best from the prime market into [that market]." He added: "We have to push products and opportunities to people who have lesser credit quality," and he praised subprime lenders as "some of the best marketers in financial services."[2] More subprime accolades came from the then-CEO of Freddie, Richard Syron. He stated that Freddie was redesigning its A-minus products to target families in the subprime market.[3] These words made it clear that Fannie and Freddie approved of subprime loans, whether purchased by themselves of private investment banks.

More blunt subprime advocacy came from Daniel Mudd, Ex-President and CEO of Fannie Mae. At an industry mortgage lending conference, in 2006, Mudd gave this amazing advice: "Don't reflexively ask about credit problems." This, according to Mudd, was a step "to advance diversity and fairness...."[4]

According to Peter Wallison and Charles Calomiris, Fannie and Freddie "found it easy to stimulate production in the private sector by letting it be known in the market that they would gladly accept loans that would otherwise be considered subprime," and it is likely that the "huge increase in commitments to junk lending was largely the result of signals from Fannie and Freddie that they were ready to buy these loans in bulk."[5] As reported in Mortgage Banking, "The top executives of Freddie Mac and Fannie Mae made no bones about their interest in buying loans made to borrowers formerly considered the province of nonprime and other niche lenders."[6]

---

1   Ibid.
2   Neil J. Morse, "Looking for New Customers," AllBusiness.com (December 1, 2004), http://www.allbusiness.com/sales/customer-service/299226-1.html.
3   Ibid.
4   Daniel H. Mudd, "Mortgage Lending Industry Diversity and Emerging Markets Conference," (Arlington, VA: Fannie Mae, September 28, 2006), http://www.fanniemae.com/media/speeches.
5   Wallison and Charles Calomiris, "The Last Trillion-Dollar Commitment: The Destruction of Fannie Mae and Freddie Mac."
6   Morse, "Looking for New Customers."

F&F designed the subprime loans of private lenders

> Fannie Mae's suite of Community Lending mortgage products and options are designed to help borrowers overcome the two primary barriers to homeownership — lack of down payment funds and qualifying income.
>
> – Fannie Mae, 2000[1]

Many apologists for F&F like to say that the duo was reluctantly dragged into the subprime market, in an effort to stay competitive with private lenders. In fact, the opposite is true: In their zeal to meet multi-trillion-dollar affordable housing commitments, Fannie and Freddie tried to inspire and cajole private lenders to make subprime loans — loans that could then be purchased by F&F (after being misclassified as "prime"). To this end, Fannie and Freddie created, for the use of small lenders and brokers, an array of subprime products, designed to turn responsible renters into irresponsible home owners. In turn, these lenders and brokers altered their own lending patterns in order to supply the particular subprime products sought by F&F.

Evidence establishing that Fannie and Freddie were the initiators with respect to subprime products was produced by a House Committee in December 2008. This evidence was described by the Washington Post:

> An e-mail to Mudd [Fannie's CEO at the time] in September 2007 from a top deputy reported that banks were modeling their subprime mortgages to what Fannie was buying.[2]

Is there anything ambiguous about that statement? Fannie wasn't conforming to the banks: They were conforming to Fannie.

F&F designed these risky, irresponsible products, and then they pushed the products on every lender and broker in the market. For example, by the year 2000, Freddie had already rolled out its "Freddie Mac 100" product line:

> For many families, the largest barrier to homeownership is lack of funds for a down payment. To help alleviate this problem, Freddie Mac introduced the Freddie Mac 100 mortgage product in 2000. It allows a 100 per-

---

1   "Housing and Community Development," (Washington, DC: Fannie Mae, 2000), http://www.fanniemae.com/global/pdf/housingcommdev/affordable/solutionstoughestproblems.pdf.

2   Zachary A. Goldfarb, "Internal Warnings Sounded on Loans at Fannie, Freddie," The Washington Post (December 9, 2008), http://www.washingtonpost.com/wp-dyn/content/article/2008/12/08/AR2008120803570.html.

cent LTV [loan to value] ratio and requires only that the borrower has
sufficient funds to pay closing costs.[1]

The "Freddie Mac 100" loans were designed for borrowers who
couldn't come up with a single dollar of equity. All they needed was
enough to pay the closing costs. But, wait! People who can't afford closing costs should also have a crack at the American dream. For these
people Freddie came out with something even better: the "Affordable
Gold 100" line. These loans required no down payment *and* no closing
costs from the borrower. The closing costs could come from "a variety of
sources, including a grant from a qualified institution, gift from a relative
or an unsecured loan."[2]

Believe it or not, loan terms became even more generous. Freddie
went on to introduce loans with total loan-to-value ratios as high as 105
percent, 40-year amortizations, and adjustable rates that required nothing more than interest payments for the first 10 years. In announcing the
new, 10-year interest-only loan, Freddie noted the impact it would have
on the lending market:

> This [loan] gives originators using Loan Prospector new marketing muscle
> by expanding the secondary market for an even wider range of interest-
> only mortgage product.[3]

Generally, Freddie pitched these products to lenders as a way to
"meet your Community Reinvestment Act (CRA) goals," and "an easy and
convenient way to expand your reach in rapidly growing markets including first-time homebuyers, move-up borrowers, retirees, and families in
Underserved Areas, new immigrants, very low and low-to-moderate-
income borrowers."[4]

Of course, each of Freddie's loan innovations was matched by something similar from its rival, Fannie Mae. In 2000, when Freddie came
out with its "Freddie Mac 100," Fannie announced its "Community 100"
product, which was also a zero-down payment loan. In 2001, Fannie's
then-CEO, Franklin Raines, boasted that his company had achieved
these affordable housing accomplishments:

---

1   "Annual Housing Activities Report for 2002," 57.

2   Ibid.

3   "Freddie Mac Expands Initial Interest Suite with 3/1, 5/1, 7/1 Arms with 10-
     Year Interest Only," (Washington, DC: Freddie Mac, February 17, 2005),
     www.freddiemac.com/news/archives/singlefamily/2005/2005.html.

4   "Affordable Gold 97 - Buy a Home with Only 3 Percent Down Payment,"
     (Washington, DC: Freddie Mac, January 2005).

- Helped pioneer increasingly flexible, low down payment and even zero down payment mortgage products, nationwide;
- Pledged a total of $3 trillion in financing targeted exclusively to minority, lower-income and other underserved groups (and delivered over $1 trillion thus far)[1]

Two years later Raines boasted that Fannie's innovations had "redefined creditworthiness."[2]

It is important to understand that F&F did not actually issue these reckless loans; they simply designed them and encouraged private banks and mortgage brokers to originate and fund these loans. This was a major factor leading to the financial crisis that exploded in 2007/08, and F&F cannot escape responsibility simply because they did not directly originate and fund the loans and, in some cases, did not even buy them.

Fannie and Freddie misled the market about subprime

As reported by Fannie's former Chief Credit Officer, Edward Pinto, the company accidentally (on purpose) classified billions of dollars of subprime investments as "prime." In the opinion of Peter J. Wallison, this misrepresentation was, in itself, "a principal cause of the financial crisis:[3]

> Market observers, rating agencies and investors were unaware of the number of subprime and Alt-A mortgages infecting the financial system in late 2006 and early 2007. Of the 26 million subprime and Alt-A loans outstanding in 2008, 10 million were held or guaranteed by Fannie and Freddie, 5.2 million by other government agencies, and 1.4 million were on the books of the four largest U.S. banks[4]

In other words, the government held most of the junk but, due to lies and misleading statements by Fannie and Freddie, investors and rating agencies grossly underestimated the number of subprime loans and, thus, underestimated the implication they held for future default and foreclosure rates. Here's an example of a flat-out lie made by Fannie on page 129 of its 2008 SEC filing: "Subprime mortgage loans, whether held in our

---

1 "Chairman's Message," in 2001 National Housing Survey (Washington, DC: Fannie Mae, 2001).
2 "Chairman's Message," in 2003 National Housing Survey (Washington, DC: Fannie Mae, 2003).
3 Peter J. Wallison is an American Enterprise Institute Scholar and a former Treasury Department counsel.
4 Peter J. Wallison, "The Price for Fannie and Freddie Keeps Going Up," The Wall Street Journal (December 29, 2009), http://online.wsj.com/article/SB1 0001424052748703327860457462468187342757574.html.

portfolio or backing Fannie Mae MBS, represented less than 1% of our single-family business volume in each of 2007, 2006 and 2005."

Unfortunately, by the time Fannie and Freddie began to 'fess up (in September 2009), the public had been thoroughly indoctrinated. They had been told by academics, bureaucrats and Nobel Laureates that the GSEs didn't buy or promote subprime loans. Supposedly, they couldn't even if they wanted to. Then the story was modified a bit. Perhaps the GSEs did buy a little subprime, after all. But, this was only after being forced to by competitive pressures from the private sector.

When I first wrote this chapter I assumed these false notions would be firmly entrenched for at least 100 years. But there is a ray of hope. Now that the SEC has charged 6 ex-officers of Fannie and Freddie for concealing material subprime acquisitions, maybe the truth will be more widely reported.[1]

F&F redefined "conforming" to include subprime

> Let me begin by telling you about a 34-year old single mom with four kids whose story illustrates why we're here today. Her name is Jill and ... she doesn't have much spare cash. And her credit wasn't so good because it took her a while to pay off some medical bills. ... Jill put $500 down [on a $129,000 house] and First Federal approved her mortgage. Best of all, Jill — even without perfect credit — got a prime rate mortgage.
>
> – Daniel Mudd, Ex-President and CEO of Fannie Mae (2006)[2]

Words matter. Once upon a time, the term, "prime" loan, had a special meaning: It was a loan made to a "prime" borrower (i.e., a person with solid credit). Because these were the only loans that qualified for purchase by Fannie or Freddie (F&F), they were called "conforming" loans (as in, they conformed to the legal standards for purchase). Starting in the 1990s, however, F&F gradually broadened the terms "prime" and "conforming" to include loans to people with imperfect credit, as long as the rate of interest on the loan was moderate. Indeed, these riskier loans were the kind that Fannie and Freddie most wanted to buy, and they let that fact be known. This affected the entire industry because, in a

---

1   "SEC Charges Former Fannie Mae and Freddie Mac Executives with Securities Fraud."

2   Daniel H. Mudd, "Mortgage Lending Industry Diversity and Emerging Markets Conference," (Washington, DC: Fannie Mae, September 28, 2006).

capitalist system, when there is a demand for a particular type of product, suppliers try their best to meet that demand.

In 2009, the Center for Community Capital of the University of North Carolina prepared a study of 1.3 million 2006 private-label loan securitizations, using a national sample known as Columbia collateral file."[1] Based upon the classifications of remittance reports of the mortgage pool trustees, it was determined that about 90,000 of the loans were classified as "conforming" and another 21,000 were classified as "Alt-A." It was the normal practice of Fannie and Freddie to buy loans within these two classifications.

The Center analyzed and summarized various characteristics of loans, including the 4 risk factors listed in Table 7:

Table 7 – Four loan risk factors

Loan Risk Factor
Borrower FICO score less than 620*
Interest-only mortgages or negative amortization mortgages with payments are so small that loan principal increases (suggests inadequate borrower income level)
Down payment less than 10% (suggests inadequate borrower cash for down payment)
Limited or no documentation loans

Note: The study used a relatively lax FICO standard of 620 rather than the preferred 660 standard.

For the conforming loan category, the Center found that 79.5 percent had at least one feature associated with subprime borrowers. For example, 28.8 percent were interest-only loans (no principal payment required), 68.6 percent were low or no-documentation loans, and 72.1 percent had original down payments that were less than 10 percent.[2] The Center also found that, for some of the conforming loans, borrowers had FICO scores of less than 620, which is a score substantially less than the more traditional 660 level used by bank regulators. (The percentage of loans between 620 and 660 was not analyzed.) Thus, nearly 80 percent of

---

1   Roberto Quercia and Lei Ding and Janneke Ratcliffe, "Loan Modifications and Redefault Risk - an Examination of Short-Term Impact," (Chapel Hill: Center for Community Capital of the University of North Carolina, March 2009), 7.

2   It appears that additional loans (home equity, "silent seconds," and "piggybacks") were not necessarily considered by the Center for Community Capital researchers. If they had been, an even higher percentage of loans would have had at least one subprime characteristic.

these "conforming" loans, the kind bought by F&F (or backing securities purchased by F&F), could be considered risky and, arguably, subprime.[1]

Alt-A loans were also purchased by F&F, and for this category the risk level was even higher. Over 92 percent of such loans had at least one risky factor, including 22 percent that did not require principal payments, 76.1 percent that had low down payments, and 76.2 percent with little or no documentation. Thus, nearly all of these loans were risky and, arguably, subprime.

What can we conclude from this study of 1.3 million securitized loans in the Columbia collateral file? First, we learn that many of the loans bundled into private-label securitizations qualified, ostensibly, as Fannie and Freddie "conforming or Alt-A loans." Second, we learn that, although they met F&F underwriting standards, these conforming and Alt-A loans were mostly junk. Many analysts won't blame Fannie and Freddie for these junk loans, but they should. At the minimum, Fannie and Freddie share responsibility because, as noted by the Lending Tree company, "they set the standard for conforming loans ... [and] are very influential in the mortgage industry due to their great size and their relationship to the federal government."[2]

Fannie Mae's Meat

If you question the culpability of Fannie and Freddie with respect to subprime lending, consider this analogy. Assume there is a huge, quasi-governmental meat distributor that purchases meat products from companies such as Hormel and Tyson. We'll call the quasi-governmental distributor "Fannie Mae's Meat" (FMM). In 1992 FMM was given a regulatory mandate to promote "affordable hotdogs" (so that no one would be excluded from the American dream of eating lots of hotdogs). To fulfill its mandate, FMM promised a financial subsidy to Hormel and Tyson, provided they produced an ultra-inexpensive dog. In addition, FMM advised Hormel and Tyson to ignore certain traditional quality and safety standards regarding, for example, additives, bacteria levels, and general cleanliness. In the opinion of FMM, those standards were unnecessary, redundant, obsolete, or (in some way) discriminatory.

Hormel and Tyson produced the cheapo hot dog, and sold many of them to FMM. FMM could or would only buy some of the dogs, so the rest were sold to private distributors by Hormel and Tyson. Before long, the new hotdog dominated the market, and competitors struck back with their own low-cost, substandard frankfurters. Many consumers

1   Quercia and Lei Ding and Janneke Ratcliffe, "Loan Modifications and Redefault Risk - an Examination of Short-Term Impact," 23.

2   "Conforming Loans," Lending Tree, 2010, http://www.lendingtree.com/smartborrower/glossary/c/conforming-loan/.

became violently ill after eating the cheap meat from Hormel, Tyson, and the various competitors.

If this scenario existed, who would be primarily responsible for the ensuing epidemic of illness? It would be FMM for three reasons: 1) FMM was the largest entity in the meat industry and had the most economic clout, 2) FMM had a certain level of authority due to its connection to the federal government, and 3) FMM was the entity that initiated the move to cheaper hot dogs (because of its "affordable hotdog" mandate).

When the federal government enters into the business arena, it is not just one additional company selling and buying products: It implicitly sets the standards for the entire industry. A government-backed entity has size and clout that affects the rest of the industry, so it must accept greater responsibility.

Fannie and Freddie were, by far, the two largest players in the lending industry, and they had special influence over the rest of the industry due to their implicit federal backing. It is a historical fact that the entire notion of relaxed underwriting standards can be traced back to 1992, when Fannie and Freddie were given their special, affordable housing mandates.

The GSEs fought predatory lending laws

It is hard to believe, but Fannie and Freddie and their funded lobbying arm, Homeownership Alliance,[1] openly fought some of the efforts to curtail predatory lending. Why? F&F feared that such laws could negatively impact subprime lending. In 2000 Homeownership Alliance proclaimed: "protecting borrowers from predatory sub-prime lenders may overshoot the mark and cut the greater flow of *good sub-prime* loans for those who might not otherwise be able to afford shelter" (emphasis added).[2] The Alliance and its benefactors, Fannie and Freddie, thought most subprime was "good" for us, and feared that predatory lending laws could be misapplied against that good subprime.

To be fair, Fannie and Freddie were opposed to predatory lending, but only certain aspects of it. They wanted lenders to charge reasonable fees and interest rates, and to properly explain the terms of the loans to the borrowers. However, they also wanted lenders to push the envelope, so to speak, with regard to alternative products and loan approvals. This

---

1   The founding members of the Homeownership Alliance included Fannie, Freddie, the National Association of Home Builders, the National Urban League, the National Bankers Association, and the National Association of Real Estate Brokers.

2   Broderick Perkins, "New Alliance Confronts Fm Watch, Champions Existing Housing Finance System," RealtyTimes (October 5, 2000), http://realtytimes.com/rtpages/20001005_fmwatch.htm.

---

was noted in Fannie's 2002 Annual Housing Activities Report: "Fannie Mae's Mortgage Consumer Rights agenda is about lenders saying yes to more borrowers."

To say "yes to more borrowers" Fannie committed to "offering lenders a broad range of alternative responsible products." We now know that saying "yes" is not always the right thing to do because a loan approval can even be, in itself, a predatory act. On this point even Congressman Barney Frank seems to agree:

> It was a great mistake to push lower-income people into housing they couldn't afford and couldn't really handle once they had it. I had been too sanguine about Fannie and Freddie.[1]

A brief history of F&F, subprime, and politics

Affordable housing becomes official policy

Once upon a time, Fannie and Freddie (F&F) were well-run entities that set the standards for prudent lending. That started to change in 1992 when Congress enacted the Federal Housing Enterprises Financial Safety and Soundness Act (Title XIII of the Housing and Community Development Act of 1992). Although this legislation was intended, ostensibly, to increase regulatory oversight of Fannie and Freddie, it also mandated that HUD impose goals on Fannie and Freddie for the purchase of minority and lower-income housing loans. By mandating affordable housing goals for these two massive entities, the Democratically-controlled Congress was able to tap into a huge, off-budget pot of gold to use for the social engineering it desired. The primary mission of F&F became the issuance of affordable housing loans. As for prudent underwriting standards ... RIP.

In 1994, Fannie made a commitment to buy $1 trillion in low-income and minority loans. Do you suppose that a trillion dollar commitment might garner the attention of private lenders?

HUD issued tougher affordable housing mandates in February 1995. These were issued in response to community activists who were concerned that Fannie and Freddie were not doing everything possible to benefit residents of underserved communities. The new rules stated that Fannie and Freddie were "expected to be 'Leaders in the Field'" — in

1   Barney Frank as cited by Lawrence Kudlow, "Barney Frank Comes Home to the Facts," rasmussenreports.com (August 21, 2010), http://www.rasmussenreports.com/public_content/political_commentary/commentary_by_lawrence_kudlow/barney_frank_comes_home_to_the_facts.

other words, they were to lead the private lending market towards their affordable housing goals. Numerical quotas were set for housing in the central cities, rural areas, other underserved areas, and minority lending. F&F were required to "establish innovative products and create new lender relationships in order to expand their purchases of mortgages for working class families, first-time homebuyers, and residents of underserved communities."[1] Thus, by 1995 HUD was putting major pressure on F&F with regard to the financing of affordable housing. In turn, F&F were asserting significant pressure on the rest of the lending industry.

Fannie and Freddie were soon designing products that loosened down payment and other underwriting standards. In addition, they aggressively tried to promote these lower standards within the private lending community. Fannie showcased its innovative new products in its "Showing America a New Way Home" program, which was committed to provide homeownership to millions of families via partnerships with others in the industry. Freddie tried to entice private lenders with the extraordinary profits they would have (supposedly) if they gave out the low-grade loans. This was itemized in its publication, *Discover Gold Through Expanding Markets*.

Another major policy change was made by HUD in 1995: Fannie and Freddie would be allowed to meet affordable housing goals via the purchase of mortgage-backed securities — provided those securities included loans to low-income borrowers. This virtually guaranteed that private securitizers would mix some crappy loans into every single security subsequently issued. Remember, Fannie and Freddie directly or indirectly purchased most of the housing loans in the United States market. Like the former brokerage firm, E. F. Hutton, when they spoke, lenders listened. This fact was well known and understood by the two GSEs. In his book, *Showing America a New Way Home* (same name as the lending program), written in 1996, James A. Johnson, former CEO of Fannie Mae, almost bragged of Fannie's ability to shape the entire lending market:

> The proper role of Fannie Mae in fighting discrimination is not in law enforcement but in providing economic incentives. Every actor in the mortgage finance system, from real estate agents to banks to mortgage bankers, wants to do more business. All of them are anxious to originate a loan if Fannie Mae will agree to buy it. We have made it clear that we

---

1   Carole Norris, "New Rules for Fannie and Freddie," NHI (National Housing Institute), no. 80 (April 1995), http://www.nhi.org/online/issues/80/fanny. html.

accord a high priority to providing more service to African Americans and Hispanics.[1]

In 2000, 8 months ahead of schedule, Fannie fulfilled its trillion-dollar commitment and launched a new American Dream initiative — a $2 trillion ten-year pledge for affordable housing. Freddie matched that with its own $2 trillion commitment, so there was a total of $5 trillion in past and future commitments to low-income and minority loans. That is a heck of a lot in a $12 trillion house lending market.

Pressure to push an affordable housing agenda did not just come from the Clinton Administration. The Bush Administration enthusiastically embraced the crusade for affordable housing. In 2004, Bush's HUD ordered Fannie and Freddie to considerably increase their purchases of affordable housing loans — to 52 percent in 2005, 53 percent in 2006, 55 percent in 2007, and to 56 percent in 2008. These unrealistically-high targets virtually guaranteed that the GSEs would be forced to buy risky subprime and Alt-A loans.

The Accounting Scandals require a distraction

> Everybody understood that we were now buying loans that we would have previously rejected, and that the models were telling us that we were charging way too little, but our mandate was to stay relevant and to serve low-income borrowers. So that's what we did.
>
> – Former Senior Fannie Executive interviewed by the New York Times[2]

As noted in Chapter 5, in 2003 Freddie had to fire three top officers after auditors found that earnings had been seriously overstated. Eventually, a $5 billion adjustment to the books was required. Meanwhile, Freddie's big sister, Fannie, was making a soufflé with her books. In 2004, the Office of Federal Housing Enterprise Oversight (OFHEO) reported that, between 1998 and 2004, Fannie overstated income by about $6.3 billion. According to OFHEO, this was done deliberately to maximize executive compensation.

In response to these scandals, the Bush administration and Congressional allies introduced tough reform legislation that would have prohibited F&F from acquiring loan portfolios, and would have given their regulators greatly expanded powers. Michael Flynn, Director of Govern-

---

1   Johnson, Showing America a New Way Home, 108.09.
2   Duhigg, "Pressured to Take More Risk, Fannie Reached Tipping Point."

ment Affairs at the Reason Foundation, explained why the reform measures failed:

> The measure came very close to passing, but Fannie and Freddie cut a deal. They would refocus on expanding mortgages for low-income borrowers if the feds kept out of their operations. The bargain worked. Virtually all the Democrats and a few Republicans backed the two companies and the reform effort failed.[1]

The most ardent defender of Fannie and Freddie was Congressman Barney Frank, the ranking Democrat on the Financial Services Committee. He claimed that the problems of F&F were "exaggerated," and he lamented that "the more pressure there is on these companies, the less we will see in terms of affordable housing."[2] In Frank's view, it would be a shame to have affordable housing goals take a back seat to prudent lending standards. Economist Charles Calomiris and AEI Fellow Peter Wallison feel that Frank and his Congressional allies made a huge mistake by opposing reform legislation:[3]

> If the Democrats had let the 2005 legislation come to a vote, the huge growth in the subprime and Alt-A loan portfolios of Fannie and Freddie could not have occurred, and the scale of the financial meltdown would have been substantially less. The same politicians who today decry the lack of intervention to stop excess risk taking in 2005-2006 were the ones who blocked the only legislative effort that could have stopped it.[4]

Thus, Fannie and Freddie were caught cooking the books but still had enough clout in Congress to avoid increased regulation. This came at a price, however. They now had to prove their worth by showing their affordable housing bona fides. According to Cambridge Scholar Helen Thompson:

> [Fannie and Freddie] created a language of political justification for their expansion around affordable housing, especially for minorities, that was

---

1   Michael Flynn, "The Roots of the Crisis," Reason Magazine (October 1, 2008), http://reason.com/archives/2008/10/01/the-roots-of-the-crisis.
2   Staff, "Who's Really to Blame for the Banking Meltdown?," Originator Times (now National Realty News) (October 22, 2008), http://www.realestatethedarkside.com/TheMortgageMeltdown.htm.
3   President Obama, who was a Senator at the time, did not take an active position on the bill. He "remained silent," according to the Wall Street Journal.
4   Charles and Peter Wallison Calomiris, "Blame Fannie Mae and Congress for the Credit Mess," The Wall Street Journal (September 23, 2008), http://online.wsj.com/article/SB122212948811465427.html.

tied closely to the political concerns of many in Congress, especially significant sections of the Democratic Party.[1]

As reported in 2006 by their regulator, OFHEO, Fannie and Freddie used affordable housing as a shield, and they labeled would-be reformers as being opposed to the national housing interest.[2] To prove their point, F&F pushed subprime lending even harder, a fact that has now been confirmed by many sources.

Conservatorship

In 2008, after the housing market in the United States collapsed, Congress passed legislation creating the Federal Housing Finance Agency (FHFA). The primary purpose of the FHFA was to oversee Fannie and Freddie. The FHFA was appointed conservator of both entities in September 2008.[3]

As conservator, FHFA's main function is to minimize GSE losses and keep credit available to the general public via new or modified mortgage loans. In February 2012, after more than 3 years of conservatorship, FHFA issued a proposed strategy for the "next phase" of its conservatorship. The three-part plan calls for the building of a "new infrastructure for the secondary mortgage market," a "shrinking" of the role of Fannie and Freddie in the mortgage marketplace, and maintenance of foreclosure prevention activities while supporting the availability of new and refinanced mortgages.

The plan is vague, but it appears that the proposed "new infrastructure for the secondary mortgage market" would be some sort of public utility that could be utilized by lenders for the purpose of securitizing their loans. The role of Fannie and Freddie would eventually be lessened or eliminated.

---

1   Helen Thompson, "The Political Origins of the Financial Crisis: The Domestic and International Politics of Fannie Mae and Freddie Mac," The Political Quarterly 80 (2009).
2   "Report of the Special Examination of Fannie Mae," 3.
3   With regard to organizations, "conservatorship" is usually established by statute or regulation for the purpose of providing management to an entity that is unable or unwilling to properly manage itself. It is usually established for a finite period of time.

CHAPTER 8: THE COMMUNITY REINVESTMENT ACT (OR DR. JEKYLL AND MR. HYDE)

> Dr. Henry Jekyll ... is an apparently respectable man who contains within him a potential for profound wickedness, released in the shape of Mr. Hyde. He is a moral and decent man but he has always been leading a double life and he is doing that because he has aimed so high.
>
> – From analysis of *The Strange Case of Dr. Jekyll and Mr. Hyde* by Robert Louis Stevenson

The Community Reinvestment Act (CRA) has its ardent supporters and fervent critics because it is really two distinguishable programs: the one created before President Bill Clinton and the one created by President Bill Clinton. Some people have only experienced or studied the former version — the nice Dr. Jekyll version. Most likely, they have seen prudent underwriting standards applied by small local banks as they attempt to provide loans to people in underserved neighborhoods. Other people have seen what happens when large banks (and in many cases, nonbanks), eager to gain expansion or merger approval, hastily create lending programs in conjunction with local governmental housing departments or community organizers (a.k.a. blackmailers). They have probably seen an erosion of underwriting standards and soaring delinquency rates. The first goal of this chapter is to describe and distinguish the two CRAs, and to explain which banks and metropolitan areas are likely to have one or the other.

A second objective for this chapter is to discuss the shameful (and, perhaps, deliberate) lack of direct government review of CRA performance (i.e., what percentage of CRA loans default?). Very little information is available, and the little that exists is often grossly misrepresented. In this chapter those misrepresentations are exposed.

A third goal is to evaluate the various attempts that have been made to quantify aspects of CRA lending programs. Estimates have been produced, and they suggest that, contrary to the contention of its supporters, the CRA significantly increased lending to subprime borrowers.

Finally, there is a brief discussion of some myths specific to the CRA issue (see "Torture").

What is the Community Reinvestment Act and how did it change?

During the 1970s community activists and governmental housing officials decided that the lending practices of many banks and thrifts were contributing to the decline of America's inner cities. They alleged that lending institutions were unlawfully "redlining," meaning they refused to extend credit to people within certain geographic areas even though they were credit-worthy. These assertions led to passage of Community Reinvestment Act (CRA) in 1977.

As originally enacted, the CRA required banks and thrifts to make an effort to lend throughout the entire market in which they were located. More specifically, banks and thrifts were required to ascertain the credit needs of their communities, to offer and market appropriate credit services throughout the nearby communities, and to finance, where appropriate, local community development and redevelopment programs. Quantitative targets were not included as part of the original Act; however, lending institutions were expected to "define their communities, make available information about how they serve the financial needs of these communities, and post notices requesting public comments on their CRA performance."[1] Regulatory agencies were mandated to assess an institution's record and consider it when "evaluating its application for deposit facilities, e.g., charter, branch, deposit insurance, office relocation, merger, or acquisition applications." It is fair to say that the original Act forced banks and savings associations to describe their efforts to extend credit to all areas of their market; however, they were not forced to allocate credit to any specific areas, or to otherwise meet quotas or lending targets.

---

1   Vern McKinley, "Community Reinvestment Act: Ensuring Credit Adequacy or Enforcing Credit Allocation?," (Regulation, 1994), 27, http://www.cato.org/pubs/pas/pa354.pdf.

A bogus Fed study is the foundation for CRA changes

In 1992 the Boston Federal Reserve studied bank lending patterns, and found no significant overt discrimination. However, it concluded that blacks and Hispanics were more likely than whites to be denied credit, even after controlling for 30 variables that were related to the lending decision. According to the study, blacks suffered a denial rate of 17 percent, while whiles were denied credit only 11 percent of the time.[1] This study became a motivating force for those who wanted more aggressive Community Reinvestment Act (CRA) enforcement. The fact that the study was soon discredited mattered little to the community activists who were bent on bringing banks to their knees.

In 1994, an economist at the Federal Deposit Insurance Corporation (FDIC), David K. Horne, re-analyzed the 70 FDIC-supervised institutions included within the Fed study. As reported by Vern McKinley, Horne found that significant mistakes had been made by the Boston Fed:

> Overall, 57 percent of all applicant files contained data errors, including critical information that could not be verified, debt that was underreported, inaccurate income figures, and assets that could not be verified. The FDIC analysis concluded that it is not possible to establish whether the racial discrepancies identified in the Boston Fed Study reflect racial bias or methodological problems with the study's statistical approach.[2]

Other studies also contradicted the Fed results. In 1993, Ted Day and Stan Liebowitz found crucial data entry errors that affected the integrity of the Fed study.[3] In 1997, Harold Black applied the Boston Fed methodology to black and white-owned banks. Surprisingly, he found that black loan applicants were significantly more likely to be denied credit by black-owned banks than white-owned banks.[4] And, in 1997, David K. Horne reported that, according to the Fed study, sixty-nine of the applicants had negative net worth, yet 57 of them were approved for loans.[5]

---

1   George J. Benston, "The Community Reinvestment Act: Looking for Discrimination That Isn't There," in Policy Analysis (Washington, DC: CATO Institute, October 6, 1999), http://www.cato.org/pubs/pas/pa354.pdf.

2   McKinley, "Community Reinvestment Act: Ensuring Credit Adequacy or Enforcing Credit Allocation?."EndNote›

3   Harold A. and M. Collins and Ken Cyree Black, "Do Black-Owned Banks Discriminate against Black Borrowers?," in Journal of Financial Services Research (New York: Kluwer Academic Publishers, 1997), http://www.cato.org/pubs/pas/pa354.pdf.

4   Benston, "The Community Reinvestment Act: Looking for Discrimination That Isn't There," 5.

5   Ibid.

The Fed made no formal response to these challenges, and decided that no new studies were needed. It then took swift action to utilize its questionable study. As noted by Stan Liebowitz:

> No sooner had the ink dried on its discrimination study than the Boston Fed, clearly speaking for the entire Fed, produced a manual for mortgage lenders stating that "discrimination may be observed when a lender's underwriting policies contain arbitrary or outdated criteria that effectively disqualify many urban or lower-income minority applicants."
>
> Some of these "outdated" criteria included the size of the mortgage payment relative to income, credit history, savings history and income verification. Instead, the Boston Fed ruled that participation in a credit-counseling program should be taken as evidence of an applicant's ability to manage debt.[1]

Despite its obvious flaws, the Clinton Administration embraced the Fed report, and used it as justification for sweeping regulatory changes.

Meet Mr. Hyde

> Today's actions demonstrate that we will tackle lending discrimination wherever and in whatever form it appears. No loan is exempt, no bank is immune. For those who thumb their nose at us, I promise vigorous enforcement.
>
> – Attorney General Janet Reno, in 1994, announcing a fair-lending discrimination settlement with the First National Bank of Vicksburg and the Blackpipe State Bank

From the day he took office, President Clinton had been eager to dramatically expand housing opportunities for lower income Americans. His initial strategy had been to fight bank loan "discrimination" using the Department of Justice. During Clinton's first year as President, Attorney General Janet Reno filed charges against the Blackpipe State Bank in South Dakota. Allegedly, the bank had discriminated against Native American Indians, in violation of the Equal Credit Opportunity and Fair Housing Acts. That was the opening salvo in an onslaught of legal filings against banks. By 1995, Ms. Reno could brag of bringing "hundreds of cases" on behalf of minorities "who have been denied housing or have been rejected for a loan because of their race, gender or national origin."[2]

---

1 Stan Liebowitz, "The Real Scandal," New York Post February 5, 2008.
2 "Attorney General Says Banking Bill Would Cripple Investigations," The New York Times (June 16, 1995), http://www.nytimes.com/1995/06/16/business/attorney-general-says-banking-bill-would-cripple-investigations.html.

These weren't necessarily difficult cases to file because the old fashioned necessity of showing racial or gender prejudice was discarded by Clinton and Company. The new definition of discrimination was based on something the Administration called, "disparate impact." Under this standard it was not enough that a bank applied its lending policies in a fair and equal manner. Discrimination existed if the bank's policies "disproportionately and adversely" affected the poor or the usual protected groups.[1] In other words, the outcomes had to be equal.

Faced with these unreasonable standards and threatened with the considerable power and resources of the federal government, banks invariably offered to settle with Janet Reno's Department. But, this was not enough for the radical, young Clinton Administration. (This was before President Clinton famously decided that "the era of big government is over.") The President wanted a much bigger club, and that would materialize in the form of a ramped up, quantified version of the Community Reinvestment Act (CRA). The flawed, 1992 Boston Federal Reserve lending study would serve as a justification for this aggressive new CRA enforcement.

Clinton ordered his banking regulators to propose major CRA improvements. Some of the proposals became law in 1994, but the bulk of them were adopted as regulatory changes in 1995. The changes were extensive and, ultimately, very destructive. Henceforth, banks and thrifts would be evaluated based on the number and amount of loans issued within their assessment areas, the geographical distribution of those loans, the distribution of loans based on borrower characteristics, the number and amount of community development loans, and the amount of innovation and flexibility they used when approving loans. President Clinton wanted banks to demonstrate results — not just process. In 2000, before Clinton left office, Howard Husock, Scholar with the Manhattan Institute, described these changes in a prescient critique:

> The new regulations de-emphasized subjective assessment measures in favor of strictly numerical ones. Bank examiners would use federal home-loan data, broken down by neighborhood, income group, and race, to rate banks on performance. There would be no more A's for effort. Only results — specific loans, specific levels of service — would count.[2]

In addition to the de facto quotas, there were two other important features of the CRA regulations:

---

1   Schweizer, Architects of Ruin, 60.

2   Husock, "The Trillion-Dollar Bank Shakedown That Bodes Ill for Cities."

- Lenders were urged to use underwriting "flexibility," if necessary to achieve their CRA goals.
- Banks examiners were instructed to evaluate how well banks and thrifts responded to complaints from community activists.

What did underwriting "flexibility" mean? In 1992 the Boston Fed issued a little "Guide" to explain it. Banks were told to consider making loans to "applicants with relatively high obligation ratios ..." and to applicants "with no credit history or problem credit history...."[1] In neighborhoods with revitalization projects banks were told to appraise house values based on their "potential as well as their existing condition." According to the Fed, "length of stay in a particular job ..." was no longer an essential underwriting requirement, and banks were told that a borrower's income potential should include more sources such as welfare and unemployment benefits.[2]

All of this information — the de facto quotas, the new underwriting "flexibility," and the responsiveness to community activists — would be used by regulators to evaluate requests for bank and thrift mergers, expansions, etc. For many banks — especially those in the spotlight and subject to attack by community activists — these changes transformed a fairly reasonable program into a highly destructive one. This was a factor that that significantly contributed to the erosion of underwriting standards that took place after the mid-1990s. Some observers watched with alarm:

> The Clinton push for numerical guidelines "will result in quotas," Kevin Kane, the president of CRA Consultants, told Mortgage Banking. "[Banks] will throw away credit criteria."... Lawrence B. Lindsey, then a governor of the Federal Reserve Board, warned, "A total reliance on statistics in credit enforcement will ultimately lead to a complete replacement of bank judgment and reason regarding loan approval with statistical rules."[3]

Consider Lindsey's words carefully because they were prophetic: "A total reliance on statistics in credit enforcement will ultimately lead to a *complete replacement of bank judgment and reason ...*" (emphasis added). Isn't that exactly what happened?

U.S. Patent no. 5,689,650

---

1 An obligation ratio would be debt, lease, child care, and other required payments as a percentage of income.
2 "Closing the Gap: A Guide to Equal Opportunity Lending," ed. Federal Reserve Bank of Boston (U.S. Government, April 10, 2000), 13-15.
3 Schweizer, Architects of Ruin, 61.

"It is extremely difficult for many institutions to prudently meet their CRA requirements through the traditional means of originating and holding portfolios of individual loans. ... The CRA apparatus compiles investor needs for CRA qualified assets, creates portfolios of assets that would be recognized by regulatory agencies as meeting the requirements of the CRA and allocates CRA credits separately from the financial return of the portfolio of assets. The CRA apparatus can acquire CRA eligible loans from the secondary market, directly from private or governmental agencies, and/or directly from loan originators. The CRA apparatus determines whether an asset meets CRA qualifying parameters from demographic and statistical data regarding the borrower and/or financial asset. The apparatus determines, by using CRA qualification factors as well as investor requirements, whether a loan should be acquired. In a parallel accounting process, the apparatus creates a pool of CRA eligible 'credits' from the assets in each portfolio and then tracks and allocates specific CRA credits associated with specific assts to specific portfolio investors ... etc., etc., etc."

I just thought you might want to know that, no matter what crap the government creates, some enterprising fellow will step forward in an attempt to clean up the mess. This excerpt, from a real patent, also gives me an excuse to discuss another aspect of the Community Reinvestment Act (CRA): the heavy compliance costs. Many banks found it necessary to maintain CRA departments, with personnel devoted to CRA on a full-time basis. For example, an ex-loan officer for a medium-sized Cleveland-area bank told me that his bank took CRA very seriously, and had 4 or 5 people devoted to it on a full-time basis. That commitment requires substantial financial cost that has to affect bank profits and, ultimately, bank user fees and interest rates.

In general, the 1995 Clinton CRA regulations were destructive, but for many banks in small metropolitan statistical areas (MSAs) — especially those without expansion plans, the regulations were more of a nuisance than a threat. These lending institutions operated in areas too small to attract the attention of activists, such as ACORN or NACA, and the CRA loans they underwrote were, in many cases, loans they would have made without the CRA. This is only a theory, but it is supported by some research.

After studying CRA lending patterns in various metropolitan statistical areas (MSAs) Economist Neil Bhutta concluded that "the effect [of CRA] appears to be *entirely concentrated in large MSAs where banks are most likely to be heavily scrutinized*" (emphasis added).[1] Based on county-level CRA performance data, Economists Raphael Bostic and Breck Robinson

---

1   Neil Bhutta, "Giving Credit Where Credit Is Due? The Community Reinvestment Act and Mortgage Lending in Lower-Income Neighborhoods," ed. Division of Research & Statistics and Monetary Affairs (Federal Reserve Board, 2008), 21-22.

noted that "the effectiveness of CRA agreements in increasing lending activity is ultimately determined by the persistence and sophistication of community groups in monitoring compliance with CRA agreements."[1] Since the small MSA banks were not subject to excessive pressure by community activists, the loans they made probably performed fairly well. However, in the large MSAs things were (and are) quite different.

Large Metropolitan Statistical Areas are more likely to have banks that contemplate mergers or other types of expansions. Also, large MSAs are likely to have well-organized and aggressive community housing activists. Since the CRA invites activists to comment and complain regarding bank lending patterns, and since these comments and complaints are considered by regulators in deciding whether to approve bank merger/ expansion plans (even including the location of new ATM machines), CRA is a much more salient factor in large MSAs. In addition, any deviations from CRA guidelines invite private discrimination lawsuits. In these circumstances, banks can be stampeded into giving large numbers of CRA loans, even if it means lowering their lending standards to do so. Or, they may simply turn over the lending process to an activist entity, such as ACORN.

After the creation of CRA-the-Sequel, several community housing organizations terrorized banks into issuing hundreds of billions worth of reckless and irresponsible loans. A great example of this is NACA — the Neighborhood Assistance Corporation of America. Journalist David Hogberg describes how NACA used the Community Reinvestment Act to pressure banks into irresponsible lending:

> Under the new [1995 Clinton] rules CRA now allowed community activist groups to file complaints against banks that could affect a bank's CRA rating. A bad CRA rating could affect whether the Federal Reserve would approve a bank's proposed merger with another bank, and this let groups like NACA legally extort huge sums from financial institutions, sometime by merely threatening to file a complaint.[2]

The tactics used by NACA and its CEO, Bruce Marks, were unpleasant, but effective. Sometimes, Marks and hundreds of his cohorts would dump broken furniture onto the front lawns of the homes of banking executives. With regard to the Fleet Financial Group of New England,

---

1   Raphael Bostic and Breck Robinson, "Do CRA Agreements Infuence Lending Patterns," Real Estate Economics 31, no. 1 (2003): 25.

2   David Hogberg, "NACA: Neighborhood Assistance Corporation of America - Acorn's Rival in Shakedown Tactics," in Organization Trends (Washington, DC: Capital Research Center, April 2009).

against which NACA was supporting several law suits, tactics were particularly rough:

> It became commonplace for Marks and his shock troops, often dressed in yellow shirts, to disrupt speeches and analysts' meetings, and to vocally protest Fleet press conferences. Marks would steer supposed victims of Fleet loans toward newspaper and TV reporters, who often ran heart-wrenching stories about them. ... The culmination of the anti-Fleet campaign came in 1995 when NACA activists disrupted a Harvard Business School event at which Fleet CEO Terrence Murray was supposed to speak. Murray agreed to meet with Mark's four days later.[1]

After that meeting between Marks and Murray, NACA agreed to stop its legal and protest actions against Fleet. In exchange, Fleet agreed to create an $8 billion (yes, BILLION) loan program for low-income neighborhoods, and Fleet agreed to give NACA $140 million for its own programs.

NACA used that money to go after its next victim, First Union Bank of North Carolina. On its own Web site, NACA describes how it went after "Fast Eddie," the nickname it gave First Union's CEO, Edward Crutchfield:

> NACA hounded Fast Eddie at every turn. Thousands of post cards were sent to his home and neighbors, informing them of First Union's practices. NACA drafted the "Fast Eddie Report," which contained Crutchfield's personal information, and sent it to all of his neighbors and the neighbors of First Union's directors and top officers.[2]

NACA also spread stories about an alleged Crutchfield love affair, and NACA sent protesters to the school of Crutchfield's children. In 1996, First Union settled with Marks by giving his organization $150 million. Other victims paid as well. Bank of America made $3 billion loan commitments twice: in 1999 and 2003. In 2003, Citigroup made a $3 billion, 10-year commitment.[3]

In most cases, NACA brokered the loans funded by these banks. In other words, it found and screened the people who would end up borrowing the funds. To its credit, NACA's efforts were focused on low-income borrowers, and NACA insisted that the banks give very generous loan terms. But, that was exactly the problem: The terms were far too generous, and many of the borrowers selected by NACA were credit deadbeats.

---

1   Ibid.
2   Ibid.
3   Ibid.

NACA-brokered loans required no down payments and no closing costs, and 65 percent of NACA borrowers had credit scores below 620 — the lower limit for most banks. (Indeed, nearly 50 percent had credit scores below 580, according to Marks.) As a result, NACA loans did not perform well.

Loan performance is a touchy subject with NACA, which has a strict policy against releasing such data. But, some information is available. In a 1999 Boston Globe article, Lynnley Browning reported: "A bank executive said yesterday that industry officials believe NACA's delinquency rates top 10 percent ... far above the 2 to 3 percent common for traditional loans."[1] In other words, NACA's rates were about 4 times higher than the prevailing rates at the time. John Anderson, a Boston real-estate analyst, calculated that Fleet loans, brokered by NACA in 1994 and 1995, also had foreclosure rates of 4 times that of the industry.[2] We also know that Bank of America, one of NACA's largest victims, reported in 2008 that its CRA portfolio, which constituted only 7 percent of its owned residential mortgage portfolio, was responsible for 29 percent of all losses.[3] Beyond this there is not much information because Marks "has steadfastly declined to disclose delinquency rates — that is, how many NACA borrowers are behind in their loan payments."[4] He even refused to give delinquency rates to the Massachusetts Community Banking Council, a group of bankers and housing advocates. "They aren't relevant," according to Marks. Apparently, NACA thinks lenders should be accountable ... unless the loans they make are brokered by NACA.

We can only speculate as to the current sky-high NACA delinquency rates, and what they did to our economy. As for NACA, however, don't worry: It is doing just fine. After it created billions of dollars of junk loans, NACA started a new crusade: It is championing the fight against foreclosures. It is almost a comedy: NACA pushed banks to make crappy loans; now it warns those same banks that they dare not foreclose on those crappy loans. And, as usual, NACA makes lots of money in the process.

NACA, the mega-rich "charity"

1   Lynnley Browning, "A $3b Welcome Mat: Marks' Group Lands Huge Mortgage Pact with Bank of America," The Boston Globe August 11, 1999.
2   John Hechinger, "Gadfly Mortgage Firm Feels Surge in Growth and Sting of Scrutiny," The Wall Street Journal September 13, 1999.
3   Edward Pinto, "Yes, the CRA Is Toxic," City Journal Autumn, 2009.
4   Hechinger, "Gadfly Mortgage Firm Feels Surge in Growth and Sting of Scrutiny."

Let's digress for a bit to consider the state of NACA's finances. As a promoter of "affordable housing" junk loans, NACA made money hand-over-fist in various ways. As noted, it intimidated banks into giving it money. For example, in 1998 Bank of America agreed to give NACA $750,000 per year in cash gifts, through 2009, to use for setting up additional offices throughout the country. As a mortgage broker, NACA made money for the loans it originated. Bank of America paid NACA $2,000 for each loan, and Fleet paid NACA 2.75% of the mortgage amount for each loan. In many cases, NACA also took a percentage of the real estate brokerage fee. According to the Wall Street Journal (back in 1999) this amount was about $1,000 per loan. Finally, people who got loans through NACA were required to pay into a NACA fund at the rate of $600 per year for 5 years, and to participate in at least 5 "actions" on behalf of NACA each year. Required actions ranged from "making phone calls to full-scale 'mobilizations' against target banks ..."[1]

These activities led NACA to accumulate nearly $16 million in net worth by the end of 2005. That's the amount of extra money left over after paying all salaries and other expenses, and after all "charitable" activities. Later, after the start of the 2007/08 financial crisis, the wheels fell off the subprime train. What would NACA do now that it was much harder to sell subprime loans?

NACA simply put on a new hat, turned the train around, and started its "Save the Dream" tour. Starting in 2008, NACA counselors descended upon various large American cities, setting up shop in convention halls and arenas. Thousands of people came to two or three-day events to learn how they could reduce their mortgage payments or, in some cases, slip out of their mortgage obligations entirely. Sometimes, Bruce Marks (NACA's CEO) would prance around these venues, yelling words of encouragement via a megaphone.

For these efforts, NACA received absolutely nothing from the attendees. But, from the Obama administration NACA received $38 million for its foreclosure mitigation efforts. This pumped up NACA's net worth to about $23.5 million by the end of 2009. Isn't it nice to know that someone did well in the recession?

By the way, even though we, the taxpayers, have given NACA $38 million, don't expect any accountability. Bruce Marks refuses to disclose the success rate of his counselors and, incredibly, this information is not required by the federal government.[2] But, we do have some feedback — mostly negative and too voluminous to recite here. Here is some of the feedback, from an article in the St. Louis Beacon:

One year after the NACA "Save the Dream Tour" stopped in Cleveland, a local nonprofit advocacy group that offers foreclosure counseling in Ohio has posted a note on the front page of its website ... "Did NACA drop the ball on your case and leave you twisting in

---

1   Husock, "The Trillion-Dollar Bank Shakedown That Bodes Ill for Cities."

2   NACA and other counseling agencies are required to report how many people they counsel, but not the ultimate results of those counseling efforts. And, the information that is reported to the government is not disclosed to the public.

the wind?" reads the message on the website of Empowering and Strengthening Ohio's People (ESOP). "Did they make promises they didn't fulfill? Did they lose your paperwork or were impossible to reach?"[1]

According to ESOP's executive director, Mark Seifert, more than 400 homeowners turned to his organization after first seeking, but not getting, help from NACA. The same story was heard after NACA's St. Louis tour. The president of a local St. Louis housing agency said that over 100 homeowners came to him after complaining of the difficulty they had communicating with NACA once it left St. Louis. He added:

They say, "I went to them [NACA] and now no one calls me back. They said, do all these things, and I did them, and now I don't know what to do because they won't call me back. They told me, don't talk to my servicer, just talk to them. I don't know what to do, and I don't know where my case is.[2]

So far, the foreclosure mitigation efforts of the Obama administration have been abysmal. Perhaps, we just need to pay NACA more. Say, $58 million instead of a mere $38 million?

Of course, NACA is only one of hundreds of housing organizations that promoted loans for subprime borrowers. The most famous, or notorious, community housing organization was probably ACORN Housing Corporation. As noted by Stan Liebowitz in 2008, ACORN also pushed banks to lower underwriting standards:

On the Web, you can still find CRA loans available via ACORN with "100 percent financing ... no credit scores ... undocumented income ... even if you don't report it on your tax returns." Credit counseling is required, of course.[3]

Regarding undocumented income, the Consumer Rights League, a now-defunct tax-exempt organization, asserted that ACORN had issued these instructions to staff loan counselors:

Undocumented income is a feature that allows ACORN Housing counselors to capture the applicant(s) total household income. Primarily observed in minority and immigrant communities, this type of income is not reported to the IRS and is *also known as under-the-table* (emphasis added).[4]

1   Mary Leonard, "Local Housing Counselors Say They Are Helping Homeowners Left in Wake of Naca's "Save the Dream Tour"," St. Louis Beacon July 28, 2010.
2   Ibid.
3   Liebowitz, "The Real Scandal."
4   "Acorn's Hypocritical House of Cards," (Tampa: Consumer Rights League, 2008), http://www.docstoc.com/docs/2036034/ACORN%E2%80%99s-Hypocritical-House-of-Cards---How-One-%E2%80%9CCommunity%E2%80%9D-Group-Helped-the-Housing-Crisis-Harm-Taxpayers.

ACORN has also advocated loans to "undocumented Mexican immigrants,"[1] interest-only loans, non-amortized mortgages, and reverse mortgages. And remember, in many cases, ACORN effectively took over the underwriting process from the CRA lender, as noted in an internal ACORN document:

> ACORN Housing counselors establish the amount, source and conduct verification of such income, without questioning from [Bank of America] underwriters ...

CRA's low underwriting standards

On page 127, I note the very low CRA underwriting standards recommended by the Boston Fed. ACORN and NACA also advocated low underwriting standards, which were fairly typical of the prescribed standards of the hundreds of other community-based housing organizations. Six hundred such organizations form the National Community Reinvestment Coalition (NCRC), so it is instructive to look at the general standards and guidelines of that umbrella organization.

In a publication titled, "CRA Commitments," the NCRC gives general guidance regarding underwriting standards, and describes some of the specific Community Reinvestment Act commitments made by banks (at the prodding of the activist organizations). Here is CRA underwriting guidance from the NCRC's booklet:

- Reduce or eliminate down payments, or fund those down payments with "sweat equity" (meaning that the new house owner promises to improve the house with his personal efforts, in lieu of the down payment).
- "...offer loans to applicants with 'marginal' credit scores."
- Consider all sources of income "including social security, unemployment benefits, public assistance (*including welfare benefits*), self employment, and part-time employment" (emphasis added).
- Relax employment requirements.
- Increase the allowable ratio of debt to income for new loan applicants.[2]

Regarding the last point (the increase in the allowable ratio of debt to income) a Cleveland-area banker told me that he just could not un-

---

1   For the unenlightened, "undocumented" means illegal.
2   "CRA Commitments," (Washingtion, DC: National Community Reinvestment Coalition, 2007), 31-33, http://www.ncrc.org.

derstand how the CRA department of his bank could justify allowing a higher ratio of debt to income for poorer borrowers than borrowers with high income. Of course, that is exactly the problem with any reduction of standards for the purpose of affordable housing. If banks can relax underwriting standards for low-income borrowers, they ultimately have to lower them for all borrowers.

A lender incorporating these low standards in the mid-2000s, just before housing values dropped, would now be facing massive defaults and foreclosures. Yet these CRA standards were broadly accepted and advocated by the federal government and by 600 activist organizations belonging to the NCRC.

The CRA-community connection

In Chapter 4 there is a discussion of the insane affordable housing programs of some state and local governments. In many cases lenders cooperated with those programs in the hope that they would get Community Reinvestment Act (CRA) brownie points. Most of the examples given in Chapter 4 had to do with reasonably affluent California neighborhoods, but here is an example from the poorer side of Cleveland, and it has a CRA connection. As a result of an investigation, the Cleveland Plain Dealer issued a scathing report in December 2009:

> The city of Cleveland has aggravated its vexing foreclosure problems and has lost millions in tax dollars by helping people buy homes they could not afford, a Plain Dealer investigation has found.
>
> The city provided mostly low-income buyers with down payment loans of up to $20,000 through the federal funded Afford-A-Home program, but did little to determine whether the people could actually afford to keep their homes.[1]
>
> Through 2004, the first-lien mortgages for Afford-A-Home buyers typically came from local banks fulfilling federal requirements to lend money in poorer neighborhoods.[2]

Translation: These local banks (and in some cases non-banks) were fulfilling CRA commitments (or, in the case of non-banks, alternative CRA commitments).[3]

---

1   Mark Gillispie, "How Cleveland Aggravated Its Foreclosure Problem and Lost Millions in Tax Dollars - All to Help People Purchase Homes They Couldn't Afford," Cleveland Plain Dealer December 31, 2009.

2   Ibid., 3.

3   As noted in Chapter 4, many nonbanks were subject to alternative CRA commitments.

Loans to people living in cars

The Cleveland Plain Dealer noted that the lack of oversight persist-ed for years, even as hundreds of borrowers defaulted on their loans. In many cases the Afford-A-Home loans went to people who had no chance of repaying those loans. For example, a loan went to a woman who "was homeless and living in a car with her children...." Another loan went to jobless couple on food stamps.

For many lenders, especially those located in areas with aggressive housing activists or left-leaning local governments, the CRA monster created by Bill Clinton was a major headache that led to imprudent loan decisions. Some lenders may have believed that they could make money as they complied with CRA; others probably saw CRA compliance as a losing proposition — a cost of doing business. Either way, we should not underestimate the detrimental impact of CRA-the-Sequel on underwrit-ing standards. An attempt to estimate the detrimental impact of CRA is found at the end of this chapter.

The government refuses to produce reliable CRA data

There is a paucity of CRA loan performance data. Activists, such as NACA, steadfastly refuse to publish statistics related to the loans they broker. Despite a mandate requiring the Federal Reserve to produce CRA default and delinquency rates, it has resisted the production of meaningful information. The Financial Services Modernization Act of 1999 required the Federal Reserve to deliver to Congress by March 15, 2000 a "comprehensive study" of CRA loan performance. Belatedly, the Fed released a laugher of a report, based on a voluntary questionnaire sent to 500 bankers. Only 34 of these bankers responded with quanti-fied information. Think about it: Our federal government has no problem subpoenaing bank records and hauling bank CEOs to Washington DC to embarrass them with all sorts of questions concerning their profits, bonuses, taxes, and private jet usage. However, the federal government was oh-so-timid when it came to requesting CRA default rates. I wonder why.

Even though there were few responses, a clear pattern did emerge: The delinquency rate of CRA home purchase and refinance loans was more than twice the rate of non-CRA loans. However, this significant fact was, effectively, covered up by the Federal Reserve. In a speech titled, "The Community Reinvestment Act and the Recent Mortgage Crisis,"

Federal Reserve Governor Randall Kroszner characterized the findings of the Fed's bank survey in the following manner:

> [The bank survey] found that lending to lower-income individuals and communities has been nearly as profitable *and performed similarly* to other types of lending done by CRA-covered institutions. Thus, the long-term evidence shows that the CRA has not pushed banks into extending loans that perform out of line with their traditional business (emphasis added).

"Performed similarly"? Does Mr. Kroszner think that a two-to-one ratio of delinquency is similar? If so, perhaps he'd like to by a $25,000 car from me from the low, low price of just $50,000. After all, $50,000 must be similar to $25,000, given the Kroszner thought process. This sole study, performed pathetically in 2000, is the only official government CRA evaluation performed almost 20 years. It is an often-cited report, and it is almost always mischaracterized (by people regurgitating Kroszner or other Fed economists). The lack of meaningful CRA performance data is a disgrace.

The dearth of feedback on Community Reinvestment Act (CRA) loan performance has been noted by Ed Pinto, the former Fannie Mae officer (1987-89):

> Taxpayers deserve to know why not one regulator had the common sense to track the performance of the CRA loans. They also deserve to know why the Federal Reserve, the Office of the Comptroller of the Currency, the Office of Thrift Supervision, and other regulators appear to have no idea how trillions of dollars in CRA loans are performing now.

Stuck on stupid

There is another type of CRA misinformation that is even more disgraceful. Several esteemed members of government show appalling stupidity with regard to CRA and its relationship to subprime lending. As noted on page 87, a meaningful definition of the term "subprime" is based on the creditworthiness of the borrower. Unfortunately, most loan data bases do not have information that can be used to distinguish prime from subprime borrowers. In lieu of that information, some researchers use a convenient proxy: the loan interest rate. They assume that, if a loan's interest rate is more than 3 percent over a certain base interest rate, the borrower must have subprime credit. The assumption is that the lender is charging a higher rate of interest to compensate for the subprime risk. If the rate of interest is not excessively high, the borrower is assumed to be prime. In certain cases it may be OK to use this proxy, but never to compare private lending to the lending associated with government programs, such as CRA.

The problem, of course, is that many of the loans made in CRA or affordable housing programs have moderate or even ultra-low interest rates, *by design*. The government never encourages lenders to charge a higher rate of interest for people who are credit risks. To the contrary, the government is more likely to pressure lenders to give such people loans with extra low interest rates. Isn't that the way government usually works: The more financially insecure you are, the *less* you pay? Therefore, when the high-interest rate paradigm is used to compare conventional vs. CRA lending, CRA and other affordable housing loans always appear to be mostly prime (even when the loans are made to deadbeats). Conclusions made on this basis are silly and self-serving.[1]

Here are a few examples showing that CRA loans often have low interest rates — even for borrowers with the very worst credit histories:

- NACA has brokered billions of dollars worth of loans, and each and every one of them has a *moderate or low interest rate*. Yet, none of the NACA loans requires a significant down payment, and nearly half of NACA's borrowers have FICO credit scores below 580 — a credit score that is below the level of most septic tanks. Indeed, NACA expressly caters to the subprime borrower. This policy is embodied in a statement by its CEO, Bruce Marks: "You can't pay your bills on time. You don't have perfect credit. That shouldn't prevent us from being homeowners." Would you label the typical NACA borrower as "prime" simply because NACA makes sure he gets a low interest rate from the bank it terrorizes?
- The loans in the Cleveland-based Afford-A-Home program (previously mentioned) carried low interest rates yet those loans were made to homeless and unemployed people, and even a woman living in a car. Would you label such people as "prime" credit risks simply because the Afford-A-Home program gave them loans with low rates of interest?
- As part of its 2003 CRA pledge, CitiMortgage offered borrowers "with past credit difficulties" a *two percent reduction in loan interest rates*. Would you call people "with past credit difficul-

---

1   This is not to say that high interest rates cannot be used to identify subprime borrowers in studies that are limited to private sector, conventional loans.

ties" prime borrowers simply because the bank gave them a special low interest rate deal?

You get the picture. It isn't complicated, yet here are some governmental scholars who are "stuck on stupid" with regard to this matter. They use the phrase "higher-priced loans" as a proxy for "subprime loans." Then, they draw erroneous conclusions based on that proxy. Obviously, these government bureaucrats are quoting each other. It is not clear who started this nonsensical line of reasoning (emphasis added):

- John C. Dugan, Comptroller of the Currency: "CRA is not the culprit behind the subprime mortgage lending abuses.... Banks subject to CRA and their affiliates originated or purchased only *six percent* of the reported *high cost* loans...."

- Randall Kroszner, Federal Reserve Governor: "Only *six percent* of all the *higher-priced* loans were extended by CRA-covered lenders.... This result undermines the assertion by critics of the potential for a substantial role for the CRA in the subprime crisis."

- Janet Yellen and Eric Rosegren, Presidents of the Federal Reserve Banks at San Francisco and Boston, respectively (in a jointly-signed statement): "We also address the critics of the [CRA] act who have pinned blame for the subprime mortgage crisis on the CRA. ... only *six percent* of all *higher-priced* loans were extended by CRA-covered lenders...."

- Richard Neiman, Damon Silvers and Elizabeth Warren on a Congressional Oversight Panel that reviewed the foreclosure crisis: "Only *six percent* of *higher-priced* loans were originated by banks subject to the CRA. Of course, originating loans is not the only way in which banks could be involved in *higher-priced* or subprime lending."

- Congressman Luis V. Gutierrez, Chairman of the Financial Institutions Subcommittee: "Republicans have long tried to take the easy way out by pointing the finger at the Community Reinvestment Act and other government-sponsored affordable lending programs; but these programs did not cause our foreclosure crisis. The fact that only *six percent* of *high-cost loans* in our communities came from CRA institutions proves the true worth and value of the CRA to our neighborhoods."

We could go on and on. If you Google "only six percent" and "CRA" you will get hundreds of thousands of hits quoting lemmings who feel CRA has been completely vindicated because, by design, it is more likely to involve reduced-interest rate loans. The fact that the borrowers may have 400 FICO scores, be unemployed, and live in cars is of no consequence to these Mensa members.

In short, there is a disgraceful lack of solid information about CRA loan performance. Community activists, such as NACA, refuse to disclose it, and the Fed has only conducted one survey in many years and the results of that half-assed survey have been distorted. Finally, thousands of pundits and bureaucrats parrot a canard about "high-priced" loans being the same as "subprime" loans, and this confusion conveniently leads to a beatification of CRA. I won't insult anyone's honesty in regard to this line of reasoning — just his intelligence.

What is the best estimate of CRA's impact on the crisis?

Before we attempt to assess the volume and performance of CRA loans, let's step back to view the entire forest, rather than the individual trees. We need to view CRA lending in the context of all governmental programs designed to promote affordable housing (usually via the promotion of subprime lending). In his dissent to the Financial Crisis Inquiry Commission, Peter Wallison describes the destructive interaction of these separate programs:

> ... the gradual increase of the AH [affordable housing] goals, the competition between the GSEs and the FHA, the effect of HUD's Best Practices Initiative,[1] and bank lending under the CRA ensured a continuing flow of funds into weaker and weaker mortgages. This had the effect of extending the life of the housing bubble as well as increasing its size. The growth of the bubble, in turn, disguised the weakness of the subprime mortgages it contained ...[2]

Thus, the affordable housing programs, including the Community Reinvestment Act, increased the size and life of the housing bubble. This caused house values to rise quickly and made shaky borrowers less likely to default on their loans (because they did not want to lose homes increasing in value). Because of the low default rates that resulted, private lenders underestimated the riskiness of subprime loans.

---

1   The Best Practices Initiative was a voluntary agreement signed by HUD and the Mortgage Brokers Association of America. It was the model agreement after-which Countrywide and numerous other mortgage brokers (non-banks) agreed to CRA-like goals and standards. These separate agreements were known as "Declarations of Fair Lending Principles and Practices."

2   Wallison, "Dissent from the Majority Report of the Financial Crisis Inquiry Commission," 23.

The bubble created by the interaction of CRA with other affordable housing programs had an additional destructive effect, as described by Wallison:

> ... as housing prices rose in the bubble, it was necessary for borrowers to seek riskier mortgages in order to afford the monthly payments on more expensive homes. This gave rise to new and riskier forms of mortgage debt ...[1]

This was a double-edged bubble, so to speak. It gave borrowers an incentive to avoid default. However, the high house prices also made it necessary for borrowers to seek out the riskiest types of loans.

Regarding specific performance data for CRA loans, "[t]here has been no systematic study, by either the Government Accountability Office or the Federal Reserve, of the performance of loans cited by banks in their CRA filings."[2] As noted, much of the information disseminated by government bureaucrats is worthless due to the conflation of "subprime" with "higher-priced" loans. What information is available? A study that is often cited (mostly by left-leaning analysts) is one produced by the University of North Carolina.

Research by the Center for Community Capital

Researchers analyzed about 9,000 mortgage loans originated in a special CRA program, and they reached conclusions that are reasonable, but widely misunderstood. They compared a group of CRA loan borrowers, many of whom had subprime credit histories, with a group of non-CRA borrowers, who were picked because they had similar credit histories. About 40 percent of each group had FICO scores under 620, the lowest level under any definition for a prime borrower. The CRA borrowers (in this particular special lending program) had favorable "thirty-year fixed-rate loans amortizing with prime-level interest rates, no prepayment penalties, no balloons, with escrows for taxes and insurance, documented income, and standard prime-level fees." On the other hand, the non-CRA borrowers mostly had adjustable rate loans (often with high interest rates), and the loans had prepayment penalties and were generally originated by mortgage brokers (who may not be as diligent as a bank would be with regard to verification of a borrower's credit background). The researchers found that the group with the broker-originated, ARM loans had serious delinquency rates of 19.81 percent, while the group

---

1   Ibid.
2   Husock, "The Financial Crisis and the CRA."

with the CRA loans had serious delinquency rates of only 9 percent. The difference in these two rates is significant, but it should be interpreted in light of the following facts:

- The non-CRA loans were picked in such a way that 40 percent had very low FICO scores (similar to the rate in the CRA loan population). We don't know that, in the geographical area of the study, 40 percent of non-CRA loan borrowers would have FICO scores that low.

- All of the CRA loans were originated in a special lending program called the Community Advantage Program (CAP). The CAP program is assisted by a well-funded nonprofit entity, called Self-Help, which retained full recourse for any credit losses.[1] Without this special Self-Help loan guarantee, which constitutes a significant subsidy, the banks would not be able to sell the loans to Fannie or Freddie. That would probably necessitate a change in loan terms (e.g., higher interest rates and prepayment penalties), and those new loan terms could lead to higher delinquency rates. In other words, the CAP loans had a special advantage over the non-CAP loans. In the real world, these results would not have been achieved.

- CAP constitutes a small sample of loans that is "geographically concentrated in certain markets,"[2] and appears to be primarily focused on smaller banks in medium or small metropolitan statistical areas.[3] As noted, there is some evidence that CRA performs differently in large markets. In the case at hand, there is no evidence that participating banks were being hounded by NACA, ACORN or any other housing activist group. Therefore, we would expect CRA loans to perform decently in such a setting.

- CAP focuses on "the less risky portion of the subprime market...." By design, 60 percent had FICO scores over 620. Indeed, one suspects that many of the borrowers in CAP had prime

1   Roberto G. and Janneke Ratcliffe Quercia, "The Preventable Foreclosure Crisis," in Housing Policy Debate (Virginia Tech: Metropolitan Institute, 2008), 780.

2   Lei Ding and Roberto G. Quercia and Wei Li and Janneke Ratcliffe, "Risky Borrowers or Risky Mortgages - Disaggregating Effects Using Propensity Score Models," (Detroit: Wayne State University, 2010).

3   This is author's judgment based on a review of the participating banks and based on the size breakdown of the metropolitan statistical areas used in CAP.

credit backgrounds, and would have been able to obtain reasonable financing with or without CRA.[1]

- The 9 percent delinquency rate of this special CAP program was much better than the delinquency of the control group, and this is to be expected because CAP borrowers had less onerous repayment terms. However, the 9 percent CRA delinquency rate was very high compared to the rate on prime loans in general, which was 2 percent as of the same date (March 31, 2008).[2] Thus, it appears that, even with the most favorable loan terms, banks (and potentially, taxpayers) might have to pay a high price (in terms of credit risk) when loans are given to people via the CRA guidelines.

The research performed by the Center for Community Capital shows us that the terms of the loan, and who originates it (banks vs. broker), are significant factors that affect delinquency rates. However, the research also demonstrates that, even in the most favorable circumstances (e.g., the inclusion of many prime borrowers, the use of reputable loan originators, the help of a nonprofit guarantor, and favorable 30-year fixed interest rates) CRA loans are substantially more risky than conventional prime loans.

Other research regarding CRA lending

Although Bostic and Robinson (first cited on page 131) did not report conclusions regarding the quality and performance of CRA loans, they determined that the volume of lending in specific geographical areas varied in relation to "the presence, number, introduction and expiration of CRA agreements ..." and that the effectiveness of CRA in promoting increased lending was highly correlated with the "persistence and sophistication of community groups ..." In addition, the researchers determined that lenders seem to view CRA agreements "as a form of insurance against the potentially large and unknown costs ..." of lending violations. This research, performed in 2003, tends to support the theory that CRA

---

1 Ding and Roberto G. Quercia and Wei Li and Janneke Ratcliffe, "Risky Borrowers or Risky Mortgages — Disaggregating Effects Using Propensity Score Models."

2 The loans used in the research were all originated after 2002. The prime rate given here is from the Mortgage Bankers Survey (MBS) for the first quarter of 2008, and includes loans originated in earlier years. If the MBS were limited to post-2002 loans, it is likely that the serious delinquency rate would be higher.

may function differently in large communities (with relatively well-organized community activists) than in small communities.[1]

The 2008 research of Neil Bhutta, cited on page 131, pertained to the impact of CRA on the volume of lending. CRA is designed to target low and medium income neighborhoods — specifically, census tracts where the median family income is less than 80 percent of the median family income for the metropolitan statistical area (MSA) as a whole. Bhutta analyzed lending patterns for borrowers "just above and below the cut-off" (i.e., the 80 percent dividing line) since those borrowers were essentially the same, and lending differences would probably be attributable to CRA. He found that, for large MSAs in the years between 1997 and 2002, bank lending was likely to be 8 percent greater just below the cut-off than just above the cutoff. This research suggests that CRA may have a significant impact on lending.

Bhutta found virtually no increased CRA lending in small MSAs, and that led him to conclude that the impact of CRA is found "where banks are most likely to be heavily scrutinized by regulators and community groups." This brings us back to the assertion I made at the beginning of the chapter, which is that CRA is best analyzed as two distinct programs: CRA in small MSAs where underwriting standards tend to be prudent (because the CRA lending is simply the lending that banks would do in any event) and CRA in large MSAs where underwriting may be compromised (because the banks are under pressure from community activists).[2]

Regarding delinquency rates, interesting research was performed by Demyanyk and Van Hemert. They compared neighborhoods (based on zip codes) "with the same median income and with the same loan and borrower characteristics ..." but in MSAs with different median incomes. In the case of MSAs with higher median incomes, the neighborhoods would qualify for CRA lending (because the neighborhood income levels would be below 80 percent of the MSA median income level). However, in the case of MSAs with lower median incomes, the neighborhoods would not qualify for CRA lending (even though those neighborhoods included borrowers with similar incomes). The researchers studied the years 2001 through 2007, and found that delinquency rates were higher where CRA lending was more likely to take place. The increase in delin-

1   Bostic and Breck Robinson, "Do CRA Agreements Infuence Lending Patterns."
2   Bhutta, "Giving Credit Where Credit Is Due? The Community Reinvestment Act and Mortgage Lending in Lower-Income Neighborhoods," 1-2.

quency ranged from 1.75 percent to 6.26 percent, depending on the year examined.[1]

Estimate of the volume of subprime CRA loans

Edward Pinto, the former Chief Credit Officer at Fannie Mae, used a different approach to estimating private CRA lending.[2] Pinto used financial disclosures, press reports, and commonsense assumptions. To start, Pinto utilized CRA commitments, as announced by the National Community Reinvestment Coalition (NCDR), a group of 600 community housing organizations. In its 2007 report, NCRC noted that, from 1994 to 2007, CRA commitments totaled $4.5 trillion. Pinto noted that 94 percent of these announcements were made by Bank of America, JP Morgan Chase, Citibank, and Washington Mutual, or banks and thrifts purchased or subsumed by these banks. He then tracked the annual press releases of identified lenders to see how much and when CRA lending was made. Added to these results was a commitment by Countrywide Financial, made pursuant to HUD's "Declaration of Fair Lending Principles and Practices," designed to be a companion program for mortgage bankers that were not directly subject to CRA. Again, Pinto examined subsequent press releases to determine the amount of loans actually made by Countrywide.[3]

To adjust for the 7,000 other banks for which Pinto had no CRA information, he multiplied his results by 125 percent. In other words, he assumed that the known lenders (the big 5) and their successors accounted for 80 percent of CRA loans, while the other 7,000 lenders accounted for just 20 percent — an assumption that appears on its face to be reasonable and conservative. These machinations led Pinto to estimate that, at June 30, 2008, there remained outstanding $1.56 trillion in CRA and HUD companion program loans. This appears to be a fairly reasonable estimate, give or take a few billion.[4]

1   Yuliya Demyanyk and Otto Van Hemert, "Understanding the Subprime Mortgage Crisis," (Web-based: SSRN, December 5, 2008), 27, http://ssrn.com/abstract=1020396.
2   He limited his estimate of CRA subprime loans to those that ended up in private mortgage-backed securities because he had already made estimates of GSE subprime loans, which included their CRA acquisitions.
3   Pinto, "Government Housing Policies in the Lead-up to the Financial Crisis: A Forensic Study," Memorandum 2.
4   Ibid.

It was much more difficult for Pinto to estimate the percentage of this amount that was subprime, and to divine how much of it was sitting in private bank portfolios or private mortgage-backed securities. Pinto simply guessed that, of the CRA loans on hand at June 30, 2008, 60 percent were subprime. Although it was only a guess, it was probably a reasonable one, given the following facts. First, 4 of the 5 main lenders were subprime lenders according to most published listings. Those 4 lenders were CitiMortgage, WaMU, Chase, and Countrywide. Second, the goals of CRA suggest that a high percentage of borrowers will have substandard credit, or will be given flexible loan terms that will cause the loans to perform as if the borrowers have substandard credit. As noted by the NCRC, the umbrella entity for 600 community housing organizations, CRA lenders are required to target low and moderate-income borrowers. In addition, they are encouraged to reduce or eliminate down payments, to accept "sweat equity" in lieu of down payments, to waive mortgage insurance, to accept borrowers who "lack traditional credit histories," to moderate employment requirements, and to include other sources of income, including welfare.[1] Given these goals, and given the nature of the lenders participating, it would be surprising if less than 60 percent of the CRA loans were subprime.

Finally, Pinto assumed that Fannie and Freddie bought 65 percent of these CRA loans, and those loans (the 65 percent) were already counted in estimates of their subprime acquisitions. For this reason he reduced his estimate of private CRA loans to the 35 percent that would have ended up in private portfolios or private mortgage back securities. This is also a conservative estimate, given that most estimates indicate that Fannie and Freddie bought only about 50 percent of the affordable housing loans (not 65 percent).[2]

Summarizing the Pinto conclusions, in June 2008 there were $1.56 trillion of outstanding CRA loans (or the equivalent). Of this amount, about $940 billion (about 6.7 million loans) was probably subprime. ($940 billion is 60 percent of $1.56 trillion.) This is a very large amount of subprime lending, and it must have had an enormous impact on the financial crisis. However, much of that amount was redundant with Fannie's and Freddie's "affordable housing" purchases we discussed in earlier chapters, so the amount has to be reduced if we are to consider only the subprime loans held by private lenders and investors (and, not Fannie's

1   "CRA Commitments," 32.

2   ———, "Government Housing Policies in the Lead-up to the Financial Crisis: A Forensic Study," Memorandum 2.

or Freddie's). Pinto made the reduction by assuming that, as of June 2008, private entities held about 35 percent of the totals, which would be $330 billion or about 2.2 million loans.[1]

I believe that Pinto's estimate is reasonable, but it is fair to say that some of this CRA subprime lending might have taken place, even in the absence of CRA. For that reason, the direct impact of CRA on the volume of subprime lending is not certain. If it wanted to, the federal government could obtain more accurate CRA loan performance data by surveying banks. It could ask them to estimate how much of their CRA lending was due to perceived pressure from the government or community activists, and how much was lending that would have been done under any circumstances. I have a feeling that certain members of Congress and HUD don't want to obtain this information, for two reasons. If the survey indicated that a lot of subprime lending was done because of CRA, those results would make CRA look bad, and if the survey showed that CRA was really irrelevant to bank lending decisions, that finding would also make CRA look bad. Get the picture?

Delinquency rates for CRA lending

Unfortunately, there is little performance data for either version of the CRA — Dr. Jekyll or Mr. Hyde. I suspect that the CRA delinquency rates for small banks in small metropolitan statistical areas (MSAs) are fairly moderate. On the other hand, there are some data suggesting that CRA delinquency rates may be sky-high for the larger banks in the larger MSAs. First, there are the high rates associated with NACA loans (see page 134). Also, Edward Pinto reported these findings in autumn, 2009:

> In Cleveland, Third Federal Savings and Loan has a 35 percent delinquency rate on its CRA-mandated "Home Today" loans, versus a 2 percent delinquency rate on its non-Home Today portfolio. Chicago's Shorebank — the nation's first community development bank, with largely CRA-related loans on its books — has a 19 percent delinquency and non-accrual rate for its portfolio of first-mortgage loans for single-family residence. And Bank of America said in 2008 that while its CRA loans constituted 7 percent of its owned residential-mortgage portfolio, they represented 29 percent of that portfolio's net losses.[2]

What torture teaches us about the CRA

> Overnight, he became a celebrity — but for all the wrong reasons. He was held personally responsible for Abu

---

1   Ibid.

2   ———, "Yes, the CRA Is Toxic."

Ghraib's horrors: The disgusting behaviour of U.S. service
personnel was seen as the bottom of the slippery slope down
which Yoo had started America's military sliding when he
wrote the torture memo.

– The Gazette (Montreal) March 17, 2007

Just a few years ago, many of President Bush's critics were trying
hard to blame the midnight transgressions of a bunch of prison guards
on a legal memo written in the Office of Legal Counsel, a section of the
U.S. Justice Department. It was theorized that a memo, written for the
Bush Administration, was responsible for torture and other misdeeds by
U.S. troops at Abu Ghraib. Although Attorney John Yoo simply outlined
what he believed to be the constitutional powers of the President (he did
not advocate torture), his legal advice was perceived to be so powerful
that it caused, somehow, military personnel to commit outrageous acts.

I suspect that the people who found a cause and effect relationship
between Yoo's memo and torture will not find a cause and effect relationship between the Community Reinvestment Act and subprime lending.
However, let's consider and compare the facts. Yoo's memo did not advocate conduct; it only described what Yoo thought was legally permissible. Further, the prison guards at Abu Ghraib were not threatened with
punitive actions if they failed to torture prisoners. Indeed, it is doubtful that they even saw or heard of the memo. On the other hand, CRA
regulations required results that, in many cases, could only be achieved
with subprime lending, and these regulations were well publicized and
known to banks and other lenders.

Banks that did not establish acceptable CRA credentials could face
punitive actions. They could be blocked from mergers, from installing
new ATM machines, or other types of expansions. In some cases, they
could be subject to boycotts, adverse publicity by community activists,
and private lawsuits. Nonbank lenders were not directly regulated under CRA but they were threatened with new regulations if they did not
adopt similar standards. (The threat of regulation can be as effective as
the regulation itself.)[1] Also, the nonbanks, such as mortgage companies,
had to adopt the same low underwriting standards to stay competitive
in the market. If, for example, CRA banks were offering loans with only
3 percent down payments, nonbanks had to offer the same, or go out of
business.

---

1   Numerous nonbanks (mortgage lenders) signed Declarations of Fair Lending
    Principles and Practices, patterned after the Best-Practices agreement signed
    in 1994 by HUD and the Mortgage Brokers Association of America.

Finally, Fannie and Freddie let it be known that they would eagerly purchase any and all CRA loans. With that kind of inducement, nonbank lenders such as Countrywide were eager to originate and sell (separately or in securities) CRA loans. CRA gave these lenders the "cover" they needed to engage in risky lending. The collateral damage, unfortunately, was underwriting standards:

> It was not just that CRA and federal housing policy pressured lenders to make risky loans — but that they gave lenders the excuse and the regulatory cover.

– Phil Gramm, former U.S. Senator from Texas[1]

"Proof" that CRA had nothing to do with the crisis

Despite these facts, some analysts are steadfast in declaring that the Community Reinvestment Act (CRA) had nothing to do with the subprime crisis, and they are eager to offer "proof" in support of that assertion. We have already dispensed with one silly item of "proof" — the one involving confusion between "subprime" and "high-priced" loans (page 140). We also hear of the enormous time lag between enactment of CRA (in 1977) and the financial crisis. How could a law passed in 1977 be blamed for a crisis that took place in 2007? Those who make this argument seem to see the CRA as a static law — one that never changed. As noted, there were extensive regulatory changes made to CRA in 1995 (and legislative changes in 1992, 1994, and 1999), and the regulatory changes involved the loosening of underwriting standards, and the imposition of sanctions, if necessary, to ensure that lower-income people were offered mortgage loans. A few years later, the NASDAQ collapsed and people were looking for a new place to park their money. After the 911 terrorist attack, the Fed lowered interest rates sharply. These factors, coupled with the low underwriting standards introduced by the 1995 CRA regulations, led to an explosion within the real estate market.

It is also argued that most subprime loans were originated by nonbanks — not subject to CRA. This is considered to be definitive proof that CRA did not cause the crisis. As noted, however, the new, low CRA standards spread beyond banks and throughout the entire industry. There were 3 reasons for this. First, HUD directly pressured nonbanks to adopt companion standards, similar to CRA standards. Countrywide,

---

1   Phil Gramm, "Deregulation and the Financial Panic," online.wsj.com (February 20, 2009), http://online.wsj.com/article/SB123509667125829243. html.

the world's biggest subprime lender, complied by voluntarily signing a "Declaration of Fair Lending Principles and Practices."[1] Second, Fannie and Freddie had their own affordable housing goals, and they could satisfy them by buying CRA loans. They let it be kno wn that they were eager to buy such loans, and this meant that nonbanks, not directly subject to CRA, could make a pile of money originating such loans (or aggregating them from other lenders) and then selling the loans (separately or as securities) to Fannie and Freddie. Third, non-CRA banks were forced, by competitive pressures, to loosen their underwriting standards, even if the first two reasons did not apply. This is the way capitalism works. If one gas station offers to clean your windshield the nearby competitors have to also clean your windshield, or they will face a loss of business. For these three reasons, it is specious to argue that loose underwriting standards of CRA affected only a few CRA banks.

Finally, we sometimes hear this argument, which was recently made by a blogger named, Leigh:

> In order to qualify for CRA credits the loan had to be made w/in a "red-line" neighborhood. Show me a "red-lined" neighborhood in Portland, Oregon, Las Vegas, NV, etc.[2]

First, this statement is factually false. CRA neighborhoods are everywhere in the nation. CRA expressly covers borrowers who have income under 80 percent of the area median income, and/or those living in tracts with a median income less than 80 percent of the area median. In wealthy parts of the United States, the CRA still applies; however, it covers people who may have higher absolute incomes. For example, in 2003, the median family income in San Francisco was $91,500. Therefore, CRA eligibility could extend up to $73,200 (i.e., 80% times $91,500).

Second, the impact of CRA extended far beyond those technically covered. Once a bank or mortgage lender lowered underwriting standards for a low-income borrower, he could not justify raising those standards up again for higher-income borrowers. If it is safe to use lower un-

---

1   Countrywide advertised that banks could meet their own CRA obligations by buying Countrywide affordable housing loans. Its Web site pitched: "The result of these efforts is an enormous pipeline of mortgages to low- and moderate-income buyers. With this pipeline, Countrywide Securities Corporation (CSC) can potentially help you meet your Community Reinvestment Act (CRA) goals by offering both whole loan and mortgage-backed securities that are eligible for CRA credit."

2   Leigh, Patrick.net, October 16, 2009, http://patrick.net/forum/?p=16997.

derwriting standards for the poor it should be even safer to use the lower standards for the rich.

CRA was not the only cause of the crisis, but it certainly was one of the causes. We will never know exactly how many subprime loans were originated specifically to meet the CRA requirements (because the government doesn't seem to want that information). However, we can be certain that CRA created a mind-set that led to the spread of subprime lending. In the opinion of Howard Husock of the Manhattan Institute, the spread of "CRA-type thinking" and the adoption of that thinking by Fannie and Freddie was a major factor leading to the financial meltdown:

> The crucial link [to the current crisis] was the extension of CRA-type thinking and regulation to the secondary mortgage markets through the government-sponsored enterprises (GSEs) Fannie Mae and Freddie Mac, which buy loans from banks in order to provide liquidity. Beginning in 1992, the Department of Housing and Urban Development pushed Fannie and Freddie to buy loans based on criteria other than creditworthiness ...
>
> Crucially, subprime loans didn't only allow banks to meet their CRA lending requirements; sold to Fannie and Freddie, they could also help the two secondary mortgage giants meet their affordable-housing targets.[1]

In other words, CRA-qualified loans were attractive to banks because they minimized their risks of lawsuits, punitive regulatory actions and adverse actions by community activists. In addition, CRA loans would be gobbled up by Fannie and Freddie, who had their own affordable housing goals to worry about. That combination made CRA a potent force.

If we could only get Mr. Yoo to put these thoughts into a memo! Perhaps that would convince my liberal friends.

---

1   Husock, "The Financial Crisis and the CRA."

The first 8 chapters of this book pertain to the primary cause of the financial crisis of 2007/08: governmental housing policies that led to the degradation of all underwriting standards. Subprime borrowers were given home loans, and prime borrowers soon became subprime as they used the new, loose lending standards as a means to buy houses that they could not truly afford. This led to a housing boom starting around 1998.

In Chapter 9 we deal with the secondary cause of the crisis: Federal Reserve interest rate policy. The housing boom grew much larger after 2001, when the United States Federal Reserve Bank took actions to dramatically lower the short-term borrowing rate of banks.[1] Several economists and investment managers persuasively argue that this monetary policy was a major cause, if not the major cause, of the financial crisis. They assert that, after the September 11th, 2001 terrorist attacks, Alan Greenspan's Federal Reserve took interest rates too low and for too long (about two years too long). David Malpass, President of Encima Global LLC, states:

---

1   The federal funds rate is the interest rate at which banks trade their account balances maintained at the Federal Reserve Bank. These trades usually take place on an overnight basis, and are for the purpose of meeting Federal Reserve requirements for capital balances. Banks with surplus balances lend their excess funds to banks with deficient balances. The exact trade rates cannot be controlled; however, the Fed has a federal funds target rate, which it sets once in approximately every 7 weeks. Banks can also borrow directly from the Fed at its "discount window." Funds borrowed in this way usually carry a slightly higher interest rate.

The blame for the current crisis extends well beyond the Fed — to banks, regulators, bond raters, mortgage fraud, the Bush administration's weak-dollar policy and Lehman bankruptcy decisions, and Congress's reckless housing policies through Fannie Mae and Freddie Mac and the Community Reinvestment Act. *But the Fed provided the key fuel with its 1% interest rate choice in 2003 and 2004 and "measured" rate hikes in 2004–2006. It ignored inflationary dollar weakness, higher interest rate choices abroad, the Taylor Rule* [1] *and the booming performance of the U.S. and global economies* (emphasis added).[2]

Investment manager Martin T. Sosnoff put it this way:

> Our present misery dates back to Alan Greenspan's easy money policy of a few years ago. When the risk-free rate was pegged at 1%, financial market players, starved for higher yields, moved out on the quality spectrum for long maturity goods.[3]

How far off track did Alan Greenspan take us? A great deal, according to the man who created the "Taylor Rule," which provided guidance to the Fed with respect to the setting of short-term interest rates. In his book, *Getting Off Track*, John Taylor has a chart indicating a sharp divergence between the Fed rates intended by Greenspan and the rates suggested by the Taylor Rule. A similar chart is found in Figure 12, below.

If Taylor is right, his friend, Alan Greenspan, steered the S.S. Federal Reserve far off course into an iceberg.[4]

Others have made similar claims, without referencing the Taylor Rule. They assert that there was a wide gap between the federal funds rate and the inflation indexes that realistically account for housing inflation. The Fed does not directly consider housing inflation when setting its target interest rates. Instead, it uses a substitute factor called "Owners Equivalent Rent" (OER), which is an estimate of what it would cost if owners were to rent their homes from themselves. In the view of Investment Advisor Mish Shedlock, OER was not a "valid construct of prices." He adds: "By ignoring housing prices, the CPI massively understated inflation for years." [5]

---

1   The Taylor Rule is a simple math formula that has provided guidance to the Federal Reserve with regard to the setting of its target interest rates.

2   David Malpass, "Did the Fed Cause the Housing Bubble?," online.wsj.com (March 27, 2009), http://online.wsj.com/article/SB123811225716453243.html.

3   Martin T. Sosnoff, "Blame Greenspan," Forbes.com (August 7, 2007), http://www.forbes.com/2007/08/06/sosnoff-markets-growth-oped-cx_mts_0807sosnoff.html.

4   Alan Greenspan and John Taylor were, and claim to still be, good friends, even though they have strongly and publicly disagreed regarding this matter.

5   Mish Shedlock, "CPI and Cs-CPI vs. Fed Funds Rate," Global Economic Trend Analysis, November 12, 2008, http://globaleconomicanalysis.blogspot.

Figure 12 – Fed historic rates vs. Taylor's rate[1]

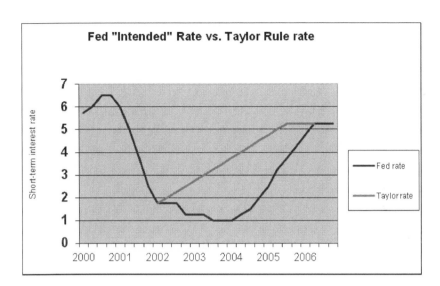

Shedlock gives this example: In the summer of 2005, when the consumer price index (using OER) was just over 4 percent, CS-CPI, which is the consumer price index with Case Shiller housing inflation added, was "near a whopping 8%." However, the federal funds rate was about 4 percent below this measure of inflation, which was "stunningly low."[2]

Chairman Greenspan and his supporters take issue with all of these assertions, and make compelling counter arguments:

- Deflation was a palpable threat, and the Fed had to keep interest rates low to defend against that threat.
- Statistics show that the housing boom began years before the Fed lowered interest rates in 2001.
- Mortgage rates started moving down 6 months before the Fed first lowered interest rates. When the Fed finally started raising rates in 2004 mortgage rates continued to fall. These facts suggest that the Fed was not the only force affecting mortgage interest rates. Most likely, the other force affecting rates was a

---

1   Taylor rates per Susan Lee, "It Really Is All Greenspan's Fault," April 3, 2009, Forbes.com; Fed rates per Federal Reserve Web site at http://www.federalreserve.gov/monetarypolicy/openmarket.htm.
2   Ibid.

world-wide savings glut. That would explain why the housing bubble was global.

- The Fed controls the overnight interest rates — not the long-term rates that normally affect mortgage loans.

I come down in the middle between the Greenspan critics and supporters. The Federal Reserve's low-interest-rate policy was a huge factor that greatly contributed to the size and destructiveness of the financial crisis. It encouraged the growth of risky adjustable rate mortgage loans, it accelerated the growth of the housing boom, and it caused investors to seek higher yields in risky investments — often derivatives or mortgage-backed securities. That said, there was genuine concern about deflation, and there were other factors, beside Fed monetary policy, that pushed mortgage interest rates lower.

Also, the destructiveness of the financial crisis of 2007 cannot be explained as the bursting of an ordinary speculative bubble. The unique and deadly aspects of this crisis are directly linked to the degradation of loan underwriting standards and to a virus of subprime loans that infected the investments that were sold across the world. In other words, the issues developed in the first 8 chapters of this book were most directly responsible for the crisis. Each of Greenspan's arguments is considered, below.

The deflation argument

Whereas inflation is the increase in the general price level of goods and services, deflation is the general level of goods and services. It occurs when the inflation rate falls below zero.

It is easy to dismiss deflation concerns now, but several economists, including some at the Federal Reserve, feared the onset of deflation in the early 2000s. Transcripts of a November 2002 Fed meeting, released in April, 2008, show that the Fed's interest rate policies were substantially driven by deflation fears. At that meeting, Greenspan said that deflation was "a pretty scary prospect, and one that we certainly want to avoid." He added:

> We are dealing with what basically is a latent deflationary type of economy, and we are all acutely aware of the implications of that economy.[1]

---

1   Martin Crutsinger, "Fed Transcript: '02 Deflation Fears Helped Drive Down Rates," ABC News (April 11, 2008), http://abcnews.go.com/Business/comments?type=story&id=4640741.

In 2002, Governor Ben Bernanke also expressed concern, stating that "central banks must today try to avoid major changes in the inflation rate in either direction."[1] That reference to "either direction" is Fed-speak for deflation.

The Fed's concerns about the risk of deflation were detailed by the Federal Reserve Bank of San Francisco:

> A substantial, prolonged deflation, like the one during the Great Depression, can be associated with severe problems in the financial system. It can lead to significant declines in the value of collateral owned by households and firms, making it more difficult to borrow. And falling collateral values may force lenders to call in outstanding loans, which would force firms to cut back their scale of operations and force households to cut back consumption.[2]

In defending the performance of Alan Greenspan, Economist Vincent Reinhart makes the following observations related to the economy in 2002:

> ...inflation was so distinctly pointed down that deflation seemed a palpable threat. Keeping the federal-funds rate low for a long time was viewed as appropriately balancing the risks to the Fed's dual objectives of maximum employment and price stability. Indeed, the Fed was seen as extending the stable economic performance since 1983 that had been dubbed the "Great Moderation."[3]

We will never know for sure how real the threat was. However, there is no doubt that the monetary policies of the Federal Reserve were affected by fears of deflation.

Exactly when did the housing bubble start?

According to real estate expert Robert Shiller, the housing boom began in 1998 — not in 2001 when the Fed lowered interest rates:

> The boom showed its first beginnings in 1998 with real (inflation corrected) home price increases first exceeding 10% in a year on the West Coast, in the glamour cities San Diego, Los Angeles, San Francisco and Seattle. ... But the boom quickly spread east, with 10% one-year real home price

---

1   Pierre Siklos, "Fed Transcript: '02 Deflation Fears Helped Drive Down Rates," Economic History Services (February 1, 2010), http://eh.net/encyclopedia/article/siklos.deflation.

2   "What Are the Goals of U.S. Monetary Policy?," Federal Reserve Bank of San Francisco, 2011, http://www.frbsf.org/publications/federalreserve/monetary/goals.html.

3   Malpass, "Did the Fed Cause the Housing Bubble?."

increases appearing in Denver and then Boston in 1999. These cities kept on appreciating at a high rate.[1]

The reason for the housing inflation in 1998 is not clear, but it was probably triggered by concerns with the stability of the growing dot com bubble, psychological (hype) factors, and by affordable housing (easy financing) programs in some of those "glamour cities" mentioned by Shiller. In Chapter 4 of this book (page 51), the rapid spread of silent second loans (i.e., undisclosed loans used to finance the required down payment) is described:

> Silent second loans spread quickly through the numerous HUD affiliates. Just two years after HUD laid out its *Strategy*, the State of California published (in June 1997) a document identifying silent second loan programs in dozens of its counties and cities.

The connection between the housing boom and silent seconds and low down payments (two instruments of affordable housing policy) is strongly suggested by the research of two academics and a Federal Reserve analyst: Matthew Chambers, Don Schlagenhauf, and Carlos Garriga. Using data from the American Housing Survey and several other sources they estimated that the availability of low-down payment loans and "combo" loans (those with silent second or piggyback loans) accounted for 56 to 70 percent of the housing boom between the mid-1990s and 2004.[2]

This is the probable sequence. In 1995 HUD laid out its "*Strategy*" for the relaxing of lending standards, by 1997 the State of California (a HUD strategy partner) could identify "silent second" programs (i.e., government-sponsored fraud programs) "in dozens of its counties and cities," and in 1998 we have the start of the housing bubble — in California no less — according to housing expert Robert Shiller. Hmmm!

The early start to the housing bubble exonerates Alan Greenspan and Company — but only partially. They did not start the bubble but, starting in 2001, misguided Federal Reserve interest rate policies almost certainly accelerated the increase in the housing bubble.

---

1   Robert J. Shiller, "Understanding Recent Trends in House Prices and Home Ownership," (Web-based: Cowles Foundation Discussion Paper No. 1630 (available at SSRN), September 14, 2007), http://papers.ssrn.com/sol3/papers.cfm?abstract_id=1017546.

2   Matthew Chambers and Carlos Garriga and Don Schlagenhauf, "Accounting for Changes in the Homeownership Rate," (Web-based: International Economic Review (available at SSRN), August 2009), http://papers.ssrn.com/sol3/papers.cfm?abstract_id=1432239.

Can the U.S. Federal reserve cause a world-wide bubble?

Asks Economist David Henderson, "...if the Fed was the culprit, why was the housing bubble world-wide? Do Mr. Greenspan's critics seriously contend that the Fed was responsible for high housing prices in, say, Spain?"[1]

The short answer is, yes, they do. Consider, for example, this Wall Street Journal Op-Ed by Economist Judy Shelton:

> The Fed owns this crisis. ... The sheer enormity of this speculative bubble, let alone the speed at which it inflated, testifies to inordinately loose monetary policy from the Fed, *keeper of the world's predominant currency*. The fact that Fannie Mae and Freddie Mac provided the "underlying security" for many of the derivative contracts merely compounds the error government intervention in the private sector (emphasis added).[2]

As noted by Shelton, monetary decisions made by the United States Federal Reserve have world-wide implications because ours is the predominant currency in the world. United States affordable housing policies also had world-wide implications for another reason: The mortgage-backed securities peddled around the world were laced with subprime loans issued in the U.S. For these reasons, the U.S. government cannot seek absolution in the fact that there was a housing bubble in many parts of the world, or in the fact that banks in other countries suffered major losses.

Shelton's view is echoed by Economist Shlomo Maital, who commented on the financial crisis gripping Ireland. He blogged:

> It was Greenspan who showed other nations like Ireland how to create a housing bubble, by slashing interest rates rapidly and irresponsibly from 6.5 percent (Fed rate) to 1 percent, in the wake of the 2000 dot com crisis. No Central Bank should ever slash interest rates so far or so fast, to the point where "real" (inflation adjusted) rates are actually negative. ("Here, borrow a ton of money! Please! We'll pay YOU if you do.")[3]

Clearly, the U.S. Federal Reserve's loose money policies had world-wide financial implications. But, it must also be stated that there was a major influx of capital from China and other countries — an influx that could not be controlled by the Fed. Those funds helped to keep mort-

---

1   David Henderson, "Did the Fed Cause the Housing Bubble?," The Wall Street Journal (March 27, 2009), http://online.wsj.com/article/SB123811225716453243.html.
2   Judy Shelton, "Did the Fed Cause the Housing Bubble?," online.wsj.com (March 27, 2009), http://online.wsj.com/article/SB123811225716453243.html.
3   Shlomo Maital, TIMnovate, October 1, 2010, http://timnovate.wordpress.com/2010/10/01/irish-crisis-is-alan-greenspan-to-blame/.

gage interest rates low. This explains, according to Tao Wu, Economist at the Dallas Federal Reserve Bank, why mortgage rates continued to fall (for most of 2004 and 2005) even after Greenspan started raising rates in mid-2004:[1]

> Faced with a rapid accumulation of dollar assets from record-high trade surpluses, Asian central banks invested many of these reserves in U.S. Treasury bonds, exerting downward pressure on Treasury yields.... Some economists estimate such pressures on the 10-year Treasury yield at 40 to 120 basis points.

> More generally, a *global savings glut* has arisen from surges in revenues for oil and commodity exporters, the rapid income growth of high-saving East Asian households and the reduction in fiscal deficits by several Latin American countries. These developments have added to the net supply of loanable funds to increasingly open world financial markets, helping hold down long-term rates in the U.S. and other advanced nations (emphasis added).[2]

The concept of a "global savings glut" is not without controversy. Indeed, Greenspan critics such as Economist John Taylor question whether there really was a world-wide savings glut. He notes that, as a percentage of world gross domestic product, savings and investment have been in decline. However, the relevance of savings and investment *as a percentage of GDP* is not clear to me: Perhaps it is the absolute amount of savings and investment that that counts. I tend to believe that the Fed had only partial control over interest rates, and it should receive only partial blame for not getting rates higher.

Fed policy doesn't affect long-term rates?

On March 11, 2009, Chairman Greenspan responded to his critics with an OP-Ed in the Wall Street Journal. One of his chief arguments concerned the mismatch between the short-term, overnight, interest rates set by the Fed and the long-term mortgage rates used for home loans. Greenspan's contention was that "the interest rate that mattered was not the federal funds rate, but the rate on long-term, fixed-rate mortgages." He added:

---

1   In June 2004 the Fed's target rate was 1 percent, but by July 2006 it had reached 5.25 percent.

2   Tao Wu, "Economic Letter - Insights from the Federal Reserve Bank of Dallas," Federal Reserve Bank of Dallas, February 2008, http://www.dallas-fed.org/assets/documents/research/eclett/2008/el0802.pdf.

No one, to my knowledge, employs overnight interest rates — such as the fed-funds rate — to determine the capitalization rate of real estate, whether it be an office building or a single-family residence.[1]

Greenspan's claim that the Fed rates did not affect mortgage rates is not credible. Gerald P. O'Driscoll, Jr., a former vice president of the Dallas Federal Reserve Bank, summarizes the problems with Greenspan's argument:

...Mr. Greenspan writes as if mortgages were of the 30-year variety, financed by 30-year money. Would that it were so! We would not be in the present mess. But the post-2002 period was characterized by one-year adjustable-rate mortgages (ARMs), teaser rates that reset in two or three years, etc. Five-year ARMS became "long-term" money.

The Fed only determines the overnight, federal-funds rate, but movements in that rate substantially influence the rates on such mortgages.[2]

O'Driscoll also notes the role of short-term rates in funding the purchase of mortgage-backed securities (the kind that lost value overnight when people realized they were laced with subprime loans):

Additionally, maturity-mismatches abounded and were the source of much of the current financial stress. Short-dated commercial paper funded investment banks and other entities dealing in mortgage-backed securities.[3]

Another Greenspan critic, George Mason University law professor Todd Zywicki, contends that the Fed's low short-term interest rates had a harmful impact on consumer behavior. He states:

Alan Greenspan's argument that the Federal Reserve's policies on short-term interest rates had no impact on long-term mortgage interest rates overlooks the way in which its policies changed consumer behavior. ... During previous times with high percentages of ARMs, the dip in short-term rates was a leading indicator of an eventual decline in long-term rates, reflecting the general downward trend in rates of the past 25 years. By contrast, during this housing bubble the interest rate on ARMs were *artificially low* and eventually rose back to the level of FRMs [fixed rate mortgages]. ... the Fed's artificial lowering of short-term interest rates and

---

1   Alan Greenspan, "The Fed Didn't Cause the Housing Bubble," online.wsj.com (March 11, 2009), http://online.wsj.com/article/SB123672965066989281.html.

2   Gerald P. O'Driscoll, "Did the Fed Cause the Housing Bubble?," online.wsj. com (March 27, 2009), http://online.wsj.com/article/SB123811225716453243. html.

3   Ibid.

the resulting substitution by consumers to ARMs triggered the bubble and subsequent crisis (emphasis added).[1]

In other words, based on past experience, consumers had reason to expect interest rates on fixed rate mortgages to eventually come down towards short-term rates. However, this did not happen because the short-term rates did not reflect economic reality. They were artificial rates set by the Fed.

The two bubble factors: monetary policy and subprime

There are at least 2 ways to create a housing bubble: by loosening lending standards so that more tenants can become house owners (or so that existing house owners can become bigger-house owners), and by lowering mortgage interest rates across the board. Both methods were in play in the years leading to the crisis. The first method started in 1995, with HUD's grand (subprime) "*Strategy*" (Chapter 1). The second method (low interest rates) began in 2001 with the Federal Reserve's low-interest monetary policies.

In the beginning of the book I cite the research performed by Atif Mian and Amir Sufi, who studied lending patterns to subprime borrowers (defined by FICO scores) in 3014 zip-codes in 166 counties. They found that lending to high-subprime zip codes (based on FICO scores) had significantly increased, and subsequent default rates for those same areas had also increased. The researchers stated "that any study seeking to understand the origins of the mortgage default crisis must explain the expansion of mortgage credit to subprime neighborhoods across the entire county."[2]

Mian and Sufi considered whether low interest policies were the cause of the growth in subprime lending. They made a fascinating observation:

> There is a possibility that historically low risk free rates from 2001 to 2005 are responsible for the subprime mortgage credit expansion; however, there is no such expansion when risk free rates drop sharply from 1990 to 1994, and there is no corresponding shift in non-mortgage consumer credit from 2001 to 2005.[3]

1   Todd J. Zywicki, "Did the Fed Cause the Housing Bubble?," online.wsj.com (March 27, 2009), http://online.wsj.com/article/SB123811225716453243.html.
2   Atif Mian and Amir Sufi, "The Consequences of Mortgage Credit Expansion: Evidence from the U.S. Mortgage Default Crisis," Quarterly Journal of Economics 124(4) (November 2009): 1449-96.
3   Ibid.

In other words, low interest rates may have contributed to a housing bubble, but there is no clear link between low interest rates and the expansion of lending to unqualified borrowers. Previous periods of low interest rates did not result in an increase in such lending.

Arnold Kling is an economist who questions if Fed policy even contributed to the housing bubble. In an October 2008 blog Kling stated:

> Today, some people continue to blame the run-up in home prices on Federal Reserve policy and low interest rates. However, I have changed my position on that, and I now believe that the bubble was speculative.
>
> A major contributing factor to the speculative bubble was the explosion in lending for home purchase with little or no money down. When the down payment is small, the buyer's equity consists almost entirely of price appreciation. When prices are rising, anyone can buy a home with a low down payment, and any mortgage loan is safe. ... Once prices stop rising, the low-down-payment loans tend to go sour rather quickly.[1]

While I believe Fed monetary policy was a factor, I believe that the low down payment, which epitomized subprime lending, was the more significant factor.

It is important to remember how we got to low-down payment loans. Down payments were anathema to housing advocates in and out of government. They questioned why banks needed to require down payments, and even created "silent second" loans to circumvent down payment requirements. Fannie and Freddie designed loan products without down payments, and community activists urged that "sweat equity" be substituted for cash down payments. That's how we got to destructive, no-down-payment loans.

Epilogue: Transcripts show a clueless Federal Reserve

In 2005, after years of super-low interest rates, the Fed started to raise its daily lending rate. In meetings held in 2006, the Fed assessed the impact of those rising rates on the economy. Based on transcripts released to the public in 2012, here are the dead-on economic forecasts made by Timothy Geithner (VP of the Federal Reserve Board at the time) and Ben Bernanke (Chairman), in 2006:

(Timothy Geithner)

---

1   Arnold Kling, "The Fantasy Testimony Continues," Library of Economics and Liberty (October 14, 2008), http://econlog.econlib.org/archives/2008/10/the_fantasy_tes.html.

We just don't see troubling signs yet of collateral damage, and we are not expecting much. The fundamentals supporting relatively strong productivity growth seem to be intact.[1]

(Ben Bernanke)

So like most people around the table, I think that a soft landing with growth a bit below potential in the short run looks like the most likely scenario.[2]

Should we buy them a Ouija board?

1   "Meeting of the Federal Open Market Committee," Federal Reserve System, September 20, 2006, http://www.federalreserve.gov/fomc/minutes/20060920.htm.
2   "Meeting of the Federal Open Market Committee," Federal Reserve System, December 12, 2006, http://www.federalreserve.gov/fomc/minutes/20061212.htm.

PART TWO: RESISTANCE TO SUBPRIME BROKE DOWN

As noted in Part One, government housing advocacy led to a break-down in underwriting standards, and the Fed's low-interest-rate policies put subprime lending, and all lending, on steroids. In other words, the restrictions on lending fell while the incentives to lend increased. Nevertheless, subprime lending should have been resisted by five economic forces. It was not.

- Borrowers should have resisted taking loans they could not repay.
- Lenders should have resisted giving loans to people with substandard credit.
- Investment banks should have feared losses associated with the bundling of subprime loans into securities.
- Investors should have resisted buying securities laced with bad loans.
- Government regulators should have ensured high underwriting standards.

Of course, the last level — resistance by government regulators — did not exist because the government was the party most interested in *promoting* the growth of subprime lending. Imagine how different things might have been if our government regulators had strived to minimize systemic risk to our banking system by insisting that loans be given only to people with adequate documentation that established that they had good credit, good income, and had provided adequate down payments. Instead, government pressure was entirely in the wrong direction.

What about items 1 through 4, involving resistance by borrowers, lenders, investment banks, and investors? Why didn't these parties resist the government's invitation to engage in subprime lending? In each case, natural market-place resistance was undermined. That phenomenon is the focus of Part Two of the book, and is represented by the shaded box in the flowchart in Figure 13.

Figure 13 – A model of the causes and other factors affecting the financial crisis of 2007/08 (The shaded box pertains to Part Two.)

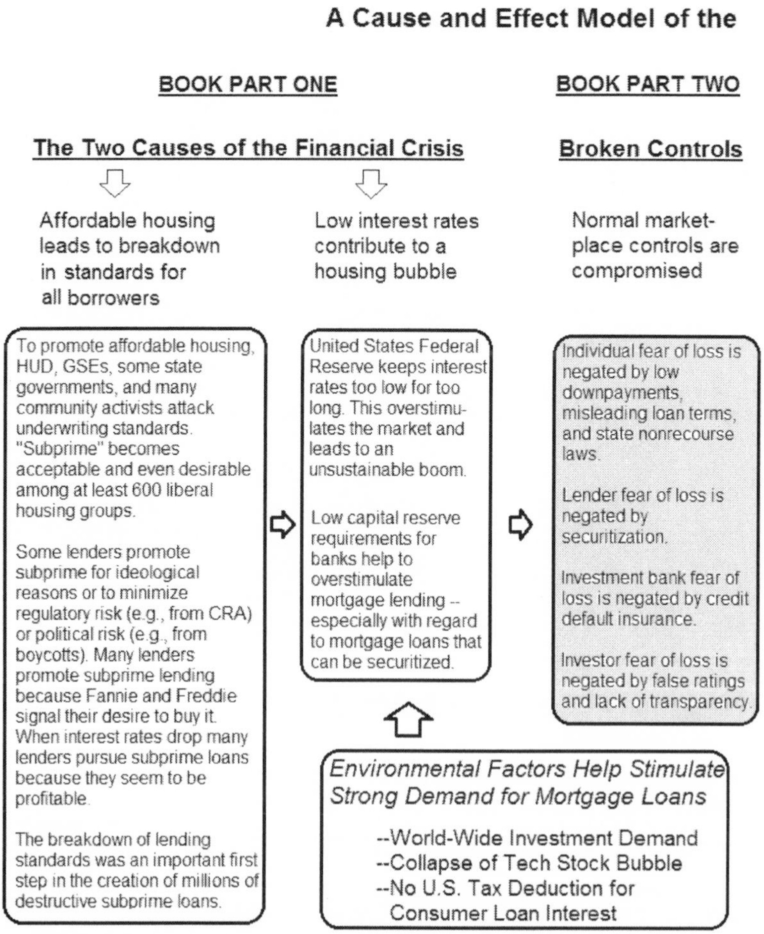

A Cause and Effect Model of the

BOOK PART ONE		**BOOK PART TWO**
The Two Causes of the Financial Crisis		**Broken Controls**
⇩	⇩	
Affordable housing leads to breakdown in standards for all borrowers	Low interest rates contribute to a housing bubble	Normal market-place controls are compromised

To promote affordable housing, HUD, GSEs, some state governments, and many community activists attack underwriting standards. "Subprime" becomes acceptable and even desirable among at least 600 liberal housing groups.

Some lenders promote subprime for ideological reasons or to minimize regulatory risk (e.g., from CRA) or political risk (e.g., from boycotts). Many lenders promote subprime lending because Fannie and Freddie signal their desire to buy it. When interest rates drop many lenders pursue subprime loans because they seem to be profitable.

The breakdown of lending standards was an important first step in the creation of millions of destructive subprime loans.

United States Federal Reserve keeps interest rates too low for too long. This overstimulates the market and leads to an unsustainable boom.

Low capital reserve requirements for banks help to overstimulate mortgage lending -- especially with regard to mortgage loans that can be securitized.

Individual fear of loss is negated by low downpayments, misleading loan terms, and state nonrecourse laws.

Lender fear of loss is negated by securitization.

Investment bank fear of loss is negated by credit default insurance.

Investor fear of loss is negated by false ratings and lack of transparency.

⇧

Environmental Factors Help Stimulate Strong Demand for Mortgage Loans

--World-Wide Investment Demand
--Collapse of Tech Stock Bubble
--No U.S. Tax Deduction for Consumer Loan Interest

Subprime Mortgage Crisis of 2007-2008

BOOK PART THREE

BOOK PART FOUR

Sparks   **Boom**   **Aggravating Factors**

These are just triggers

Bear Stearns & ML are sold, Lehman goes broke, AIG is downgraded, and Feds take over Fannie and Freddie

These factors complicate the crisis aftermath but do not cause the crisis

Mark-to-market accounting

Naked short selling

Sudden downgrades by rating agencies

Financial Crisis

Banks & borrowers are hurt because of documentation defects.

Taxpayers are hurt because bank capital reserves are deficient.

Homeowners are hurt by nearby foreclosures, which are aggravated by nonrecourse lending rules.

CHAPTER 10: SECURITIZATION — WHO NEEDS IT?

> Securitization meant the originator did not bear the cost
> of flawed mortgage products ... This was based on the idea
> that a fool is born every minute.
>
> – Jordan Eizenga, Economic Policy Analyst, Center for
> American Progress, May 18, 2010

As it pertains to home mortgages, securitization is the process of buy-ing mortgage loans, transferring them to a special entity (usually a trust), and having the special entity issue debt securities or bonds that pay prin-cipal and interest derived from the pool of mortgage loans it holds. The process creates liquidity by enabling smaller investors to buy shares of securities that reflect the earning potential and diversified credit risk of large numbers of loans.

Some economists cite securitization as a chief cause of the financial crisis. It may be a matter of semantics, but I do not think securitization caused the crisis. After all, it was around for almost 4 decades before we got into financial trouble. However, after HUD introduced lower un-derwriting standards and the Fed lowered interest rates to the extreme, securitization took on a new role. It allowed lenders to take the Fed's cheap money, use the government-recommended loan standards (or lack thereof), make subprime loans, and escape the consequences of those bad loans. Securitization made lenders much less resistant to the idea of lending to subprime borrowers because it allowed them to transfer their loans to investment banks that would bundle them into securities that could be unloaded to gullible investors across the globe.

A brief history of securitization

> Mortgage securitization has always had two major advantages. One is that it permits accounting gimmicks, such as moving mortgages off the government books and thereby lowering the official national debt. Similar accounting tricks occur with every major surge in securitization.
>
> – Economist Arnold Kling[1]

Although securitization has been endorsed by many economists of all ideological persuasions, it started out as an accounting gimmick and remains, in fact, a corruption of free market lending. Fannie Mae was created in 1938 to serve as a liquid secondary market for home mortgages; however, it did not securitize those mortgages. Securitization was born thirty years later (in 1968) when the original Fannie Mae was split into two entities: the Government National Mortgage Association (Ginnie Mae) and the current Fannie Mae. To get the massive debt of public housing off the federal books, Fannie was privatized by selling its stock to private investors. However, debt remained in the form of Federal Housing Administration (FHA) and Veterans' Administration (VA) loans. Ginnie Mae was formed to bundle these FHA/VA loans into securities so they could be sold to private investors. This made Uncle Sam's books look good, but taxpayers were still on the hook, in the event of loan default.

Freddie Mac was created in 1970 to provide competition for Fannie. It began securitizing loans in 1971, and Fannie began its securitization program in 1981. Unlike the securities of Ginnie Mae, the securities of Fannie and Freddie were not explicitly guaranteed by the U.S. government; however, they were implicitly guaranteed — a guarantee that became explicit in 2008 and subsequent years, at huge cost to U.S. taxpayers.

That is how the U.S. embarked on its securitization programs, but how did securitization come to dominate the lending market? At least part of the answer lies with (misguided) government capital reserve requirements. As noted, securitization started with Ginnie Mae, then Freddie and Fannie. These 3 entities had an enormous advantage over traditional, direct lenders: Their securities were either explicitly or implicitly guaranteed by the government, and that meant their securities were less risky, and could carry lower interest rates, thus increasing both revenues and profits.

Fannie and Freddie (F&F) had an additional advantage over investment banks in the form of lower capital reserve requirements. In the

---

1   ———, Unchecked and Unbalanced (New York: Rowman & Littlefield Publishers, Inc., 2010), 3.

early 2000s, this enabled F&F to give their shareholders more profits by means of leverage. While banks and thrifts were generally required to maintain adjusted net worth of at least 4 percent for the residential mortgage loans they held, Fannie and Freddie had a minimum capital requirement of only 2.5 percent of on-balance sheet assets.

The government rewarded securitizers

Those were the rules for retained, whole residential mortgage loans. However, by bundling thousands of loans into securities, all entities — Fannie and Freddie and private investment banks — could dramatically reduce the normal capital requirements, stated above. For triple A-rated mortgage securities — even those that included mostly subprime assets — private lenders had an effective capital requirement of only 1.6 percent (instead of 4 percent). F&F had an effective capital requirement of a mere .45 percent (instead of 2.5 percent) for the trillions of dollars of mortgage-backed securities they guaranteed.[1] The analysis became more complicated after modified standards were issued for F&F and for investment banks, but at all times the capital reserve standards imposed by regulators greatly favored securitization, and this was a driving force behind its spectacular growth.[2] Economist Arnold Kling summed up the perverse nature of these capital requirements by noting:

> The securitization process so bamboozled the regulators that ... [they] were telling banks to treat [securitized] mortgage loans with low down payments as safer than [retained] mortgage loans with high down payments.[3]

These capital requirements, and the role of regulators in setting them and monitoring them, are discussed in greater detail in Chapter 17.

Was our 40-year securitization experiment a success?

In a word, securitization was a disaster. Most of the benefits of securitization could have been achieved in other ways, and the remaining

---

1   The standard bank capital requirement was 8 percent. That was cut in half to the degree that the bank held residential mortgage loans. Thus, the effective capital requirement for a bank holding residential mortgage loans was 4 percent (.5 times 8 percent). To the degree that the bank held securitized residential mortgage loans the capital requirement was only .2, producing an effective capital requirement of 1.6 percent (.2 times 8 percent).

2   Due to their accounting misdeeds, Fannie and Freddie were required to each maintain a 30 percent capital surplus after 2004. In 2004, the capital requirements of private investment banks were modified by the SEC.

3   Kling, "The Fantasy Testimony Continues."

benefits were greatly offset by the destructive contribution of securitization to the 2007/08 subprime mortgage calamity. Securitization contributed enormously to the financial crisis by driving up the demand for housing. As Alan Greenspan put it, "The evidence strongly suggests that without the excess demand from securitizers, subprime mortgage originations (undeniably the original source of the crisis) would have been far smaller and defaults accordingly far fewer."[1]

Securitization decreased the normal resistance of lenders to the notion of giving loans to subprime borrowers. Lenders assumed that, before Armageddon, they could unload these substandard loans on private investment banks that would turn them into securities that could be unloaded on investors. It is not clear, however, that the investment banks knew just how risky their subprime-riddled securities were. If they did, why did they swallow so much of their own snake oil? That is, why did they retain so many of the securitized time bombs? Jesse Eisinger, a columnist at Portfolio.com, notes that several large companies retained billions of dollars of supersenior securities:

> These companies thought — erroneously — that the slices were so unlikely to default that they needn't set aside much capital for that eventuality. The problem was that the underlying assets propping these slices up weren't blue-chip loans but rather loans to subprime borrowers and junk companies. The supersenior slices turned out to be enormously risky, exposing these companies to huge losses.[2]

Call me naïve but I agree with Eisinger that some or most investment bank CEOs were truly in the dark regarding the (low) quality of the securities they created. Perhaps they believed Countrywide and other aggregators when they said they tested the quality of the underwriting of their loans, believed the AAA ratings of well-established companies such as Moody's and Fitch, or believed that the securities they issued were effectively insured by companies such as AIG Financial Products. The degradation of loan quality happened very quickly — over just a few years. As an auditor I know that it can take time (years) for grassroots statistical information to reach and influence the upper echelons of a large organization.

---

1   Edmund L. Andrews, "Greenspan Concedes Error on Regulation," The New York Times (October 24, 2008), http://www.nytimes.com/2008/10/24/business/economy/24panel.html.

2   Jesse. Eisinger, "The $58 Trillion Elephant in the Room," Portfolio.com (October 15, 2008), http://www.portfolio.com/views/columns/wall-street/2008/10/15/Credit-Derivatives-Role-in-Crash/.

In addition, the CEOs probably didn't see the systemic risk inherent in a national decline in home values, because almost nobody did. Indeed, most economists felt that the real estate market was regional, not national. The expectation of a major national devaluation was simply not there. Further, it was assumed that, if a national decline did take place, the upper tranches (levels) of mortgage-backed securities would be insulated from substantial devaluation because there would always be enough principal and interest collected to services those upper tranches. (It was assumed that the value of mortgage-backed securities was tied to the collection of loan interest and principal payments — not to resale values.) However, even this assumption became doubtful after the adoption of new accounting standards that took effect in 2007 (see Chapter 14).

It is interesting that conservatives and liberals share the same fallacy about the sophistication and acumen of large businesses, although their conclusions differ along ideological lines. Conservatives think large businesses can anticipate and remedy all problems, and that is good for society at large. Liberals think large businesses can anticipate and remedy all problems, and that means they can figure out how to screw the little guy. In reality, as Mitt Romney famously (and accurately) said, "corporations are people," and people can make outrageous blunders.

Research by author Michael Lewis (*The Big Short: Inside the Doomsday Machine*) seems to support the notion that investment bank CEOs were in the dark, at least partly. In an interview with 60 Minutes Lewis noted that "the CEOs of Wall Street's big investment banks ... had no clue what was going on while it was going on." When asked how many people in the world knew what was going on, Lewis estimated "between 10 and 20 investors at most and this is from the universe of tens of thousands of people...."[1]

Whether clued or clueless, investment banks were major contributors to the financial crisis, and have to take their share of responsibility. My assertion that they were more dumb than crooked is not intended to excuse their role in the crisis. Likewise, banks cannot be absolved of wrongdoing simply because the government led the way with its ridiculous assault on underwriting standards and its incompetent handling of interest rates. It is regrettable that a taxpayer-financed bailout of banks was needed. In normal circumstances it would be better to let the banks fail, rather than give them a lifeline.

---

1   "Author Michael Lewis on Wall St's Delusion," 60 Minutes (March 10, 2010), http://www.cbsnews.com/2100-18560_162-6292458.html.

Securitization did more than just drive up home demand and impregnate the market with subprime mortgages. When the you-know-what finally hit the fan, we learned that the complexities inherent in many collateralized mortgage obligations made default and foreclosure problems intractable. The magnitude of the problem was described by an executive of Pulte Homes (per Joe Nocera, Business Consultant with the New York Times):

> There are well over $1,000,000,000,000–$1,500,000,000,000 of mortgages trapped within mortgage-backed securities. These are the most risky mortgages ever issued.... Pool losses will be unprecedented.
>
> ...there has been no successful effort on a broad scale to reform these mortgages because of contractual obligations of trustees and services to bondholders. Simply put, these fiduciaries are scared of being sued by bondholders if the modify loans into affordable new mortgages.[1]

The most problematic loans seem to be those where "piggybacks" or home equity loans were added after the primary mortgage. Although "underwater," the lender of the second mortgage does not want to take a loss, so he may block efforts by the primary mortgagee to prevent the house from going into foreclosure. In addition, the bank foreclosure process was impeded by documentation problems that were created as loans were bundled and securitized. That is the subject of Chapter 16.

Mechanics of mortgage loan securitization

To fully understand the impact of securitization on the financial crisis of 2007/08, it is necessary to consider the types of products offered by loan securitizers. Loans were purchased by Fannie or Freddie or an investment bank, and transferred to a special purpose entity (SPE) — usually a trust. When the SPE received the loans they were considered to be "bankruptcy remote," meaning that they were protected from creditors of the loan originator or aggregator. The SPE bundled the loans into separate pools, and issued debt securities or bonds that would pay principal and interest derived from the cash flows attributable to that pool. Various types of mortgages could underlie the pool, including prime, subprime, Alt-A (no documentation), and jumbo-sized loans. Upon securitization, the loan originator or aggregator received and recognized the payment stream as a lump-sum. The securitized loans were called mortgage-backed securities, or MBS.

---

1   Joe Nocera, "Can Anyone Solve the Securitization Problem?," The New York Times Executive Suite (November 11, 2008), http://executivesuite.blogs.nytimes.com/2008/11/11/can-anyone-solve-the-securitization-problem/.

With a basic, "passthrough" MBS, the special purpose entity (SPE) would collect the monthly payments from homeowners. The SPE would then distribute the principal and interest, prorata, to the security investors. The more sophisticated MBSs were divided into different levels (tranches) of risk. Some people prefer to call this form of mortgage-backed security a "CMO," which stands for collateralized mortgage obligation. (You will find conflicting opinions regarding this.) The tranched MBS (or CMO) was invented by Freddie Mac in 1983, to provide investors with a choice of different risk levels. Losses due to prepayments or credit defaults are assigned first to the lower level tranches, making the upper level tranches the least risky. Each tranche is associated with its own security issuances.

You will often see references to "CDOs," which are collateralized debt obligations. A CDO is simply the generalized form of the CMO (collateralized mortgage obligation). It comprises bundles of various types of debt — not necessarily just home mortgage loans.

During the 1990s some banks, especially JP Morgan, developed something known as "synthetic CDO." Essentially, a synthetic CDO is just a collection of credit default swaps — bets, if you will, about the future performance of assets. One party bets (insures) that a component of a specified collateralized debt obligation will not default, while the other party collects those insurance premiums because he feels there will not be a default. The unique feature of the synthetic (as opposed to regular) CDO is that neither party needs to own the referenced securities. These are really just side bets about pool of assets owned (probably) by someone else. The original idea of synthetic CDOs was to help banks jettison junk off their balance sheets. As noted, however, many banks chose to retain some of the specified assets.

Securitization is not needed, but it is here to stay

Arnold Kling notes that the creation of the securitization programs was largely aimed at addressing the mismatch between savings (which was heavier in the eastern U.S.) and mortgage demand (which was greater in the western U.S.). However, this mismatch between needed and available funds was largely due to antiquated governmental regulations. One such regulation, Regulation q, put a ceiling on deposit interest rates for savings and loans associations. Another antiquated regulation restricted interstate banking:

> Freddie Mac was able to do what the thrifts themselves were not able to do because of regulation. Had Regulation q not been in effect, California thrifts could have increased interest rates on deposits to attract sufficient

funds to allow them to meet mortgage demand using the direct method of lending. Alternatively, if restrictions of interstate banking had been lifted, a multi-state holding company could have channeled excess savings from its banks in the East to be used for mortgage loans by its banks in the West — and it could have done so without resorting to indirect mortgage origination.[1]

Thus, we could have solved the mismatch of funds problem simply by letting private lenders expand and adjust interest rates appropriately, or by letting them expand to multi-state markets.

Dodd-Frank tries to curtail securitization

Title XIV of the Dodd-Frank Wall Street Reform and Consumer Protection Act has established "risk-retention" rules pertaining to the use of securitization. A securitizer (but not FHA, Fannie, or Freddie) will be required to retain 5 percent of the credit risk associated with a securitized asset, unless the securitized loan is a "qualified residential mortgage" (QRM). A QRM must ...

- Not have negative amortization or balloon payments.
- Not require fees and points in excess of 3 percent of the loan.
- Be based on verified income and financial resources.
- Not be adjustable rate unless the borrower's estimated resources are sufficient to meet all payments for a 5 year minimum period.
- Be supported by a written appraisal that conforms to established appraisal standards.
- Not be assumable.
- Contain servicing and loan default mitigation procedures.
- Require a 20 percent down payment (as presently proposed).

The last item, the 20 percent down payment, is highly controversial and is not finalized. Affordable housing advocates hate this provision, and see it as unfair to low-income borrowers and minorities. Businesses and conservatives are generally opposed to the complexities, ambiguities, and implementation costs of the legislation.

Peter Wallison of the American Enterprise Institute also questions the *effectiveness* of the Dodd-Frank provisions. He believes that the 5 percent retention requirement will not necessarily deter banks from securitizing loans during housing booms, and the new rules do not sufficiently address the securitization of subprime loans by FHA, Fannie, or Freddie — entities that will remain susceptible to political pressure.

1   Kling, Unchecked and Unbalanced, 6.

As an alternative, Wallison describes a plan that could be simpler to implement, while yielding more effective and predictable results. Under the plan, developed by the American Enterprise Institute (AEI), a "prime loan" would be defined by statute, and only prime loans could be securitized. There would be no 5 percent risk retention provision and there would be no need to define a "qualified residential mortgage." Fannie and Freddie would be phased out over a 5-year period, and FHA coverage would be limited to low and moderate-income borrowers. The AEI plan deserves serious consideration.

Conclusion

Securitization contributed to the crisis by enabling lenders to pass faulty loans to investment banks and to Fannie and Freddie, who bundled the loans into securities for sale world-wide. It is debatable that the economy needed securitization, or that we need it now. That said, securitization is here to stay.

Dodd-Frank includes a 5 percent "risk-retention" provision that may dampen the reckless use of securitization, but not necessarily during housing booms. In addition, Dodd-Frank does not adequately address the status of Fannie and Freddie, and it may provide a pathway for subprime securitization via FHA. Alternatives to these Dodd-Frank provisions should be considered.

CHAPTER 11: BORROWER RESISTANCE IS HURT BY PREDATORY
TACTICS

Mortgage fraud and predatory lending are not interchangeable terms. In the case of mortgage fraud, the lender is the victim. The FBI defines mortgage fraud as "the intentional misstatement, misrepresentation, or omission by an applicant or other interested parties, relied on by a lender or underwriter to provide funding for, to purchased, or to insure a mortgage loan."[1] On the other hand, predatory lending is, by definition, an abuse of the borrower. It involves "cases in which a broker or originating lender takes advantage of a borrower, often through deception, fraud, or manipulation, to make a loan that contains terms that are disadvantageous to the borrower.[2]" Note that predatory lending may, but does not have to, involve illegality.

No doubt, mortgage fraud and predatory lending both contributed to the financial crisis, but it can be shown that they were probably not major factors. To the extent that they were factors, however, primary blame must be given to small mortgage brokers, individual borrowers, and to Fannie Mae and Freddie Mac.

---

1   FBI, "Mortgage Fraud Report 2006," Reports and Publications (May 2007), http://www.fbi.gov/stats-services/publications/mortgage-fraud-2006.
2   Lucy Delgadillo and Luke Erickson and Kathleen Piercy, "Disentangling the Differences between Abusive and Predatory Lending: Professionals' Perspectives," review of how mortgage professionals differentiate abusive from predatory lending, The Journal of Consumer Affairs 42, no. 313-335 (Fall 2008): 316.

In the years immediately preceding the financial crisis, Democrats and Republicans each proposed anti-predatory lending legislation; however, effective legislation was not passed until after the crisis occurred.

Mortgage fraud

> To understand the problems of mortgage fraud we must also stop pretending the politically correct idea that it is being perpetrated without the knowledge of the borrower. The borrowers are almost always either actively or passively involved. Borrowers almost always know what is going on. For most borrowers, the only thing that matters is that they get the best loan or qualify to purchase the property they want.
>
> – Blogger and ex-mortgage broker Mike Volpe[1]

You probably have not even heard of the phrase, "mortgage fraud," because most politicians and journalists have little interest in exposing the misdeeds of the little guy — the guy who represents millions of potential voters, readers, or viewers. As noted, the FBI defines mortgage fraud as a crime against the lender "by an applicant or other interested parties." Let's start by discussing the culpability of those "applicants" (i.e., the borrowers); then we will discuss the criminality of those "other interested parties" (namely, brokers).

Applicants are usually little guys, like you and me, seeking to buy the best home they can with the best financing possible. A problem arises when these little guys start fibbing and misrepresenting during the loan application process. Perhaps, the borrowers are Fred and Ethel, and they are trying to buy a house that they can't quite afford. Fred and Ethel know that they are putting themselves and the lender at risk, but interest rates are exceptionally low, prices are rising fast, their friends all live in bigger homes, and they just located their "dream home." To ensure that they get loan approval, Fred and Ethel conveniently forget to tell the lender that they borrowed the down payment from Ricky and Lucy, their best friends. Or, perhaps, Fred fails to mention the alimony he has to pay to his ex-wife, Lolita, and Ethel fails to mention that her employment supervisor just gave her 2 weeks' notice.

The fraud perpetrated by Fred and Ethel seems pretty minor, but the results can be horrendous for the lender and, ultimately, for the taxpayer. Some common forms of mortgage fraud are more serious. In its

---

1   Mike Volpe, "Mortgage Fraud: The Problem and the Solutions," The Provocateur, July 17, 2008, http://theeprovocateur.blogspot.com/2008/07/mortgage-fraud-problem-and-solutions.html.

2006 "Mortgage Fraud Report," the FBI noted that the most common form of mortgage fraud (at the time) was illegal property flipping, which entails fraudulent loan documents and inflated property appraisals. The FBI gave the following illustration of a typical illegal flip that might have occurred in the run-up to the financial crisis: A property flipper buys a house for $20,000, but has it fraudulently appraised for $80,000. A friend of the flipper then "buys" the house for $80,000, and obtains an 80 percent ($64,000) mortgage on the property. The flipper and his friend now have a $44,000 profit, calculated as the $64,000 mortgage minus the original $20,000 purchase price. The bank is stuck with a $64,000 mortgage that won't be paid, and that is secured by a house worth only $20,000.

Other common mortgage fraud schemes include:

- "Silent second" loans, where the buyer of the property borrows the down payment and/or closing costs via an undisclosed loan. Incredibly, this illegal activity was widely practiced by borrowers colluding with nonprofit housing organizations and state and local governments (with the blessing of HUD). See Chapter 4.
- Fictitious identities used on loan application papers. (Get a cash-out equity loan and have the debt put in some other person's name.)
- Multiple and concurrent home equity lines of credit, where numerous lines are opened within a very short period of time. The bank searches for liens encumbering the property, but because it may take several days for a lien to be recorded, the property appears to be unencumbered.
- Occupancy fraud, where the borrower is purchasing an investment property, but claims he will live there so that the bank gives him a better interest rate.
- Cash-back schemes, where the real price of the property is inflated so that a larger mortgage loan can be obtained. The excess funding is used to give a "rebate" to the borrower.

Although these types of fraud are fairly common, they are not taken very seriously. When caught, people engaged in this kind of fraud may have their loan applications denied, but they almost never go to jail or pay a meaningful penalty. For this reason, the FBI states that "mortgage fraud is a relatively low-risk, high-yield criminal activity that tempts many."[1]

The FBI also acknowledges that it does not focus its efforts on such cases. In my opinion it should. During the run-up to the financial melt-down, a few highly-publicized arrests might have deterred some of the hundreds of thousands of people who engaged in this kind of criminal activity. As Mike Volpe (ex-broker) put it: "...the Feds need to make it clear that fraud, small or large, will no longer be tolerated. To do this, they need to make an example of someone."[2]

Mortgage fraud where the broker participates

As noted, the FBI defines mortgage fraud as a crime "by an applicant or other interested parties." These "other interested parties" are often mortgage brokers, who are independent parties who find borrowers and match them up with lenders. Although there are good and decent mortgage brokers out there, they are generally the bottom-feeders of the lending industry. In some cases, dishonest brokers collude with borrowers to defraud lenders. At the same time, these brokers may swindle the borrower by means of outrageous fees, by persuading the borrower to refinance into a higher rate loan, or by selling an adjustable-rate loan as a fixed rate loan. These illegal acts, aimed at the borrower, are discussed under "Predatory lending," below.

Overall impact of mortgage fraud

Although mortgage fraud is odious and costly, it is unlikely that it significantly impacted the financial crisis of 2007/08. In its 2006 "Mortgage Fraud Report," the FBI cites an estimate of mortgage fraud prepared by The Prieston Group, a company that administers an insurance product covering fraud losses. The company estimated that fraud losses for 2006 would reach $4.2 billion, plus another $1.2 billion required for fraud prevention tools. These amounts are not nearly high enough to have significantly impacted the financial crisis.

Predatory lending

> Is it preying on the borrower to make a bad loan? Not so much. The borrower gets a free option. If the house price goes up, it doesn't matter whether the borrower can make the payments or not — the borrower can sell the house at a profit. If the house price goes down, the borrower loses his

---

1   FBI, "Mortgage Fraud Report 2006."
2   Volpe, "Mortgage Fraud: The Problem and the Solutions."

down payment, plus moving expenses, plus a ding on his
credit rating. As down payments approached zero, the total
down side of this was pretty small.

– Economist Arnold Kling[1]

The views of Kling notwithstanding, predatory lending can be very
costly to the borrower. Predatory lending may be an illegal act aimed
at the borrower, or it may be a (normally) legal act that abuses the borrower. It is most often perpetrated by the mortgage broker (who is an
independent agent who finds the borrower and introduces him to the
lender). Predatory lending schemes include:

- Steering and coercing the borrower to take a relatively-high-
  priced loan.
- Packing the loan with excessive fees or options that are not
  needed.
- Encouraging the borrower to take loans with abnormally-
  high prepayment penalties.
- Bait and switch schemes, where the borrower is presented
  with reasonable terms that don't jibe with the terms that are
  ultimately found in the fine print.
- Equity stripping, where the homeowner is encouraged to take
  multiple equity loans until there is no more equity left in the
  home. At that point the homeowner may be left with a huge
  loan that he cannot repay, resulting in an eventual foreclosure.
- Falsifying the loan application (without the borrower's
  knowledge) so that it appears he can afford the loan when, in
  fact, he cannot.
- Concealing the amount by which interest can increase on hybrid mortgages.

The last of these schemes, involving hybrid mortgages, is the one most
often cited as a contributing cause of the 2007/08 financial crisis. A hybrid mortgage loan is one with a fixed rate for two or three years that is
then adjusted once or twice each year to reflect current market rates. The
assumption is that the subprime borrower was bamboozled into thinking that an initial, very low interest rate on her hybrid mortgage would
last indefinitely. The theory is that, when the rates reset (after two or
three years) the borrower was surprised by the amount of the increase,

---

1   Arnold Kling, "Self-Defense on Predatory Lending," Library of Economics
     and Liberty (April 27, 2010), http://econlog.econlib.org/archives/2010/04/
     self-defense_on.html.

and unable to pay the new, higher monthly payments. This theory warrants further investigation.

Low "teaser" interest rates did not cause the financial crisis

In "Economic Commentary" published by the Federal Reserve Bank of Cleveland, Economist Yuliya Demyanyk states that the notion of subprime borrowers being offered low, "teaser" rates is a "myth." Demyanyk notes:

> Hybrid mortgages were available both in prime and subprime mortgage markets, but at significantly different terms. Those in the prime market offered significantly lower introductory fixed rates, known as "teaser rates," compared to rates following the resets. People assumed that the initial rates for subprime loans were also just as low and they applied the same label to them — "teaser rates." We need to understand, though, that the initial rates offered to subprime hybrid borrowers may have been lower than they most likely would have been for the same borrowers had they taken a fixed-rate subprime mortgage, but they were definitely not low in absolute terms.
>
> The average subprime hybrid mortgage rates at origination were in the 7.3 to 9.7 percent range for the years 2001-2007.... The subprime figures are hardly "teaser rates" (emphasis added).[1]

A similar observation was made by Eric S. Rosengren, President & Chief Executive Officer of the Federal Reserve Bank of Boston. In a speech before the Boston Fed, Mr. Rosengren noted that "These 2/28 and 3/27 mortgages have suffered from several misperceptions. First, the fixed rate for the first 2 or 3 years is often referred to as the teaser rate. However ... the teaser rate was not particularly low — nationally, the average rate on a 2006 subprime 2/28 mortgage was 8.5 percent...."[2] In other words, the notion that millions of subprime borrowers were misled with very low teaser rates is a lot of bunk. For the most part, their first mortgage loan payments were at significant interest rates.[3]

---

1   Yuliya Demyanyk, "Ten Myths About Subprime Mortgages," Economic Commentary (July 23, 2009), http://www.clevelandfed.org/research/commentary/2009/0509.cfm.
2   Eric S. Rosengren, "Subprime Mortgage Problems: Research, Opportunities, and Policy Considerations," (Speech in Boston, Mass.: Federal Reserve Bank of Boston, December 3, 2007).
3   Adjustable-rate loans (also known as hybrid loans) are often described with 2 numbers – one before a slash and one after the slash. The first number is the number of years that the interest rate is fixed, and the second number is the number of years that the loan rate of interest "float" in accordance with some

Other studies showed the same. For example, data analyzed by Foote, Gerardi, Goette, and Willen, who are consultants with the Analysis Group, showed that most subprime adjustable rate mortgages never even had low teaser rates.[1] Two CATO Institute scholars, Jagadeesh Gokhale and Peter Van Doren, had these findings in October 2009:

> Commentators have also argued that the popularization of financial products such as teaser-rate hybrid loans for subprime homebuyers and credit default swaps for investors is to blame for the financial crisis. We find little evidence for this. Housing data indicate that the majority of subprime hybrid loans that have entered default had not undergone interest rate resets, and the default rate for subprime hybrid loans is not much higher than for subprime fixed rate loans.[2]

Another "myth," identified by Ms. Demyanyk, is the notion that subprime mortgages failed because of mortgage rate resets. Initially, analysts attributed high delinquency rates to the adjustable rate feature of loans:

> ...analysts compared the proportion of outstanding FRMs [fixed rate mortgages] that were delinquent to the proportion of outstanding ARMs [adjustable rate mortgages] that were delinquent. Based on that comparison, the proportion of delinquent hybrid loans had begun to skyrocket after 2006, while fixed-rate loans looked as if it was fairly stable.[3]

The problem with this analysis, according to Demyanyk, is that it involved the comparison of loans originated in different years. More specifically, the FRMs, which were mostly originated in earlier years, were compared to ARMs, which were mostly originated in recent years. This research was flawed because all recent loans — fixed or adjustable — were more likely to fail. When loans were compared after being sorted by year of origin, the "FRMs showed as many signs of distress as did ARMs."[4] In other words, there is no evidence that interest rate resets had significant impact on the financial crisis.

The above analysis notwithstanding, mortgage loans to subprime borrowers are far more likely to default than mortgage loans to prime

---

prescribed index. Thus, a 2/28 loan has a fixed interest rate for 2 years and a floating rate for 28 years.

1 Elizabeth Evans and Sushrut Jain, "Understanding the Financial Crisis: A Look Back," White Paper (April 2010), http://www.analysisgroup.com/published_work.aspx?LangType=1033&id=9934.
2 Jagadeesh Gokhale and Peter Van Doren, "Would a Stricter Fed Policy and Financial Regulation Have Averted the Financial Crisis?," CATO: Policy Analysis 648 (October 8, 2009): 1.
3 Demyanyk, "Ten Myths About Subprime Mortgages."
4 Ibid.

borrowers. Why? The primary reason is obvious. In many cases these loans were made to people who were poor credit risks — people who were given ownership of a house but who retained the outlook of tenants. That said, there is no doubt that fraud and interest reset provisions contributed at least somewhat to the crisis. That being the case, we need to find out who was directly, and indirectly, responsible.

Mortgage brokers and nonbanks were responsible for predatory lending

To the extent that predatory lending contributed to the crisis, who should we blame? The people most responsible were the thousands of small mortgage brokers — the people in the middle between the borrowers and the lenders. This is something Freddie Mac knew no later than 1999, the year in which Freddie estimated that 65 percent of its fraud cases involved "third-party originators" (brokers). That was at a time when third-party originators provided Fannie and Freddie with only about 26 percent of their mortgages. The disparity between those two percentages told Freddie that brokers were committing fraud at extremely high rates compared to banks and other direct lenders. It was also the conclusion of a study of predatory lending, published in the Journal of Consumer Affairs in 2008:

> The majority of fraud-for-profit cases involves third-party brokers, or broker networks ... who deliberately misrepresent information to mortgage lenders, underwriters, or borrowers for the purpose of increasing their profits from a transaction.[1]

Like her brother, Freddie, Fannie knew of the problem. The Fannie Mae Foundation stated: "Brokers originate over half of all mortgage loans [and an even greater percentage of subprime loans] and a relatively small number of brokers are responsible for a large percentage of predatory loans."[2] There were many reasons for this. Brokers were lightly capitalized and, in most states, lightly regulated. In fact, some states had virtually no regulations regarding mortgage brokers. Michigan, for example, was "a state where you can talk about becoming a mortgage broker over breakfast and open an office in the afternoon —

---

1   Delgadillo and Luke Erickson and Kathleen Piercy, "Disentangling the Differences between Abusive and Predatory Lending: Professionals' Perspectives," 319.

2   James Carr and Lopa Kolluri, "Predatory Lending: An Overview," (Washington DC: Fannie Mae Foundation, 2001), 13.

no license, no bonding...."[1] In addition, mortgage brokers sometimes had an incentive to abuse the borrower. They were paid something called a "yield spread premium," which is a reward for steering the borrower into a higher-than-average-rate loan. Finally, brokers rarely took ownership of the loans they sold — even briefly. If the loan was unlikely to be repaid, they didn't have to care. I think it is fair to say that, without the small army of fly-by-night mortgage brokers, mortgage fraud and predatory lending would have decrease significantly.

A few large nonbank lenders were a major secondary source of predatory lending. A particularly egregious example is the former Ameriquest, a California-regulated company that was accused of wrongdoing by many customers and former employees. In an expose written in early 2005, complaints of the former employees were itemized:

> ...32 former employees across the country say they witnessed or participated in improper practices, mostly in 2003 and 2004. This behavior was said to have included deceiving borrowers about the terms of their loans, forging documents, falsifying appraisals and fabricating borrowers' income to qualify them for loans they couldn't afford.

There were some employees who contradicted these assertions, but there is little doubt that several instances of illegal and unethical activities took place — to the detriment of the borrowers and to the detriment of the investment banks that would ultimately purchase the loans.

F&F were indirectly responsible for predatory lending

There was a time — not that long ago — when mortgage brokers were relatively rare. However, as noted on page 104 ("Fannie and Freddie promoted brokers over banks"), Fannie and Freddie (F&F) actively promoted and encouraged the growth of small, sleazy mortgage brokers at the expense of well capitalized and relatively respectable banks. I am not alleging that this was done in order to promote fraud or predatory lending; however, it was done, apparently, without regard for the consequences. We might call it, "mortgage manslaughter."

The era of the modern-day mortgage broker started in 1995, when Fannie and Freddie rolled out their new automated underwriting systems. As noted in Chapter 2, "the online technology, provided for a modest fee, has quietly fragmented the lending business and shifted power to

---

1   Kurt Eggert, "Held up in Due Course," in Predatory Lending, Securitization, and the Holder in Due course Doctrine (Web-based: Creighton University School of Law (available at SSRN), April 2002), 25, http://papers.ssrn.com/sol3/papers.cfm?abstract_id=904661.

---

brokers by allowing them to perform some of the services once provided exclusively by banks."[1]

This was no accident, and bankers and other respectable lenders repeatedly warned F&F of the risks they were taking. Starting below, you will find a chronological listing of quotations from The GSE Report, which is a bi-weekly publication that reports on activities of Fannie and Freddie. The list is long, but well worth reading. From these quotations, it is obvious that, between 1998 and 2002, Fannie and Freddie were determined to build up their army of brokers. This army eventually comprised as many as 75,000 brokers — most with little or no capital, no ultimate responsibility for the loans they sold, and many with little experience or education.

F&F actively promoted these risky companies, many of whom were sleaze-balls, at the expense of relatively experienced and highly capitalized lenders. Not only did the number of brokers increase, their relative power increased. Instead of brokers finding borrowers and submitting their loan applications to lenders for underwriting approval, the brokers were able to get advance approval via software from Fannie or Freddie (the Nintendo-like software described in Chapter 2). Once that happened, the broker could shop the loan package around until a willing lender was found. The broker was now in the driver's seat.

Some bankers theorized that Fannie and Freddie wanted to directly deal with brokers so that they could purchase their loans and put them in their loan portfolios (something that boosted F&F's profits). Banks, on the other hand, would often retain the loans on their own balance sheets. Whatever the motivation, it is clear that F&F put power in the hands of brokers at the expense of relatively stable and responsible banks and other lenders. To the extent that mortgage fraud and predatory lending were problems contributing to the financial crisis, let's give a big "thank you" to tax-subsidized Fannie and Freddie. They are the ones who armed the fraudsters. Here is a chronological listing of the contemporaneous headlines and other quotations from various issues of The GSE Report: It shows the determination of F&F with regard to this matter.

- "Both Fannie and Freddie Increase Efforts to Access and Push Their Systems on Brokers" (August 21, 1998).
- "Morgan Stanley Dean Witter recently released a report stating that Fannie Mae was aggressively pushing its point-of-sale

---

1   Barta, "Why Big Lenders Are So Afraid of Fannie Mae and Freddie Mac."

underwriting technology, Desktop Originator onto brokers" (September 4, 1998).

- "Fannie and Freddie Develop Internet Conduits so that Brokers Have Direct Access to Fannie & Freddie's AU System Without Going Through a Lender.... The GSEs [Fannie and Freddie] have virtually exhausted the lender market ... and Fannie and Freddie are now aggressively marketing their systems to brokers and bypassing lenders" (October 23, 1998).

- "First American Claims Brokers Will No Longer Need Wholesalers" (November 6, 1998).

- "Morgan Stanley Analyst States that Fannie's New Internet Conduit Linking Fannie's Automated Underwriting System Directly to Brokers Demonstrates How Fannie Could Reduce the Role of Banks and Originators to that of 'Order-Takers'...." (November 20, 1998).

- "[T]here is growing concern at the Mortgage Bankers Association (MBA) about Fannie and Freddie's new automated underwriting (AU) initiatives that are bypassing lenders and bringing automated underwriting closer to brokers enabling the brokers to shop AU scores among lenders" (January 8, 1999).

- "Fannie & Freddie Acknowledge that they will Continue to Push their Systems onto Third-Party Originators" (February 5, 1999).

- "Despite Fannie's Repeated Pronouncements that Lenders are their 'Only Customers,' Fannie & Freddie Continue to market and Build their Technology Brand Name Directly to Brokers" (June 11, 1999).

- "Are we seeing the first step by Fannie and Freddie by taking the underwriting decision out of our [banker's] hands by going direct to the broker? ... Will underwriting become fungible?" (October 29, 1999).

- "[Freddie's pilot program] allows brokers to run borrower information through Freddie's automated underwriting system, Loan Prospector, prior to a lender bidding and winning a deal" (February 11, 2000).

- "Fannie continues to expand its technology reach to brokers" (June 2, 2000).

- "Freddie provides its technology to mortgage brokers (bypassing their lender customers). Freddie to provide its automated underwriting system directly to mortgage brokers who are members of the National Association of Hispanic Real Estate Professionals...." (September 23, 2000).

- "Freddie also reduced by 75 percent to $250,000 the minimum net worth a seller must have to sell Freddie loans. Industry observers note that some big lenders interpreted this as meant to help small lenders or brokers bring loans directly to Freddie" (November 3, 2000).

- "Freddie announces that it will allow brokers automated underwriting 'portability' which will permit brokers to use Freddie's automated underwriting system to receive and underwriting decision prior to a lender bidding and winning the deal and shop the loan to various lenders" (July 6, 2001).

- "More than 11,000 brokers have signed up to use Freddie's LP on the Internet (Freddie's AU system) — Freddie expects that other groups, such as tax preparers and insurance agents, will get into the mortgage origination business.... Peterson [Freddie official] predicted that 'a host of new people' would jump into the origination market because simple-to-use AU systems available on the Internet have eliminated the barriers to entry" (August 10, 2001).

- "Mortgage brokers are by far the largest users of Freddie's Loan Prospector" [automated underwriting system]. More than 50,000 brokers representing 13,000 different firms now actively use the system — 'and more are signing up every day,' Freddie's Chairman Leland Brendsel told the National Association of Mortgage Brokers convention in Cleveland." (June 28, 2002).

- "At a recent national Association of Mortgage Brokers annual convention, both Fannie and Freddie were urging brokers to skip wholesale lenders and mortgage insurance companies by using the GSEs' [Fannie's and Freddie's] automated underwriting systems" (August 2, 2002).

This list makes it clear that Fannie and Freddie were instrumental in creating the mortgage broker beast that engaged in the most egregious and irresponsible acts of predatory lending.

Regulatory efforts with respect to predatory lending

The two types of entity most likely to practice predatory tactics — the small broker and the much larger nonbank (such as Ameriquest) — were primarily regulated at the state level, and most state regulation was pathetic. There were two reasons for this: First, legislators were afraid to do anything that might discourage homeownership within their respective states. This was true for Republicans and Democrats. Second, subprime was still seen as virtuous by those interested in promoting affordable housing and the expansion of home ownership to middle and lower income borrowers. An article on a pro-consumer Web site describes how California legislators were confronted with both of these challenges. A California senate bank committee convened in January 2007 to assess lending practices on the part of New Century Financial Corp., a large nonbank lender located in the state:

> A senior executive for mortgage lending giant, New Century Financial Corp., calmly assured California legislators that risks associated with subprime loans were entirely manageable. Lawmakers should be exceedingly careful about requiring any changes, or else Californians would be frozen out of the housing market, he warned. ... In his testimony, [Marc] Lowenthal extolled non-traditional mortgage products, saying they had made home ownership affordable and helped borrowers improve their credit ratings. Importantly, he said, this new style of lending was allowing working Californians to "build financial safety nets" for themselves.[1]

That pitch was irresistible because it had both carrot and stick. The stick was the threat of being "frozen out of the housing market." The carrot was the chance to feel that borrowers would be helped to become homeowners and would improve their credit ratings. Two months later, New Century Financial Corp. filed for bankruptcy.

Federal regulatory efforts were probably even weaker, for similar reasons. In 1994 the Home Ownership and Equity Protection Act (HOEPA) was passed in an effort to control predatory lending. Unfortunately, this legislation, written by Massachusetts Democrat Joseph P. Kennedy, did not apply to most situations. The law was triggered only when a loan's interest rate was 10 points higher than that of a treasury security of comparable maturity, or when points and fees exceeded 8 percent of the total loan amount, or $400 (adjusted for inflation), whichever was higher. Ac-

---

1   Jill Replogle, "Banking Lobby Spent Its Way around Regulation," Protect Consumer Justice.org, September 21, 2009, http://www.protectconsumer-justice.org/banking-lobby-spent-its-way-around-regulation.html.

cording to a Federal Trade Commission report issued in 2001, the law only applied to an estimated one percent of subprime loans.

Although the law gave the Federal Reserve the authority to adjust the trigger rate to as low as 8 percent (which was not done until years later), one can only guess why the legislation was written to apply so narrowly. Perhaps, sponsors of the bill simply miscalculated its impact, or they did not want to dampen the ability of subprime borrowers to obtain credit.

"Predatory" was a dirty word, but in 1994 "subprime" was not; it was seen as a boon to low-income and minority borrowers who could not otherwise get home loans. A fondness for subprime was found in Congress and in the Federal Reserve. In 2002 the Federal Reserve made modest amendments to the provisions of Regulation Z that implement HOEPA. The ten percent trigger rate was lowered to 8 percent, but this was done with the expectation that it would now impact (only) 5 percent of subprime loans, instead of 1 percent. It appears that Congress did not want to dampen the growth of the fledgling subprime loan industry.

Other modest changes were made by HOEPA to the way fees were to be calculated, and restrictions were placed on the use of balloon payments, prepayment penalties, and negative amortization. In describing the forthcoming regulatory changes to HOEPA, Edward Gramlich, one of the governors of the Federal Reserve System, spoke favorably of subprime lending, which he distinguished from predatory lending:

> In understanding the problem, it is particularly important to distinguish predatory lending from generally beneficial subprime lending.... Subprime lending ... refers to entirely appropriate and legal lending to borrowers who do not qualify for prime rates.... When considering the adjustment of the APR trigger, the Board balances the risk of diminishing [subprime] credit availability against the need to protect consumers.[1]

Mr. Gramlich was concerned about borrowers being charged excessively high rates of interest (as well he should have been) but he did not seem worried about the enormous systemic risk (to lenders) that would be generated by giving loans to hundreds of thousands of people with tarnished credit histories. This was the case even though he knew subprime lending was exploding, and so stated:

> ...the number of conventional home-purchase mortgage loans to lower-income borrowers nearly doubled between 1993 and 2000, whereas the number of loans to upper-income borrowers rose 66 percent. Also over

1   Governor Edward M. Gramlich, "Predatory Lending," in Housing Bureau for Seniors Conference (Speech in Ann Arbor, Michigan: The Federal Reserve Board, April 9, 2009).

the same period, the number of conventional mortgage loans increased 122 percent to African-American borrowers and 147 percent to Hispanic borrowers, compared with an increase of 35 percent to white borrowers.

Much of this increased lending can be attributed to the development of the subprime mortgage market.... [T]he number of subprime loans to purchase homes increased *nineteen fold*, from 16,000 to 306,000 [1993 to 2000] (emphasis added).[1]

After the Fed tweaked HOEPA in 2002, Democrats and Republicans each pushed legislation designed to curb predatory lending. The Republicans and several Democrats supported House bill H.R. 1295, "The Responsible Lending Act." Democrats (and no Republicans) sponsored H.R. 1182, "The Prohibit Predatory Lending Act." Each bill had many similar features such as new definitions of high-cost loans, dispute and error resolution mechanisms, revised requirements for prepayment penalties, and consumer counseling. A major difference, however, had to do with the preemption of state predatory lending programs. The Republican proposal would have set a uniform 50-state standard; whereas the Democrat plan would have allowed the states and localities to keep their own predatory lending laws. Neither piece of legislation passed.

The Federal Reserve deserves criticism for not lowering the 10 percent trigger sooner, and for not crafting tougher regulations sooner. However, Congress also deserves a rebuke for setting triggers (whether 8 or 10 percent) so high, and for not passing legislation that would curb both predatory lending and subprime lending. The basic problem was that neither Congress nor the Fed saw the inherent systemic danger of massive subprime lending. To the contrary, Republicans and Democrats saw subprime lending as a positive means for extending home ownership to minorities and the disadvantaged.

Dodd–Frank Title XIV

In July 2010, well-after the crisis started, the "Mortgage Reform and Anti-Predatory Lending Act" was passed as Title 14 of the Dodd-Frank Wall Street and Consumer Protection Act. It does not pre-empt state anti-predatory lending laws unless those state laws conflict or are less protective of consumers. As of mid-2012, final regulations related to The Act have not been issued; however, it appears that the legislation could produce some needed reforms — with a large compliance-cost price tag. The Act ...

---

1   Ibid.

- Establishes new minimum standards for ensuring that borrowers have the ability to repay their loans. Lenders must make a "reasonable and good faith determination based on verified and documented information that, at the time the loan is consummated, the consumer has a reasonable ability to repay the loan ..." plus taxes and related expenses.

- Establishes a "safe harbor" presumption of ability to pay if the loan is a "qualified mortgage," which is a residential mortgage loan without negative amortization or balloon payments, or fees and points exceeding 3 percent. Other characteristics of the "qualified mortgage" are specified. For example, it must be affordable on the basis of verified income and financial resources. In the case of adjustable rate mortgages, the income and resources must be sufficient to meet all payments for a period of no less than 5 years.

- Requires loan originators to be qualified and registered by their respective states.

- Prohibits "steering," which is encouraging a borrower to take a loan with terms that are more adverse than those of another loan for which he is qualified.

- Prohibits loans with "predatory characteristics." Such loans are not specifically defined, but examples given include loans with excessive fees or abusive terms. (This part of the legislation sorely needs specificity, lest it becomes an invitation to frivolous lawsuits.)

- Establishes originator compensation limits by prohibiting yield-spread premium bonuses on residential mortgage loans. (This may be difficult to enforce.)

- Requires counseling for those obtaining high-rate loans. (This needs to be controlled, lest it produces a cottage industry of counseling shops that do little more than add to lending costs.)

- Establishes new disclosure requirements (but, no one will read these).

Chapter 12: Were rating agencies victims of the copy machine?

> How the rise of the copy machine led to the fall of the ratings model. ... Originally ratings were an "investor pays" model. It was the rise of the copy machine, of all things, that made sharing prospectuses among investors easier, and threatened the industry's already thin profit margins. ... The conflict of interest inherent in the current system is the "issuer-pays-for-the ratings" model, coupled with the fact that so much of the business comes from so few clients, leaving the agencies fearful of alienating any of their customers.
>
> – CNNMoney.com[1]

For the most part, the rating agencies operated legally and in accordance with published standards and methods that were well-known to government regulators and available to the public. That said, the rating agencies were neither boy scouts nor heroes of the financial crisis. They were more deferential to the banks that paid them than to the public that needed them. Rating Agencies could have slowed the growth of subprime lending, but did not. From the perspective of the public, rating agencies were "missing in action." The many problems of the rating agencies are discussed later in this chapter. There is also a description of the less valid accusations that are frequently made against rating agencies.

---

1   Ken Stier, "The Race to Kill the Ratings Agencies," CNNMoney.com (April 30, 2010), http://money.cnn.com/2010/04/30/news/companies/kill_ratings_agencies.fortune/index.htm.

The big three rating agencies, Moody's Standard and Poors (S&P), and Fitch, have roots that go back about a century. "Moody's Manual" was first published in 1900, and contained general information about the stocks and bonds of diverse industries. In 1914 Moody's started its "Investor Services," which provide ratings for most government bonds. By the 1970s Moody's became a full-scale rating agency, rating commercial paper and bank deposits, as well as government bonds. S&P started as "Standard Statistics" in 1906, and published ratings for corporate bonds, municipal bonds, and sovereign (national) debts. In 1941 Standard Statistics merged with Poor's Publishing, and the result was Standard and Poor's Corporation. Fitch Publishing Company was founded in 1913, and introduced the alphabetical rating system (i.e., the AAA through D system) in 1924. The modern Fitch Ratings is the product of Fitch Publishing Company and several entities with which it merged during the 1990s.

Originally, the rating agencies were paid by subscribers — not the banks issuing the securities. By the 1970s, however, the copy machine made it difficult to continue this practice. Ratings could be copied and disseminated, without compensation to the rating agencies. The subscription-based revenue model ended, and concerns about conflicts of interest began. Could rating agencies objectively evaluate the banks that paid them?

Compounding the problem was the creation, in 1975, of "nationally-recognized statistical rating organizations" (NRSRO), which were a few rating agencies found to meet Securities and Exchange Commission (SEC) standards. The SEC decided that the capital requirements of financial institutions could be satisfied if they invested in securities receiving favorable (AAA) ratings from this small, elite group of SEC-blessed agencies. This effectively softened capital reserve requirements.

To ensure the safety of the deposits and other investments of their customers, banks are required to maintain funds (money) in reserve — that is, "capital." From the bank's perspective, less capital permits greater profits. However, smaller amounts of capital can put customers at risk. Because their ratings directly affected capital requirements, rating agencies, specifically NRSROs, became an important element of government regulation of financial institutions.[1]

---

1   To ensure the safety of the deposits and other investments of their customers, banks are required to maintain funds in reserve – that is, "capital." From the bank's perspective, less capital permits greater profits. However, smaller amounts of capital can put customers at risk. Because their ratings directly affected capital requirements, rating agencies, specifically NRSROs, became

The two most notorious investments

There were many products rated by the rating agencies, but the most controversial were the residential mortgage-backed security (RMBS) and the collateralized debt obligation (CDO). These are also the investments that experienced the highest rates of downgrading during the crisis.

To create an RMBS the arranger (usually an investment bank) packages thousands of separate mortgage loans into a pool, which is then sold to a newly-created trust, which becomes entitled to the interest and principal payments of the borrowers. The trust's purchase of the loans is financed by its sale to investors of mortgage-backed securities (RMBS). The principal and interest collected from mortgagors (the borrowers) by the trust is used to make the monthly principal and interest payments to the investors.

Typically, the RMBS comprises several different "tranches," which are different classes of the RMBS, each of which pays a different interest rate and each of which has different credit risk.[1] The tranches are arranged in a hierarchy, wherein the upper-most levels have the least risk and highest ratings, but pay the lowest interest rates. These high-ranked tranches are the first to be paid, and are the least affected by borrower defaults.

There may be additional forms of "credit enhancement," such as "over-collateralization" and "excess spread" (the amount by which the trust's monthly interest income exceeds monthly liabilities). Those enhancements are designed to minimize credit risk associated with all or part of the RMBS. In the years immediately preceding the financial crisis, a high percentage of RMBS comprised subprime mortgage loans.

The typical CDO has a structure similar to that of the RMBS. An arranger creates a trust to purchase bank assets; however, instead of thousands of mortgage loans the bank assets comprise hundreds of bank debt securities. CDOs are different from RMBSs in another way: They are

---

an important element in the government's regulation of financial institutions. The Dodd-Frank Wall Street Reform and Consumer Protection Act of 2010 has eliminated the requirement that money market funds use NRSRO rating agencies. Although an NRSRO firm can be used, the fund's board of directors must now make their own independent evaluation.

1   Some analysts assert that, when residential mortgage-backed securities (RMBS) have tranches, they should be called CMOs (collateralized mortgage obligations). That is not the position of the Securities and Exchange Commission, which has indicated that RMBS can have tranches.

actively managed, meaning that the underlying assets (within the supporting trust) may change over time. CDO trusts became major purchasers of subprime RMBS during the 2000s, and by 2006 subprime RMBS comprised an estimated 70 percent of CDO trusts.

Instead of purchasing RMBS, some CDOs enter into credit default swaps, designed to mimic the performance characteristics of RMBS by referencing them. These CDOs are known as "synthetic CDOs."

The credit rating process was no secret

The three major credit rating agencies had similar procedures for rating subprime RMBS and CDOs, and those procedures were known to government regulators. For an RMBS, the rating agency was given specific loan information by the arranger (the bank). That information probably would have included the loan-to-value ratio, the principal amount, the location of the property, proposed usage of the property (primary or secondary residence), the FICO (credit score) of the borrower, the amount of the borrower's equity, and the documentation in support of the borrower's claimed income and assets. After considering that information, expected loan correlations, and tranche hierarchy within the RMBS, the rating agency analyst would develop predictions of expected losses under various stress scenarios.

To get the highest (AAA) rating a tranche had to perform well under the most severe hypothetical stress level. The analyst also performed a cash flow analysis, to ensure that the principal and interest received by the trust was sufficient to meet the monthly payment obligations of the RMBS. The preliminary conclusions of the analyst were sometimes communicated to the bank (or other arranger), who could accept the proposed ratings or, perhaps, make adjustments sufficient to improve the ratings.

Ultimately, ratings recommendations would be presented to a committee comprising other analysts and senior personnel of the rating agency. A vote would be held with regard to the rating of each tranche, and the final decisions would be communicated to the bank (or other arranger) who, in some cases, could appeal the decisions. Final decisions were published and subsequently monitored.

For CDOs the methodology was similar in that there was a review of the creditworthiness of each tranche within the CDO, and there was a review of the pool of assets in the CDO trust. (Generally, those assets were RMBSs or CDOs.) There was, however, one significant difference between the ratings processes for RMBSs and CDOs: Because CDO trust assets could change frequently (due to their being actively managed), ratings were based on covenanted limits rather than the actual asset composition within the trust. In other words, the rating agency analyst considered the worst case scenarios for the minimum and maximum asset concentrations — not the actual concentrations at any given time. As with the RMBS, the analyst made his recommendations to the ratings committee, which voted on the ratings of each tranche before communicating the decision to the bank or other arranger.

The Levin hearings produce useful data — and smoke

One of the most damning critiques of the rating agencies came in the form of hearings conducted by the U.S. Senate Permanent Subcommittee on Investigations. The hearings revealed that, in some cases, practices were shoddy, methods were invalid, employees were overworked, and estimates were overly optimistic. In addition, some employee emails indicated a keen awareness that ratings made could affect business revenues. Senator Carl Levin, the Chairman of the Subcommittee, described such an email:

> ...after a Moody's analyst emailed that he could not finalize a rating until the issue of fees was resolved, an investment banker from Merrill Lynch responded: "We are okay with the revised fee schedule for this transaction. We are agreeing to this under the assumption that this will not be a precedent for any future deals and that you will work with us further on this transaction to try to get to some middle ground with respect to the ratings."[1]

Although Senator Levin's point was undermined by the analyst's response to Merrill Lynch (that the "deal analysis was independent from its fees") we can assume that analysts must have known their work could affect the revenue collections and future growth of their companies. This has led many to question the "issuer-pays" model (the business model adopted after the copy machine knocked out the subscriber-pays model).

Senator Levin also described the poor working conditions at some rating agencies. They were, at times, "understaffed and overwhelmed with complex deals that investment bankers wanted to close within days."[2] The worker shortage, which can be demonstrated with payroll statistics, may have caused employees to have a short-term, cavalier outlook.

---

1   Permanent Subcommittee on Investigations of the Committee on Homeland Security and Governmental Affairs, Wall Street and the Financial Crisis: The Role of Credit Rating Agencies, April 23, 2010.
2   Ibid.

With the following vignette, Senator Levin tried to demonstrate how "short-term profits permeated the industry":

> One of the witnesses here today will describe how when he once questioned a banker about the terms of a deal, the banker replied, "IBG–YBG." When asked what that meant, the banker explained, "I'll be gone, you'll be gone"....[1]

The strongest evidence of possible malfeasance on the part of rating agencies is the fact that their ratings have not held up. Most of their AAA ratings for securities issued in recent years have been downgraded sharply. An incident demonstrating this fact was described by Senator Levin:

> In January 2007, S&P was asked to rate an RMBS being assembled by Goldman Sachs using subprime loans from Fremont Investment and Loan, a subprime lender known for loans with high rates of delinquency. On January 24, 2007, and analyst wrote seeking advice from two senior analysts: "I have a Goldman deal with subprime Fremont collateral. Since Fremont collateral has been performing not so good, is there anything special I should be aware of?" One analyst responded: "No, we don't treat their collateral any differently." The other asked: "are the FICO scores current?" "Yup," came the reply. Then, "You are good to go." [2]

This conversation shows that the rating agency seemed to ignore the quality (or lack thereof) of the underlying subprime loans. That spring, S&P and Moody's each provided AAA ratings for 5 of the tranches of RMBS securities backed by Fremont loans. By the time Senator Levin's hearings were held, all of the AAA tranches (backed by Fremont) had been downgraded to junk. This was just a small part of a much larger pattern.

According to Senator Levin, "91% of the AAA subprime RMBS securities issued in 2007 ... have since been downgraded to junk status." The Senator is correct, and these statistics indicate a very serious problem that must be addressed. However, he was misleading in two respects: He avoided telling us the downgrade rate for prime (vs. subprime) RMBS securities, and he failed to note that the government knew (for many years) that "Rating agencies generally do not ... conduct audits or due diligence reviews of issuer-provided information."[3]

---

1 Ibid.
2 Ibid.
3 "Report on the Role and Function of Credit Rating Agencies in the Operation of the Securities Markets," ed. Securities and Exchange Commission (U.S. government, January 2003), www.sec.gov/news/studies/credratingreport0103.pdf.

By noting that 91% of 2007 AAA subprime securities were down-graded to junk, Senator Levin gave the impression that this astonishing downgrade rate was entirely attributable to the poor quality of loans underlying the RMBS securities. However, if Levin had revealed another fact — that 92% of 2007 prime fixed-rate securities were also downgraded to junk, we would realize that there must be additional factors explaining the downgrades. Indeed, the astronomical rate of prime downgrades reflects the fact that, as of December 31, 2010, unemployment was sky-high, housing values had collapsed, and the economy had gone to hell. The rating companies made plenty of mistakes, which we are about to numerate. But, let's not pile on. If a meteorite wipes out New England are we going to blame rating agencies for any resultant downgrades?

Levin's second omission had to do with the government's role in this debacle. The government may now believe that rating companies need to audit the loans underlying the securities they rate, but the government did not seem concerned with this in the past. Each of the rating agencies had published the fact that it accepts, at face value, the information provided to it by banks and lenders. That was standard operating procedure, and it was noted in several government reports. For example, in its January 2003 report on the role and function of rating agencies, the SEC noted:

> In general, the rating agencies state that they rely on issuers and other sources to provide them with accurate and complete information. They typically do not audit the accuracy or integrity of issuer information.[1]

Looking professorial, with his spectacles perched at the tip of his nose, Senator Levin gave the impression that rating companies suddenly began to omit their standard review of underlying loans in order to please their banker clients. Levin added that "they did it for the money" and for "large fees." Alas, Levin is not just a Senator, he is a politician, and at times he behaved like one. His hearings produced useful information, but they also produced plenty of smoke.

The rating agencies made many mistakes

The rating agencies could have been the heroes of the financial crisis — instead they behaved like chumps. They did not break any laws (of which I have heard), although they are the target of some lawsuits alleging they gave ratings higher than warranted by the facts as they knew

---

1   Ibid.

them, or should have known them.[1] Whether or not they are culpable under the law, the rating agencies defined their responsibilities too narrowly, did the minimum work to justify their ratings, and used suspect methodologies that ultimately failed. They were not the cause of the crisis but the rating companies could have been the Paul Reveres of this crisis. They could have warned us of the growing risk of subprime lending. Instead, they were enablers. Here is a list of the many sins of Moody, Fitch and S&P. They ...

- Were slow to react to the subprime lending that became prevalent in the years 2005-2007. "The appetite for highly rated structured securities, combined with the belief that housing prices would always rise and that securitized loans would not create risks for the originator, prompted mortgage lenders to relax credit underwriting standards and expand into higher-risk market segments (such as subprime mortgages).... This increase in risk appetite does not seem to have been detected by rating agencies or investors."[2]
- Overestimated the diversity of the loans underlying RMBSs and CDOs. "[T]here was a failure to appreciate default correlation within and across pools of assets due to common underlying economic factors such as the housing market or to contemplate declines in housing prices."[3] In other words, the rating agencies did not sufficiently appreciate the potential for systemic risk.
- Underestimated the potential for housing values to drop, and assumed that any drops would be local — not national. "One assumption [of the rating agencies] was that if housing prices declined, the declines would not be severe. Another was that

---

1   In the past the rating agencies asserted that their ratings are constitutionally-protected "free speech" – mere opinions that cannot be relied upon for investment purposes. The Dodd-Frank Wall Street Reform and Consumer Protection Act eliminated the possibility of such claims. It expressly indicates that the advice given by a rating agency is expert testimony, and subject to the standards of such.

2   Jonathan Katz and Emanuel Salinas and Constantinos Stephanou, "Credit Rating Agencies: No Easy Regulatory Solutions," (Web-based: The World Bank Group (available at SSRN), October 2009), 3, http://papers.ssrn.com/sol3/papers.cfm?abstract_id=1485140.

3   Ibid., 4.

the housing market in California was indeed uncorrelated with the housing market in Connecticut."[1]

- Didn't increase staffs enough to handle the numerous and complex RMBS and CDO securities. "The analysts in structured finance were working twelve to fifteen hours a day. They made a fraction of the pay of even a junior investment banker. There were far more deals in the pipeline than they could possible handle. They were overwhelmed."[2]

- Based their ratings models on histories that were too short. "Because rating agencies often lacked extensive historical loss experience for innovative structures or transactions based on untested assets (for example, subprime mortgages), they used different (and sometimes inappropriate) analytical tools and assumptions to determine the risk of default and losses."[3]

- Failed to adequately surveil their existing ratings. "While NRSROs are not required under the law to perform surveillance, a rating agency will generally monitor the accuracy of its ratings on an ongoing basis in order to change the ratings when circumstances indicate that a change is required. ... The Staff notes that weaknesses existed in the rating agencies' surveillance efforts...." Specifically, "resources appear to have impacted the timeliness of surveillance efforts" and "there was poor documentation of the surveillance conducted."[4]

- Did not perform due-diligence with respect to the underlying loan data. (This was in accord with their announced policies.) "While corporate debt ratings are based on publicly available, audited financial statements, structured debt ratings are based on nonpublic, nonstandard, unaudited information supplied by the originator or nominal issuer."[5] The rating agencies did not seem overly concerned with the quality of the underlying

1   Bethany McLean and Joe Nocera, All the Devils Are Here, 5th ed. (New York: Portfolio Penguin, 2010), 118.

2   Ibid., 123.

3   Katz and Emanuel Salinas and Constantinos Stephanou, "Credit Rating Agencies: No Easy Regulatory Solutions," 4.

4   "Summary Report of Issues Identified in the Commission Staff's Examination of Select Credit Rating Agencies," ed. Securities and Exchange Commission (United States, July 8, 2008), 21.

5   ———, "Credit Rating Agencies: No Easy Regulatory Solutions," 4.

loans, as they believed that the structure of the RMBS or CDO was of greater importance to creditworthiness.

- Relied on new math models and neglected experience and judgment. "S&P ... and Moody's substituted theoretical mathematic assumptions for the experience and judgment of their own analysts. ... If the old rating methods were like Rembrandt's portraiture, with details painted in, the new ones were Monet impressionism, with only a suggestion of the full picture."[1]

- Didn't retroactively apply important methodological changes. "By 2006, Moody's and Standard & Poors knew their ratings of residential mortgage-backed securities (RMBS) and collateralized debt obligations (CDOs) were inaccurate, revised their rating models to produce more accurate ratings, but then failed to use the revised model to re-evaluate existing RMBS and CDO securities, delaying thousands of rating downgrades and allowing those securities to carry inflated ratings that could mislead investors."[2]

- May have undermined standards by providing consulting services to those for whom they provided ratings services. By providing these services, "the rating agencies may have served not just as monitors and evaluators of existing structures, but rather as architects and creators of new securities. Providing such models to issuers potentially led to the creation of CDOs with the minimum possible collateral needed to obtain an AAA credit rating."[3]

- Failed to make all necessary disclosures regarding their methods. "The rating agencies stated to the [SEC] Staff that, prior to being registered as NRSROs, they disclosed their ratings process. It appears, however, that certain significant aspects of the ratings process and the methodologies used to rate

---

1 Elliot Blair Smith, "Bringing Down Wall Street as Ratings Let Loose Subprime Scourge," Bloomberg.com (September 24, 2008), http://www.bloomberg.com/apps/news?sid=ah839IWTLP9s&pid=newsarchive.

2 Wall Street and the Financial Crisis: The Role of Credit Rating Agencies, Hearing 3.

3 John Lounsbury, "The Alchemy of Securitization," Seeking Alpha (October 21, 2010), http://seekingalpha.com/article/231248-the-alchemy-of-securitization.

RMBS and CDOs were not always disclosed, or were not fully disclosed...."[1]

A very tepid defense of the rating agencies

Many people question if it is possible for a rating agency to fairly evaluate the companies that provide its revenue. It is a reasonable question, and it is one that applies equally to my profession: auditing. Accountants are usually paid by the businesses that they audit, and in such situations maintaining independence is a concern. In my view, high quality, objective work can be produced if the proper safeguards are in place. One huge safeguard is the threat of lawsuits: Auditors never forget that they can be sued if work is not thorough and objective. In addition, we are peer-reviewed at least once every three years. During the peer review process, samples of our audit reports and workpapers are re-evaluated by other CPAs, who are potential competitors. Auditors sometimes get it wrong, but it is usually due to mistakes — not dishonesty.

In the case of rating agencies, lawsuits were deflected by the specious assertion that a rating is constitutionally-protected free-speech. Further, there was no meaningful and consistent peer review process, and internal audit procedures were not always adequate.[2] Nevertheless, it is not clear that the agencies lacked the independence required to fairly perform their function in the years prior to the crisis. After the SEC Staff conducted an exhaustive review of the rating industry it reported, in July 2008, that "there is no evidence that decisions about rating methodology or models were made based on attracting or losing market share...."[3] This conclusion contradicts the implication of Senator Levin, et al.

The rating agencies did not review detailed loan documentation related to the securities they evaluated, but this fact was not concealed, and was well-known to government regulators. For example, in a July 2003 SEC report on rating agencies it is stated:

> Rating agencies generally do not ... conduct audits or due diligence reviews of issuer-provided information.[4]

Until the financial crisis unfolded, government regulators simply saw no need for rating agencies to review underlying loan documentation. If

---

1 "Summary Report of Issues Identified in the Commission Staff's Examination of Select Credit Rating Agencies," 13.
2 Ibid., 29.
3 Ibid., 25.
4 "Report on the Role and Function of Credit Rating Agencies in the Operation of the Securities Markets," 26.

they had, such due-diligence would have been required, and would have been performed.[1]

The agencies failed to appreciate default correlation within and across pools of assets. Specifically, they saw housing as a collection of disconnected regional markets — not a national market. However, this fallacious reasoning was shared by most economists and financiers. In testimony to Congress in 2005, Former Federal Reserve Chairman Alan Greenspan stated:

> The housing market in the United States is quite heterogeneous, and it does not have the capacity to move excesses easily from one area to another. Instead, we have a collection of only loosely connected local markets.[2]

In addition, billionaire investor Warren Buffet acknowledged, to the Financial Crisis Inquiry Commission, that Moody's erred in giving such high ratings to mortgage-related bonds. But, he stressed that millions of other Americans made the same mistake. In his June 2010 testimony he added this statement:

> Look at me. I was wrong on it too.... In this particular case, I think they [rating agencies] made a mistake that virtually everybody in the country made.[3]

After his statement, critics noted that Warren Buffet's company, Berkshire Hathaway, Inc., owns a nice chunk of Moody's. Some analysts seem to suspect that he made his comments in an effort to boost the value of Moody's stock (a view I don't share).

It is hard for me to believe that the agencies recognized (but simply ignored) the massive systemic risk of the U.S. housing market. If they appreciated the risk they would have seen the likelihood of a financial

1   In late 2010, D. Keith Johnson, a former president of Clayton Holdings, told the Financial Crisis Inquiry Commission that his former company had analyzed mortgage pools for investment banks, and found numerous underwriting deficiencies in the loans. He claimed that he took those results to S&P, Moody's, and Fitch, but none of them had interest in the findings. A week or so later, Johnson's testimony was flatly contradicted by a written statement released by Clayton Holdings. That statement indicated that "at no time did Clayton share any client reports or data, much less the beta Trending Reports, with any rating agency." It also claimed that each of Johnson's meetings with the rating agencies took place "after the securitization market had collapsed" (emphasis as in original statement).
2   David Levy and Sandr Peart, "An Expert-Induced Bubble: The Nasty Role of Ratings Agencies in the Busted Housing Market," Reasonline (September 30, 2008), http://www.reason.com/news/show/129116.html.
3   Aaron Lucchetti, "Buffett Defends Moody's Management," online.wsj.com (June 2010), http://online.wsj.com/article/SB123491508784704057.html.

crisis that could destroy their own reputations and the rating industry, as a whole. This view is implicitly supported by Michael Lewis, who is author of numerous books about Wall Street and who is a critic of rating agencies. Lewis expressed the belief that the CEOs of big investment banks had no clue what was going on with regard to the risks leading up to the crisis.[1] If the investment banks were clueless, and the rating agencies were basing their work on representations from those investment banks, it is not surprising that the rating agencies failed to recognize the threat posed by the subprime lending epidemic.

Rating agencies have been criticized for not downgrading quickly enough when their cash flow models seemed to be failing. However, downgrades have to be made very cautiously because they can trigger a vicious cycle that destroys a company. This risk is aptly described by Malay Bansal, Managing Director of Capitalfusion Partners:

> The downgrade increases cost of financing as investors demand more yield reflecting lower rating. The downgrade may also result in existing investors having to sell holdings, further increasing the yields in the market. It can become a vicious circle increasing the likelihood of default. The downgrade reflects rating agency's *opinion* of the outcome, but it also becomes a *causal factor* in determining that outcome. The rating agencies in effect become the judge, jury, and the hangman for the company (emphasis as in original).[2]

Rating agencies are not investment advisors. They are not in the business of making of investments or assigning values to investments. As stated by Vickie Tillman, S&P's Executive Vice President, rating agencies make a judgment as to "how much cash we believe the underlying loans are likely to generate." After 2007, many RMBS securities became illiquid, and they lost most of their market value. In many cases, however, those investments could still generate substantial cash flows, as predicted by rating agency models.

Finally, it is possible that the importance of rating agencies to the financial crisis has been slightly overstated. After analyzing investment bank balance sheets and their capital reserves, economists Viral Acharya and Matthew Richardson made the following surprising statement:

> ...we believe that the rating agencies' role in marketing asset-backed securities to investors can be overestimated as a factor in the crisis, because,

---

1   "Author Michael Lewis on Wall St's Delusion."

2   Malay Bansal, "Rating Agency Reform:The Real Problem That Has Not Been Recognized," Seeking Alpha (June 28, 2010), http://seekingalpha.com/article/212142-rating-agency-reform-the-real-problem-that-has-not-been-recognized.

in fact, investors were not the chief purchasers of these securities: banks themselves were. Instead of acting as intermediaries between borrowers and investors by transferring the risk from mortgage lenders to the capital market, the banks became primary investors.[1]

The banks did not need the services of rating agencies to ascertain the risks associated with their own products. If they bought and held onto their mortgage-backed securities it is their fault — not the fault of the agencies. In all likelihood, the banks were holding these securities because they were trying to minimize their capital reserve requirements under the rules established by the government. (There is more detail regarding capital reserve requirements in Chapter 17.)

The future of rating agencies

Changes were already underway prior to the financial crisis. In 2006, the Credit Rating Agency Reform Act was passed. Although the law prohibited SEC from regulating NRSRO rating methodologies, it gave SEC responsibility for establishing the rules used to determine which rating agencies qualified as Nationally Recognized Statistical Rating Organizations (NRSROs). The legislation also gave SEC the authority to regulate internal policies with respect to record-keeping and conflicts of interest.

The Dodd-Frank Wall Street Reform and Consumer Protection Act, passed in mid-2010, creates a new Office of Credit Ratings, within the SEC, to "administer the rules of the Commission (i) with respect to the practices of NRSROs in determining ratings, for the protection of users of credit ratings, and in the public interest; (ii) to promote accuracy in credit ratings issued by NRSROs; and (iii) to ensure that such ratings are not unduly influenced by conflicts of interest." SEC will have the right to suspend or revoke NRSRO registration if an agency's ratings are substantially inaccurate or if the agency lacks the financial or human resources necessary to produce quality ratings.

Disclosure requirements are extensive and include the initial rating (as well as subsequent ratings), the information, procedures and methods used to produce any rating, limitations relative to the ratings, and potential volatility of the estimates.

Formerly, it was difficult to successfully sue a rating agency because their ratings were considered to be constitutionally-protected free speech. (At least, that was their contention.) This has been explicitly changed by the Dodd-Frank legislation. Ratings are now subject to the

---

1   Viral Acharya and Maattlew Richardson, "Causes of the Financial Crisis," Critical Review Foundation May 12, 2009, 200.

SEC's fair disclosure rule, and rating agencies are subject to so-called expert liability.

Dodd-Frank requires the removal of statutory references to credit ratings in federal and state law. The idea is to lessen the importance of NRSRO ratings, and to encourage the development of alternative standards of creditworthiness.

To minimize the likelihood of conflicts of interest, Dodd-Frank requires the complete separation of the analyst function and the sales function, within each agency.

Finally, the legislation calls for a 2-year study of the rating process with respect to RMBSs and CDOs, and with regard to conflict of interest inherent with the "issuer pays" model. It is specifically noted that the outcome of the 2-year study could be the creation of a system in which rating agencies are assigned to rate companies by some yet-to-be-formed public or private utility, or self-regulatory entity.

CHAPTER 13: THE BET THAT DIDN'T BLOW UP WALL STREET?

> Senator Jack Reed: So the perception that this
> London operation was some rogue sort of group that were
> unsupervised, that you had no access to, that your regulatory
> authority did not reach there, is not accurate?
>
> Scott Polakoff: Correct. That would be a false statement.
> ... [W]e were clearly responsible as the consolidated regulator
> for FP [AIG's London Financial Products division]. We in
> 2004 should have taken an entirely different approach than
> what we wound up taking regarding the credit default
> swaps....
>
> – Testimony before the Senate Banking, Housing and
> Urban Affairs Committee on March 5, 2009

For months, the nation had been told that regulators were barred from reviewing credit default swaps, due to sneaky legislation promoted by Republican Phil Gramm 8 years earlier. Indeed, 60 Minutes told millions of viewers that credit default swaps were "totally unregulated." But here is this guy, rudely interrupting testimony of a Federal Reserve officer, to make a startling confession.

In front of the Senate Banking Committee, Scott M. Polakoff, Acting Director of the Office of Thrift Supervision (OTS), said that his agency had responsibility for a major regulatory failure related to the credit default swaps (CDSs)[1] sold by AIG's London investment office. After indicating that AIG Financial Products (AIGFP) was "part of the overall con-

---

1   Credit default swaps are defined on page 215 .

solidated regulator responsibilities of OTS," Polakoff detailed many specific actions taken by OTS with respect to AIG. Here are some of them:

> OTS conducted continuous consolidated supervision of the AIG group, including an on-site examination team at AIG headquarters in New York. Through frequent, on-going dialogue with company management, OTS maintained a contemporaneous understanding of all material parts of the AIG group, including their domestic and crossborder operations. ...

> OTS held monthly meeting with AIG's Regulatory and Compliance Group, Internal Audit Director and external auditors. In addition, OTS held quarterly meetings with the Chief Risk Officer, the Treasury Group and senior management, and annually with the board of directors. ...

> In 2005, OTS conducted several targeted, risk-focused reviews of various line of business, including AIGFP....[1]

A couple weeks later, Polakoff repeated his assertions before a committee of the House of Representatives, where he conceded that OTS should have and could have stopped AIG's sale of CDS in 2004. He also had this exchange with Rep. Jeb Hensarling:

> Rep. Hensarling: So, again, in retrospect, it wasn't the lack of authority. It wasn't the lack of resources. It wasn't the lack of expertise. You just flat made a mistake. Is that a correct assessment?

> Polakoff: In 2004, we failed to assess how bad the mortgage economy, the real estate economy would become in 2008. Yes, sir.[2]

To be specific, the mistake made by OTS was to concentrate "too narrowly on the perceived creditworthiness of the underlying securities...." The regulator had been lulled into complacency by the fact that AIGFP's credit default swaps were guaranteeing "the safest portion of the security," and that there had been no related credit losses. What OTS (and AIG and many others) failed to consider was the possibility of a liquidity crisis. In his prepared statement for the Senate Banking Committee, Polakoff said:

> No one predicted, including OTS, the amount of funds that would be required to meet collateral calls and cash demands on the credit default swap transactions. In retrospect, if we had identified the absolute mag-

---

1 Senate Committee on Banking, Housing, and Urban Affairs, Statement of Scott M. Polakoff, Acting Director, OTS, March 5, 2009, 10-11.

2 Declan McCullagh, "Treasury Admits It Could Have Stopped Aig Years Ago," CBSNEWS (March 20, 2009), http://www.cbsnews.com/8301-503983_162-4878325-503983.html.

---

nitude of AIGFP's CDS exposures as a liquidity risk, we could have requested that AIGFP reduce its exposure to this concentration.[1]

Under post-Enron accounting rules (as interpreted at the time), it was necessary to rapidly mark-down investments to market value, even though most mortgagors were still paying their loans and there was absolutely no collection risk for the upper layers (tranches) of the mortgage-backed securities referenced in the credit default swaps. Nevertheless, AIG had to write down its portfolio of mortgage-backed securities, and when it did, all hell broke loose. The write-down of the investments led to a decrease in AIG capital reserves, which led to lower ratings by the rating agencies (Moody's, et al), which led to calls by CDS counterparties (the "insured" parties) for more collateral. AIG couldn't come up with the money fast enough and it was sort of a modern-day "run on the bank."

Scott Polakoff was something of a whistleblower who deserved credit for candor, but he wasn't invited to appear on 60 Minutes or any other mainstream news program. To be fair, CBSNews.com did write about him, but the piece was titled, "Did AIG find the dumbest regulator in town?" Polakoff can also forget about doing college lectures, *The Daily Show*, or *Saturday Night Live*. You see, his testimony was not appropriately anti-Bush or anti-Wall Street. Indeed, it was the opposite. It obliterated the myth that AIGFP got into trouble because of deregulation, an absence of governmental oversight, or a lack of regulatory authority or resources.

A few days after Polakoff testified about the government's regulatory failures, he received his reward. The Obama administration suspended him — ostensibly to investigate if he was involved in the backdating of capital infusions by some banks. On June 19, 2009 the Treasury Department announced that Scott Polakoff had resigned, and in a subsequent interview Polakoff said there was no correlation between his decision to retire and the backdating investigation.

What are Credit Default Swaps (CDS)?

A credit default swap (CDS) is a financial product that enables the purchaser to transfer default risk related to his corporate bond to the seller of the CDS. For example, if a bank owns a $100,000 GM bond, and is worried about default by GM, it might purchase a CDS from a hedge fund for, say, $500 per year. In return, the hedge fund would guarantee

---

1   Statement of Scott M. Polakoff, Acting Director, OTS, 6.

payment of the bond, in the event of default by GM. The deal is attractive to both sides: The bank receives a relatively low-cost form of insurance and the hedge fund receives some easy money.

In many cases the CDS purchaser does not even own the investment referenced (insured, so to speak) by the CDS. For example, the late Lehman Brothers might have bought a CDS guaranteeing payment in the event of default on mortgage-backed securities owned by Morgan Stanley. In such cases, the investment is more like gambling than insurance.

CDSs started to become popular in the late 1990s, and grew to a market of a few trillion dollars by 2007.[1] Problems then developed due to the inclusion of subprime mortgages in mortgage-backed securities, collateral call features in the CDS, and new accounting rules that appeared to require the rapid write-down of investments to market value. Even these problems, however, did not pose a major challenge to most CDS sellers because they generally hedged any potential losses with their own CDS purchases. In other words, they were on both sides of the deal. AIG was the unfortunate exception. It sold CDS but did not buy them.

In September 2008, AIG had $440 billion in CDS on its books. As the real estate market sagged and some mortgage-backed securities racked up defaults, investors became worried about AIG's ability to pay. Moody's lowered AIG's credit rating, collateral calls were triggered, and AIG could not produce the needed collateral. In that same month (September) the U.S. Federal Reserve established a liquid credit line for AIG, secured by its assets. In exchange for the credit line the U.S. government was given substantial (majority) equity position in AIG. In mid-2012 the Federal Reserve announced that AIG had repaid its governmental credit line. The government plans to eventually sell its AIG stock on the market.

The early controversy regarding CDS, derivatives, and regulation

Credit default swaps are a form of derivative, meaning that they *derive* their value by referencing the changes in value of other investments — usually bonds or other forms of debt securities. There are trillions of dollars of derivatives in the world, although most are for the purpose of

---

1   The size of the credit default swap market is often wildly exaggerated. For example, it was estimated at $45 trillion by George Soros, and it was reported as being "more than $50 trillion" on the 60 Minutes program. These estimates are of the gross notional amounts that include great redundancy. A good analysis is provided by Peter Wallison of American Enterprise Institute, who estimates that the net notional amount is more likely below $3 trillion ("Credit Default Swaps are not to Blame," AEI, June 1, 2009).

protecting the buyer against fluctuations in interest rates — not credit default.

The exact amount of derivatives, types, and ownership are not known, and this fact has been a matter of substantial concern and controversy. Several years ago, Warren Buffet famously declared that derivatives were "financial weapons of mass destruction, carrying dangers that, while now latent, are potentially lethal."

The former Federal Reserve Chairman, Alan Greenspan, did not feel that there was a need to regulate derivatives because he assumed that the buyers and sellers were sophisticated enough to protect themselves against fraud and abuse. This view was shared by President Clinton's financial team, including former Treasury Secretary, James Rubin, and his deputy, Lawrence H. Summers.

On the other side was Brooksley Born, the Chairwoman of the Commodity Futures Trading Commission (CFTC), a federal agency that regulates futures trading. In the late 1990s she advocated greater disclosure of derivative trades and larger capital reserve requirements because she was concerned that derivative trading could "threaten our regulated markets or, indeed, our economy without any federal agency knowing about it."[1]

In April 1998 federal regulators convened to discuss Born's recommendations. At that time, Rubin and Greenspan implored her to reconsider. When she refused, Rubin and Greenspan recommended that Congress suspend the CFTC of authority over derivatives. It did this, and Ms. Born soon departed the agency.

Thus, derivatives remained unregulated, and this was the case before George W. Bush set foot in the White House, and before passage of the much maligned (and much misrepresented) Commodity Futures Modernization Act (the legislation that, supposedly, Bill Clinton was tricked into signing).

Credit Default Swaps and the Commodity Futures Modernization Act

When the financial crisis unfolded in 2007 and 2008, the Commodity Futures Modernization Act (CFMA) became a battle cry of the left. It was portrayed as Republican deregulation that led directly to the crisis. This was a gross misrepresentation.

---

1   Peter S. Goodman, "Taking Hard New Look at a Greenspan Legacy," The New York Times (October 9, 2008), http://www.nytimes.com/2008/10/09/business/economy/09greenspan.html?pagewanted=all.

The CFMA was enacted in 2000 (while Bill Clinton was President) with bipartisan support and little controversy. The ostensible goal of the legislation was to provide legislative clarity with regard to the regulation of derivatives (such as credit default swaps), thus enabling the United States to remain competitive with respect to this important financial product. The day after it passed, Democratic Senator Tom Harkin stated that, although he disliked parts of the legislation, he recognized "the overall importance and positive features of this legislation."[1] He also praised Republican Senators Phil Gramm and Richard Lugar for their help and "outstanding work." A little while later, Democratic Senator Paul Sarbanes was filled with praise for the law and its authorization of "a new financial product, the 'security future,' to be traded under a regulatory scheme that protects investors against fraud, market manipulation and insider trading." On that same day (Jan. 2, 2001) Senator Sarbanes submitted to the Congressional Record a letter from the President's Working Group (that is, President Clinton's Working Group) "strongly supporting the Commodity Futures Modernization Act of 2000." The letter reads (in full):

> Dear Senator Sarbanes:
>
> The Members of the President's Working Group on Financial Markets strongly support the Commodity Futures Modernization Act. This important legislation will allow the United States to maintain its competitive position in the over-the-counter derivative markets by providing legal certainty and promoting innovation, transparency and efficiency in our financial markets while maintaining appropriate protections for transactions in non-financial commodities and for small investors.
>
> Sincerely,
>
> Lawrence Summers, Secretary, Department of the Treasury
> Alan Greenspan, Chairman, Board of Governors of the Federal Reserve
> Arthur Levitt, Chairman, Securities and Exchange Commission
> William J. Rainier, Chairman, Commodity Futures Trading Commission[2]

The key words in the letter from the President's Working Group were "legal certainty." CFMA did not change the regulatory treatment of credit default swaps, but it provided a legal safe harbor for the treatment already in effect. The legislation clarified that non-retail, over-the-counter (OTC) credit default swaps were not securities subject to regulation

---

1   Congressional Record, V. 146, Pt. 18, November 1, 2000 to January 2, 2001
2   Senator Paul Sarbanes, "Submission of Letter from the President's Working Group," Congressional Record 146, no. 156 (January 2, 2001).

by the Security and Exchange Commission or the Commodities Futures Trading Commission. However, they were subject to the antifraud, anti-manipulation and anti-insider trading provisions of the 1933 and 1934 Security laws. Legislators on both sides of the aisle recognized this to be a benefit.

The Democratic praise for the CFMA ended a year or so later when the Enron scandal broke. Suddenly there were stories of the "coordinated trickery" used to get the bill passed "without undergoing the usual committee hearings and preliminary votes." Supposedly, Senator Gramm had slipped in an "Enron Loophole," and that led to rampant oil speculation. (If this Democratic 180-degree turn-around sounds familiar, think Democratic flip-flop on support for Iraq War.) However, it was later shown, in an email retrieved from Enron, that President Clinton's Treasury Department was solidly behind the so-called Enron loophole. Enron lobbyist, Chris Long, described to his bosses the Treasury Department's support, as expressed to him by Laurence Summer's lieutenant, Lee Sachs:

> I told Lee that we shared his desire to move the legislation as long as it contains a full exclusion for all non-agriculture commodities (including metals). He said that we would have a difficult time defending the metals provision politically. But, Lee said, *"we would not find Treasury opposition to the House Commerce Committee language" (which includes favorable language on energy and metals).* This is a positive development, because it isolates the CFTC from its key defenders and I hope ensures no veto threat on our issues. However, I do not expect Treasury to be vocal in support of our position (emphasis added).[1]

Thus, it appears that Clinton's Treasury Department understood and supported the Enron loophole, and this was at least 4 months prior to the law's adoption.

Phil Gramm — Sorcerer!

A new round of outrage materialized after the 2007/08 financial debacle. Now, Phil Gramm's powers of sorcery reached almost mythical heights, while Democrats were, at worst, trusting rubes. "Who's to blame for the biggest financial catastrophe of our time?" asked pundit David Corn. It's Phil Gramm. You see, said Corn, "eight years ago, as part of a decades-long antiregulatory crusade, Gramm pulled a sly legislative maneuver that greased the way to the multi-billion dollar sub-

---

1   Kevin Connor, "Celebrating Ten Years of Derivatives Deregulation," The Huffington Post, December 21, 2010, http://www.huffingtonpost.com/kevin-connor/celebrating-ten-years-of_b_799981.html.

prime meltdown." Corn seemed to believe that Gramm tricked Congress and President Clinton by slipping language, related to the deregulation of credit default swaps, into the CFMA just before it was voted upon. That's the reason it passed with a huge, bipartisan margin and that is why it was signed into law by Democratic President Bill Clinton. In his 1500-word conspiratorial tome, named "Foreclosure Phil," Corn mentioned President Clinton's name exactly once, and only to note that he had been tricked by a "wily senator." The nation was doomed, and it was all the fault of Republican Gramm, bosom buddy of John McCain — the man opposing Barack Obama in the 2008 presidential election.[1]

At least Corn mentioned Clinton's name once. In an 8,800-word rant in Rolling Stone, Matt Taibbi managed to indict and convict Phil Gramm without even hinting at the words, "Bill" or "Clinton." (You probably thought that President Clinton was a fairly important person in the United States, but Taibbi knows that the real power resided in the hands of this lone, Republican Senator.)[2]

Countless Democratic pundits and journalists joined the chorus, shouting their disgust at Republican deregulation. But, now you know the rest of the story: that the CFMA became law when Bill Clinton was the head honcho, and that Democratic indignation materialized much, much later, and only after scandals unfolded. You also need to know that CFMA had almost no impact on AIG and its financial troubles.

CFMA had little or nothing to do with AIG

> Cassano's outrageous gamble [to create a credit default business] wouldn't have been possible had he not had the good fortune to take over AIGFP just as Sen. Phil Gramm — a grinning, laissez-faire ideologue from Texas — had finished engineering the most dramatic deregulation of the financial industry since Emperor Hien Tsung invented paper money in 806 A.D.
>
> – Matt Taibbi, Teller of Tall Tales[3]

You have to love the enthusiasm of the Left, even if their facts get a bit snarled. Matt Taibbi seems to think that AIG Financial Products (AIGFP), which is AIG's credit default swap business located in London,

---

1   David Corn, "Foreclosure Phil," (May 28, 2008), http://motherjones.com/politics/2008/05/foreclosure-phil.

2   Matt Taibbi, "The Big Takeover: How Wall Street Insiders Are Using the Bailout to Stage a Revolution," Rolling Stone March 22, 2009.

3   Ibid.

"wouldn't have been possible ..." were it not for Grinning Gramm's sneaky Commodity Futures Modernization Act. Perhaps Matt has been watching 60 Minutes too much. Eric Dinallo, the ex-insurance superintendent for the state of New York, argued on 60 Minutes that "existing gambling and bucket shop laws" (state laws) could have controlled Wall Street's sale of credit default swaps, were it not for the Commodity Futures Modernization Act. He also told the CBS news magazine that AIGFP's credit default business could have been regulated as insurance. According to Dinallo, state insurance regulators in the United States would have ensured that AIGFP had adequate capital reserves in support of the swaps.[1]

There is one possible flaw in these theories: Last time I checked, London was not located in the United States, and probably would not have been subject to state regulation of any kind. However, for the sake of argument let's assume that London is situated in New York State — just east of Buffalo — and let's further assume that AIGFP has been selling credit default swaps from its London, New York office. Even if this were the case, there is no evidence to suggest that the New York Attorney General was about to apply antiquated gambling and bucket shop laws to anyone, including AIGFP. This assertion easily withstands the fact that, according to Dinallo, credit default swaps would have been "...very illegal 100 years ago" (not just illegal, mind you, very illegal).

As for the strategy of treating the swaps as insurance, there was a significant problem (aside from the small venue problem): In the year 2000, just before the CFMA was passed, the New York Insurance Department (Dinallo's department) specifically decided that credit default swaps were not insurance (a decision Dinallo now says was "incomplete"). It doesn't seem that state insurance regulators had any plans to scrutinize credit default swaps — with or without the CFMA.

Finally, let's remember what was said by Scott Polakoff, the Acting Director of the Office of Thrift Supervision (OTS). His agency did, in fact, review the credit default swap operation of AIG, due to the fact that it could impact the savings and loan company within the larger holding corporation (AIG). He testified to Congress that his agency had the authority and resources to review all of AIG, including its London office. He candidly acknowledged that OTS simply screwed up and overlooked the liquidity risks associated with the swap business.

---

1   "The Bet That Blew up Wall Street," 60 Minutes (October 26, 2008), http://www.cbsnews.com/2102-18560_162-4546199.html?tag=contentMain;contentBody.

Thus, there is no credible evidence that CFMA affected the regulation of AIG's London operations. That said, the CFMA did have an impact on CDSs, in general. Undoubtedly, the legal certainty provided by the legislation led to increased world-wide production of credit default swaps. This, in turn, probably led to increased sales of mortgage-backed securities, many of which were laced with subprime loans.

Are credit default swaps beneficial or harmful?

> ...if A.I.G., instead of selling protection on the portfolios, had bought the portfolios themselves, commentators would have merely clucked about the company's poor credit judgment. For some reason, the fact that it did substantially the same thing by selling protection on these securities through credit-default swaps has caused hysteria about the swaps that insured the securities. Regardless of how it was insured, however, the real risk was created when banks borrowed the funds necessary to assemble a portfolio of subprime mortgage-backed securities.
>
> – Peter J. Wallison, American Enterprise Institute[1]

The words of Peter J. Wallison, above, are extremely important to a proper evaluation of credit default swaps. Wallison notes that the risk of a credit default swap (CDS) is "no different from the risk of making the underlying loan. CDSs allow risks to be spread among more parties instead of being concentrated at vulnerable points, but they do not add to the total amount of risk."[2]

The following analogy puts this into perspective, and demonstrates why the root cause of the financial crisis was subprime lending — not the packaging of the loans into securities, or the insuring of the loans with CDSs.

Let's say that there are certain minimum standards for building a home. The joists and rafters have to be of a minimum thickness, the concrete has to have steel reinforcement, etc. However, these features result in more expensive homes that many people cannot afford. Since politicians on both sides of the aisle want to promote home ownership, they encourage builders to use less stringent standards. In some cases they even require the builders to use mediocre building standards.

---

1   Peter J. Wallison, "Credit Default Swaps Are Not to Blame," (Washington, DC: American Enterprise Institute, June 1, 2009), http://www.aei.org/article/economics/financial-services/credit-default-swaps-are-not-to-blame/.

2   Ibid.

Thousands of these lousy homes are sold by a few large real estate companies, and the homes are insured by State Farm Insurance. As the homes start falling apart, the cost of insurance claims is staggering, State Farm is teetering on the edge of bankruptcy, and taxpayers are forced to "bail out" State Farm.

We could argue that the real estate companies should not have sold the homes. Rather, they should have avoided them after researching construction building methods. We could castigate State Farm for insuring the homes: It should have inspected them carefully before offering insurance. However, the main culprits would be the builders who made the lousy homes and the politicians who encouraged them to do so.

Critics of the CDS claim that it is "a mechanism through which the failure of one financial institution could be transmitted to others," and this is true — theoretically. However, as AEI's Peter Wallison asserts, "there is no evidence that the failure of Lehman or AIG — both of which were major players in the CDS market — caused any other financial institution to fail."[1] Indeed, CDSs can actually be helpful, when used properly, because they spread risk. They are, and should remain, an important tool of finance.

The above notwithstanding, I believe that Brooksley Born was right: Credit default swaps should have been monitored and regulated more carefully. Alan Greenspan's belief that sophisticated bankers and counterparties would be protected by their own self-interests did not prove to be true — at least with respect to AIG.

Using the authority granted to it by the Dodd-Frank Wall Street Reform and Consumer Protection Act (2010), the SEC has issued a series of regulations related to credit default swaps. Among them is the requirement that derivative sellers register with the SEC, and the so-called "Volker rule," which (with great ambiguity) prohibits banks from using CDSs to make speculative bets with their own funds. In addition, the Federal Reserve retains the right to set capital reserve requirements for swap entities that are banks. Let us hope that these regulations are administered competently. Last time they were not.

---

1 ———, "The Error at the Heart of the Dodd-Frank Act," (Washington, DC: American Enterprise Institute, August-September 2011), http://www.aei.org/article/economics/financial-services/the-error-at-the-heart-of-the-dodd-frank-act/.

SPARKS THAT LIT THE FUSE

Did accountants cause the meltdown? Hardly. But, the 2007 introduction of mark-to-market accounting, an accounting standard that was
widely misunderstood and misapplied, served to trigger and accelerate
the crisis.

A second crisis trigger was provided by naked short selling. While traditional short selling can be beneficial to the markets, naked shorts are a different matter. This abusive practice probably accelerated the demised of Lehman Brothers, and possibly other companies as well.

Figure 14 – A model of the causes and other factors affecting the financial crisis of 2007/08 (The shaded box pertains to Part Three.)

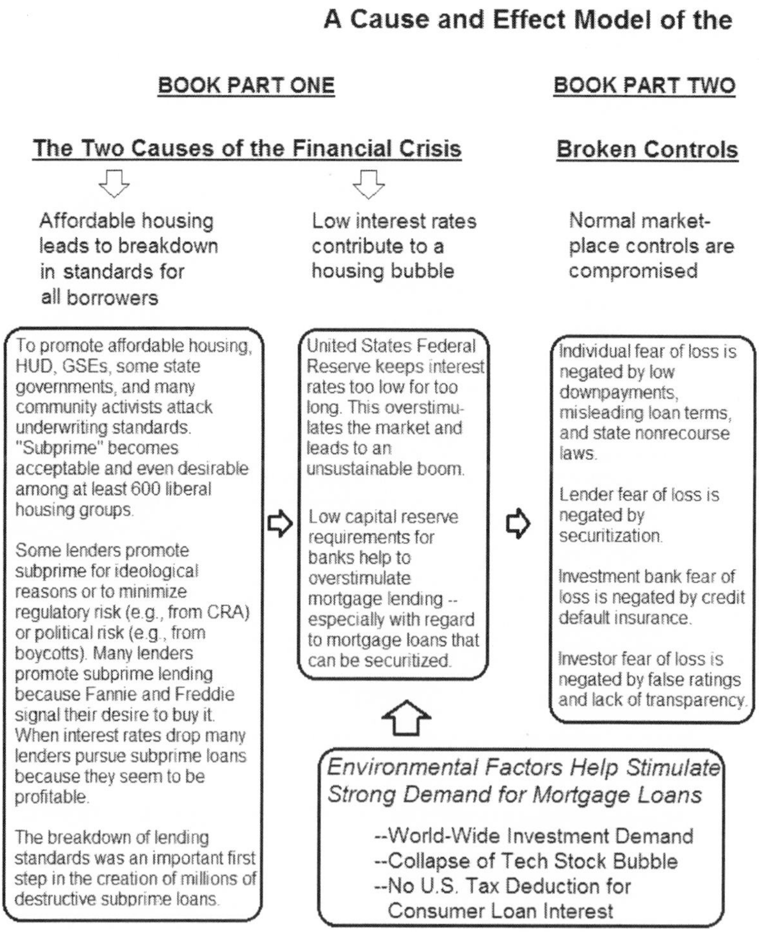

A Cause and Effect Model of the

BOOK PART ONE

BOOK PART TWO

The Two Causes of the Financial Crisis

Broken Controls

| Affordable housing leads to breakdown in standards for all borrowers | Low interest rates contribute to a housing bubble | Normal market-place controls are compromised |

To promote affordable housing, HUD, GSEs, some state governments, and many community activists attack underwriting standards. "Subprime" becomes acceptable and even desirable among at least 600 liberal housing groups.

Some lenders promote subprime for ideological reasons or to minimize regulatory risk (e.g., from CRA) or political risk (e.g., from boycotts). Many lenders promote subprime lending because Fannie and Freddie signal their desire to buy it. When interest rates drop many lenders pursue subprime loans because they seem to be profitable.

The breakdown of lending standards was an important first step in the creation of millions of destructive subprime loans.

United States Federal Reserve keeps interest rates too low for too long. This overstimulates the market and leads to an unsustainable boom.

Low capital reserve requirements for banks help to overstimulate mortgage lending -- especially with regard to mortgage loans that can be securitized.

Individual fear of loss is negated by low downpayments, misleading loan terms, and state nonrecourse laws.

Lender fear of loss is negated by securitization.

Investment bank fear of loss is negated by credit default insurance.

Investor fear of loss is negated by false ratings and lack of transparency.

Environmental Factors Help Stimulate Strong Demand for Mortgage Loans

--World-Wide Investment Demand
--Collapse of Tech Stock Bubble
--No U.S. Tax Deduction for Consumer Loan Interest

Subprime Mortgage Crisis of 2007-2008

BOOK PART THREE

Sparks   **Boom**

These are   Bear Stearns & ML
just triggers   are sold, Lehman
                 goes broke, AIG is
                 downgraded, and
                 Feds take over
                 Fannie and Freddie

BOOK PART FOUR

Aggravating Factors

These factors complicate
the crisis aftermath but
do not cause the crisis

Mark-to-
market
accounting

Naked short
selling

Sudden
downgrades
by rating
agencies

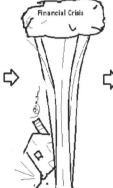

Banks & borrowers
are hurt because of
documentation
defects.

Taxpayers are hurt
because bank capital
reserves are
deficient.

Homeowners are hurt
by nearby
foreclosures, which
are aggravated by
nonrecourse lending
rules.

CHAPTER 14: ACCOUNTANTS GET BLAMED — IT'S GREAT!

> "...Don't mark our love to market ... don't kiss our love goodbye ... You're still the one I dream of ... please give me one more try ..."
>
> – Merle Hazard, in song dedicated "to the courageous men and women of the FASB" [Financial Accounting Standards Board]

I never thought I'd live long enough to hear a song written about an accounting rule. As a CPA, I've got to admit that it makes me kind of teary-eyed and melancholy. Finally, someone notices the lowly bean-counters ... even if we are being blamed for the financial collapse of the world!

In truth, CPAs deserve some blame for the financial crisis of 2007/08 because, just before the crisis broke, we created an accounting standard so poorly defined that businesses couldn't figure out how to apply it in a market of collapsing mortgage-backed security prices. The standard is called FAS 157. Accountants refer to this as "fair value" accounting; however, the rest of the world likes to call it "mark-to-market" accounting.

Many investors and economists believe that FAS 157 helped to trigger the financial crisis of 2007/08. For example, here is the view of First Trust Portfolios Chief Economist Brian S. Wesbury and colleague, Bob Stein

It is true that the root of this crisis is bad mortgage loans, but probably 70% of the real crisis that we face today is caused by mark-to-market accounting in an illiquid market.[1]

William Isaac, a former FDIC Chairman, was even harsher in his assessment:

> The SEC [Securities and Exchange Commission] has destroyed $500 billion of bank capital by its senseless marking to market of these assets for which there is no marking to market, and that has destroyed $5 trillion of bank lending.[2]

Mr. Isaac justified his viewpoint by comparing the 2007/08 crisis to an earlier crisis:

> During the 1980s, our underlying economic problems were far more serious than the economic problems we're facing this time around. ... It could have been much worse. The country's 10 largest banks were loaded up with Third World debt that was valued in the markets at cents on the dollar. If we had marked those loans to market prices, virtually every one of them would have been insolvent.[3]

A brief mark-to-market history

Historically, accountants valued most assets at original cost, adjusted downward by depreciation, amortization, or impairment. Market fluctuations did not matter. The cost (or adjusted cost) method was far-from-ideal but accountants liked it because it was less subject to manipulation. Investors, however, wanted values that were more reflective of market realities.

In response, the profession took a significant step towards fair value ("mark-to-market") accounting. In 1993 the Financial Accounting Standards Board (FASB), which is an SEC-endorsed private, nonprofit organization that promulgates accounting standards, declared that "fair value" should be used for certain debt and equity securities. The fair value prescribed by FASB was based upon quoted market prices, where available. In other cases it was to be estimated using a "variety of pricing tech-

---

1   as cited by Newt Gingrich, "Suspend Mark to Market Now!," Forbes.com (September 29, 2008), http://www.forbes.com/2008/09/29/mark-to-market-oped-cx_ng_0929gingrich.html.
2   "Former Fdic Chair Blames SEC for Credit Crunch," cnbc.com (October 9, 2008), http://www.cnbc.com/id/27100454/Former_FDIC_Chair_Blames_SEC_for_Credit_Crunch.
3   Gingrich, "Suspend Mark to Market Now!."

niques, including, but not limited to, discounted cash flow analysis, matrix pricing, option-adjusted spread models, and fundamental analysis."[1]

Additional changes to fair value accounting came in September 2006, when FAS 157 was issued. This new accounting standard does not stipulate new situations where fair value accounting is required; however, effective for years beginning after November 15, 2007, it requires changes in the way fair value accounting is applied. As originally promulgated, the new FASB standard has made several important changes:

- Created a hierarchy of the information sources to be used in fair value measurements.
- Emphasized a market-based rather than entity-specific fair value.
- Defined "fair value" as the price paid by market participants in an "orderly" transaction in the principal market used by the reporting entity at the measurement date.
- Clarified that changes in credit risk must be factored into the valuation.
- Expanded disclosure requirements.

Unlike the 1993 standards, FAS 157 emphasizes market-based rather than entity-specific fair values. In situations where there is little or no market activity for a given asset, other methods, such as discounted cash flow analysis, may be used to estimate fair value. However, in all cases there has to be an adjustment for any risk that market participants perceive. If, for example, the market perceives that future cash flows are in jeopardy, it is necessary to use a lower asset value to reflect that risk assessment (even if there is no history of payment default).

The pros and cons of mark-to-market

Criticisms of mark-to-market accounting center around two issues:

- It doesn't seem to produce good valuations when there is no active market for a particular type of asset — particularly income-generating assets. Losses can be overstated, and this can lead to the premature triggering of margin calls or to the failure of banks to meet regulatory requirements for capital reserves. This can force businesses to make distress sales of assets in an effort to raise cash.

---

1   Accounting Standards as of June 1, 2005, ed. Financial Accounting Standards Board, vol. 2, Current Text (New York: John Wiley & Sons, Inc., 2005), 27637.

- The method tends to be pro-cyclical, meaning that it magnifies economic fluctuations in the business cycle.

The first criticism is largely unfair because, as noted, FAS 157 has always allowed for the use of other estimation techniques in markets that were inactive. Alternative valuations, such as the present value of expected cash flows, could have been used, provided those estimates were adjusted for market perceptions of future default risk. Arguably, the real problem was the failure of some businesses to apply FAS 157 correctly. After the crisis (in September 2008) the SEC and the Financial Accounting Standards Board "clarified" that, under the "orderly" transaction standard of FAS 157, alternative methods could be used.

In April 2009 FASB made three explicit changes to FAS 157. First, FASB gave businesses more discretion in deciding if a formerly active market has become inactive. Where they deem the market to be inactive they are able to use alternative estimation methods in lieu of market value. Second, FASB increased the frequency with which businesses must disclose valuation techniques for assets that are not shown at market value.

FASB should have stopped with the second change, but it made an additional modification to FAS 157. This third change was (and is) controversial, and passed in a close, 3-2 vote of the FASB Board. Under heavy pressure from politicians and bankers, FASB changed the way businesses have to report certain investment losses in their financial statements. Henceforth, losses deemed to be temporary would not have to be recorded in the statement of profit and loss. Instead, accountants would deduct them directly against net worth, thus bypassing the income statement. Essentially, this change makes banks appear more profitable by letting them defer recognition of some of their mortgage-backed securities losses.

"I think it's a mistake. If it's too cold in the room, you don't fix the problem by holding a candle under the thermometer," said William Poole, former president of the St. Louis Federal Reserve Bank.[1] Jack Ciesielski, a CPA and former FASB member complained that "investors lost on this vote,"[2] while former SEC Chairman Arthur Levitt expressed deep

---

1   Al Yoon, "U.S Rulemaker Eases Mark-to_Market Bite," Reuters. com (April 2, 2009), http://www.reuters.com/article/2009/04/02/ us-marktomarket-fasb-idUSN0235590020090402.

2   Maatthew G. Lamoreaux, "Fasb Approves New Mark-to-Market Guidance," Journal of Accountancy (April 2, 2009).

concern "about the apparent FASB succumbing to political pressures."[1] I concur with these critics: The change in the method of reporting investment losses should not have been made. This was not FASB's finest hour.

The other major problem of mark-to-market accounting, in the view of many economists, is its pro-cyclical economic impact. When a company marks up its assets to higher market values, its net worth automatically increases. Research suggests that, when net worth increases (or appears to increase) businesses are likely to "search for uses of their surplus capital." For example, they search for more borrowers for their mortgage loans. On the other hand, as the asset values of a business fall, its net worth also falls. The business now has less capital surplus, and is less interested in finding borrowers for its loans. In this manner, mark-to-market tends to reinforce and exaggerate the economic fluctuations caused by changes in asset values.[2]

Is this pro-cyclical characteristic of mark-to-market necessarily bad? In the view of many economists it is. However, Warren Coats (CATO Institute) believes that the criticism is misguided.

> The pro-cyclical behavior of asset values is an economic reality. No good policy purpose would be served by attempting to hide the fact by corrupting accounting standards. Full transparency is desirable.[3]

Mr. Coats believes we should keep mark-to-market accounting, and supplement it with a system of bank capital requirements that vary with the business cycle. In his view capital requirements should increase during business upswings and decrease during the down side of the business cycle. This proposal is worth studying, but might lead to overly-complex capital reserve requirements. Exactly when would we require increased capital reserves, and by how much?

Another view, articulated in testimony to the U.S. House of Representatives by the Chairman of the SBCC Group, Inc., is that multiple measures should be used to prevent market participants from acting "in concert." This would soften the pro-cyclical impact of asset price fluctuations. Financial statement disclosures would be expanded to include

---

1   Ian Katz, "Fasb Eases Fair-Value Rules Amid Lawmaker Pressure " (April 2, 2009), http://www.bloomberg.com/apps/news?pid=newsarchive&sid=agf rKseJ94jc.

2   Tobias Adrian and Hyun Song Shin, "Liquidity and Leverage," (FRB of New York Staff Report No. 328, January 1, 2009), http://papers.ssrn.com/sol3/papers.cfm?abstract_id=1139857.

3   Warren Coats, "Mark to Market Accounting - What Are the Issues?," (CATO. org, October 29, 2008), http://www.cato.org/publications/commentary/mark-market-accountingwhat-are-issues.

an appropriate explanation of any significant valuation differences resulting from the use of different methodologies. This view is also worthy of study, but the use of multiple measures and expanded financial statement disclosures could make financial statements difficult to comprehend (even more than now).

In any event, the procyclical nature of mark-to-market accounting was not an issue with respect to the financial crisis. As of 2007/08, the method had not been in force long enough to affect the lending decisions of banks.

Conclusion

Mark-to-market accounting, as embodied in FAS 157, was not a direct cause of the financial crisis of 2007/08. That calamity was caused by subprime lending and, secondarily, by inappropriately-low Federal Reserve interest rates. However, confusion regarding the initial application of FAS 157 probably led some financial institutions to overstate their losses, and this helped to accelerate and aggravate the crisis.

The mark-to-market rules are still in effect; however, in April 2009 FASB modified FAS 157 in an apparent effort to placate politicians and bankers. One of those modifications enables financial institutions to defer recognition of part of their mark-to-market losses. This was not helpful, and will only confuse investors who are trying to interpret the financial statements of banks and investment companies.

Most importantly, as a result of mark-to-market accounting, a Country Western song was finally written about accountants. It kind of chokes me up.

CHAPTER 15: THE BARE TRUTH ABOUT NAKED SHORTS

> As Lehman Brothers Holdings Inc. struggled to survive
> last year, as many as 32.8 million shares in the company
> were sold and not delivered to buyers on time as of Sept. 11,
> according to data compiled by the Securities and Exchange
> Commission and Bloomberg. ... The SEC has linked such
> so-called fails-to-deliver to naked short selling, a strategy
> that can be used to manipulate markets.... "We had another
> word for this in Brooklyn," said Harvey Pitt, a former SEC
> chairman. "The word was 'fraud.'"[1]

Few financial subjects stir as much controversy as something known as the "naked short" stock sale ("naked shorts"). Some see naked shorts as fraudulent transactions that were partly responsible for the financial crisis of 2007/08, while others see them as necessary, harmless, or even beneficial. In this chapter we explore both positions. First, however, it is necessary to examine short selling, in general.

The normal (traditional) short sale

If a stock trader feels that a particular stock is about to drop in price he may short-sell the stock. Let's say the stock presently sells for $50 per share but the trader believes it may soon drop to $40. In a normal (traditional) short sale the trader would "borrow" the stock (via his broker) and immediately sell it for $50 per share. Assume he sells 1,000 shares for a total of $50,000. A few days later, when the price has (he hopes)

---

1   Gary Matsumoto, "Naked Short Sales Hint Fraud in Bringing Down Lehman," (March 19, 2009), http://www.bloomberg.com/apps/news?pid=newsarchive &sid=aBljlqmFOTCA.

dropped to $40 per share, he would buy 1,000 shares of stock for $40,000, and return those shares to the lender from whom he borrowed the stock (when it was selling for $50). In this manner the trader would make $10,000, less transaction costs.

Most economists and financiers (and the U.S. Securities and Exchange Commission) see plenty of benefit associated with normal short sales. In an article titled, "The Economics of Naked Short Selling," Christopher Culp and J.B. Heaton (a professor of finance and an attorney) note:

> Prices are socially valuable signals. Short selling can correct irrational overpricing if and when it occurs and, for that reason, financial economists usually object to regulatory constraints on short selling. ... The potential social benefit of short selling is that it forces prices today closer to the amount that reflects the intersection of supply and demand later, if we assume that the current demand is excessively optimistic and will shift to a more rational (i.e., lower) level.[1]

In other words, it is beneficial for sales to be initiated by people at both ends of the spectrum: those who are bullish on the stock and those who are bearish. For this reason, there is widespread acceptance of the normal (as opposed to naked) short sale.

The naked short sale

Today, naked short selling is mostly illegal in the United States. However, many types of naked short sales were legal during the financial crisis and for several years before. The legal and regulatory status of naked short selling is more fully described later in this chapter.

Unlike normal short sales, naked shorts involve no preliminary act of borrowing. After selling the stock in a naked short transaction, the trader typically fails to deliver the shares when they are due (because he has none — owned or borrowed).[2] Eventually, the trader will acquire the shares he sold (assuming he is able to) and turn them over to the purchaser. In our example, those shares were sold for $50 per share. If the price per share unexpectedly increases to, say $60, the trader will be stuck with a $10,000 loss. If the trader won't or can't complete the transaction, his broker will buy the shares, give them to the purchaser (for $50,000) and charge the trader's account for the $10,000 loss incurred, plus transaction costs.

---

1   Christopher. Culp and J.B. Heaton, "The Economics of Naked Short Selling," CATO: Regulation Spring (2008): 47-48.

2   Typically, the buyer does not know that the stock is being sold "short," and he may not even know (initially) that there has been a failure to deliver the shares.

There is not a great deal of difference, economically, between normal and naked short sales of stock. In a naked stock sale the buyer of the stock may have to wait longer to get the stock he purchased; however, he will eventually get the shares at the agreed-to price, plus interest on his purchase funds for the period between purchase and stock delivery. Despite the economic similarities, views regarding normal and naked shorts can be starkly different.

The majority of financial economists and stock owners feel that short sales of the naked type are undesirable. Indeed, years before the financial crisis, most investors thought they were fraudulent. Responding to a December 2005 Harris Interactive survey, 76 percent of investors said that people who naked-short stocks should face civil or criminal penalties, and the same percentage said that the penalties should be as tough or tougher than those for counterfeiting. In other words, they would throw these people in prison — not a place where a naked short guy wants to be.

Despite these strong criticisms, there is a small minority of economists and investors who see the naked short as something harmless or even socially useful. Let's review some of their arguments. Culp and Heaton (previously cited) praise the liquidity provided by the naked short. They point out that the normal short sale is not always workable.

> For securities that are heavily demanded for short selling, locating securities for delivery at settlement of a short sale can be very difficult and costly. Unlike deep and centralized markets for long positions in common stocks, no such deep and centralized markets exist to match those willing to lend their securities for short selling.[1]

In other words, the naked short provides liquidity by working in situations where stocks are difficult to borrow.

Researchers affiliated with the University of Oklahoma analyzed a random sample of 300 New York Stock Exchange securities, and found that "naked shorting leads to significant reduction in positive pricing errors, the volatility of stock price returns, bid-ask spreads, and pricing error volatility." They also found little evidence that naked shorts caused the financial crisis of 2007/08:

> ...we analyze naked short selling in Bear Stearns Companies Inc. (Bear Stearns), Lehman Brothers Holdings Inc. (Lehman), Merrill Lynch & Co. Inc. (Merrill), and American Insurance Group (AIG). We find that, except for one instance in June 2008 of possible stock price manipulation through naked shorting in relation to Lehman Brothers Holdings Inc., most of the

---

1   Culp and J.B. Heaton, "The Economics of Naked Short Selling," 50-51.

time naked short selling was too low to reasonable "cause" significant stock price distortions, and when naked shorting did become abnormally heavy, it was after dramatic price declines, not before....[1]

The Oklahoma researchers conceded that naked shorts can be used to manipulate the market but they believe that the potential to manipulate was sharply reduced by regulations established in 2005. They concluded that "the impact of naked short selling on market quality ... is very positive overall."[2]

Naked and ugly

> If short sellers could be rounded up and roasted as heretics to the true bull market religion, there'd be a rush of people from Lehman and Merrill fighting to add wood to the fire. And Mack [John Mack, CEO of Morgan Stanley] would bring the gasoline.[3]

I can't buy the pro-naked arguments. Perhaps I don't have enough financial sophistication, but I'd rather have integrity and honesty than a little extra market efficiency and liquidity. Further, it is hardly reassuring to know that "...except for one instance in June 2008 of possible stock price manipulation through naked shorting in relation to Lehman Brothers Holdings Inc. ..." the volume of naked short selling was too low to significantly screw things up. If defenders of naked shorts have to concede that the technique could have contributed to the demise of Lehman, I have heard enough.

Richard Fuld, CEO of the now-defunct Lehman Brothers Holdings Inc., told a Congressional panel that a combination of naked shorts and unsubstantiated rumors contributed to the fall of Lehman Brothers and Bear Stearns. This is a view shared by Susanne Trimbath, president of a financial consulting firm. As reported by Bloomberg, she estimated that failed trades (strongly associated with naked short sales) were "enough to account for 30 to 70 percent of the declines in Bear Stearns, Lehman and other stocks...." in 2008.[4]

---

1   Veljko Fotak and Vikas Raman and Pradeep Yadav, "Naked Short Selling: The Emperor's New Clothes?," (Web-based: SSRN, May 22, 2009), 4, http://papers.ssrn.com/sol3/papers.cfm?abstract_id=1408493.
2   Ibid., 30.
3   Bill Saporito, "Are Short Sellers to Blame for the Financial Crisis?," Time Business (September 18, 2008), http://www.time.com/time/business/article/0,8599,1842499,00.html.
4   Matsumoto, "Naked Short Sales Hint Fraud in Bringing Down Lehman."

Trimbath describes how failing to deliver sold shares can lower the market value of a company's stock:

> [It is like] "issuing new stock in a company without its permission. You increase the number of shares circulating in the market, and that devalues a stock. The same thing happens to a currency when a government prints more of it.[1]

Of course, naked shorts do not account for each and every failure to deliver sold shares. Deliveries can fail due to computer hang-ups and misunderstandings. But, naked shorts probably account for the vast majority of delivery failures. This was particularly true with respect to Lehman Brothers stock, which was easy to borrow. As Trimbath said, "You can't have millions of shares fail to deliver and say, 'Oops, my dog ate my certificates.'"[2]

As of September 11, 2008, about 33 million shares of Lehman Brothers stock had been sold, without being delivered. That was 57 times more than the number of delivery failures for Lehman Brothers as of the previous July, and constituted about 5 percent of all available Lehman shares. No doubt, there were innocent explanations for some of the delivery failures. However, to the extent that the failures were due to naked shorting, they were, in effect, counterfeit shares of stock (sold shares that did not exist). Just ponder these questions: If someone printed and distributed massive quantities of U.S. greenbacks, do you think those counterfeit dollars might dilute the value of the currency? What if the massive counterfeiting became widely known? What psychological (negative) impact would be produced? What if we threw in a rumor that the U.S. government was about to default on loans to China? What would be the combined impact of the counterfeiting and rumors on the value of the dollar? The answer is, gigantic.

The above notwithstanding, it is not even important that we prove that naked shorts hastened the demise of Lehman, Bear Stearns, or any other company. A company has the right to know that the integrity of its stock is respected, an investor has the right to know that he is buying stock that actually exists, and we all have the right to a financial market that is run in a sound manner. Period. The entire controversy reminds me of the voter identification efforts in the United States. Do we really need to prove massive voter fraud before we require a common-sense verification of identity, such as a driver's license or utility bill? If people are

---

1   Ibid.
2   Ibid.

to believe in an election system (or in the financial markets) the system must have integrity — both in fact and *appearance*.

The naked shorts regulatory smack-down

It could be said that the first serious restriction on naked shorts came in 1733, when Great Britain banned them after a major scam involving stock of the South Sea Company, an importer/exporter. Based on claims that the company had a trading monopoly, the price of stock in South Sea rose dramatically, only to collapse once the public learned that the company was making virtually no profit. Many people lost their lifetime fortunes, and naked shorting was implicated.

A mere 271 years later, the U.S. sprang into regulatory action. In 2004 the Securities and Exchange Commission announced the issuance of Regulation SHO, which required daily publication of a list of securities having significant numbers of delivery failures (more than .5 percent of the company's outstanding shares). The idea was to reduce the number of naked shorts by shining a light on the practice. In addition, SHO put a time limit on delivery failures. After 13 days, brokers were required to close-out open fail-to-deliver positions. Finally, the new regulation prohibited brokers from accepting short sale orders before they identified the stock being sold.

Research suggests that Regulation SHO, as originally issued, was somewhat effective, and may have reduced manipulative naked shorting during the 2007/08 crisis. Proxies for the impact of manipulative naked shorting (namely, the speed at which negative pricing errors dissipate) declined after the introduction of Regulation SHO, which became effective on January 1, 2005.[1] Nevertheless, Regulation SHO had some broad exemptions, which could be described as "loopholes":

1. Short-sellers only had to have "reasonable grounds" to think they could obtain the shares needed to consummate the sales transaction.

2. "Market makers"[2] were afforded the "Madoff exemption," whereby they could naked short sell in order to facilitate liquidity.[3]

---

1   Fotak and Vikas Raman and Pradeep Yadav, "Naked Short Selling: The Emperor's New Clothes?," abstract, 4,30.
2   A market maker is defined by Investopdia .com as "a broker-dealer firm that accepts the risk of holding a certain number of shares of a particular security in order to facilitate trading in that security. Each market maker competes for customer order flow by displaying buy and sell quotations for a guaranteed number of shares. Once an order is received, the market maker immediately sells from its own inventory or seeks an offsetting order.
3   The exemption was named in honor of Bernie Madoff, who was well-respected by the SEC prior to his Ponzi pioneering.

These loopholes enabled the naked shorting of Lehman and other financial companies in the summer and fall of 2008. In September of that year Regulation SHO was modified by Christopher Cox and his SEC to "make it crystal clear that the SEC has zero tolerance for abusive naked short selling."[1] A "Hard T+3 Close-out Requirement" was added, establishing penalties unless short sale securities were delivered to the buyer by the close of business, three days after the sale date. In addition, the Madoff exemption was eliminated. These steps were wise, but belated.

Regulation SHO and the "Uptick Rule"

We can't conclude this chapter without discussing the elimination of something known as the "uptick rule." As part of its Regulation SHO, the SEC ended a rule that had affected all short sales — normal and naked — for about 70 years. In 1938 the SEC created Rule 10a-1(a)(1), which provided that short sales of a security were not permissible unless they were made at a price higher than the last sale price of the security, or at a price as high as the last sale price of the security if that last price was higher than the previous sale price. The purpose of the rule was to prevent a group of speculators from driving down the price of a stock with a high-frequency barrage of coordinated, low-ball short sales.

Elimination of the uptick rule was not particularly controversial, and was done in July 2007 after a long period of analysis (commencing in 2004) that included a pilot study, designed to test the impact of the uptick rule on market prices. In rescinding the uptick rule the SEC said that it reduced market liquidity and was not needed to prevent short sale manipulation.

After the financial crisis of 2007/08, several investors, financial analysts, politicians, and regulators strongly urged the SEC to reinstate the uptick rule. The general belief was that reinstatement of the rule would help to stabilize the market.

Surprisingly, the SEC has not reinstated the rule (as of mid-2012), although it created an alternative form of the uptick, which is triggered for any security that drops in value by more than 10 percent in a single day of trading. This alternative rule, which became effective in early 2011, is not adequate. The uptick rule needs to be fully reinstated.

---

1   "SEC Issues New Rules to Protect Investors against Naked Short Selling Abuses," ed. Securities and Exchange Commission (U.S. government, September 17, 2008), http://www.sec.gov/news/press/2008/2008-204.htm.

Conclusion

Naked short selling did not cause the financial crisis of 2007/08, but it is likely that this abusive practice aggravated the crisis by hastening the demise of some businesses. The first serious effort to regulate naked short selling (in modern times) took place in 2004, with the announcement of Regulation SHO. Although research suggests that Regulation SHO had some positive effects, naked short selling was widespread in 2008, as major investment banks failed. Additional regulations, implemented in September 2008, have made most naked short selling illegal in the United States.

Elimination of the uptick rule did not cause the financial crisis but probably increased volatility of the market during the financial crisis of 2007/08. The uptick rule served the market with some positive effect for about 70 years, but the SEC and many of its supporters argued that the rule was unnecessary to prevent short sale manipulation. Nevertheless, that rule is needed, at the minimum, to maintain the appearance that a stock's price is not affected by abusive short selling.

Part Four: Aggravating factors

These were not causes of the crisis, and they did not trigger the crisis. However, these factors, shown in the shaded box on the right side of Figure 15, intensified the crisis and made its resolution more difficult and painful — especially for taxpayers and homeowners.

Figure 15 – A model of the causes and other factors affecting the financial crisis of 2007/08 (The shaded box pertains to Part Four)

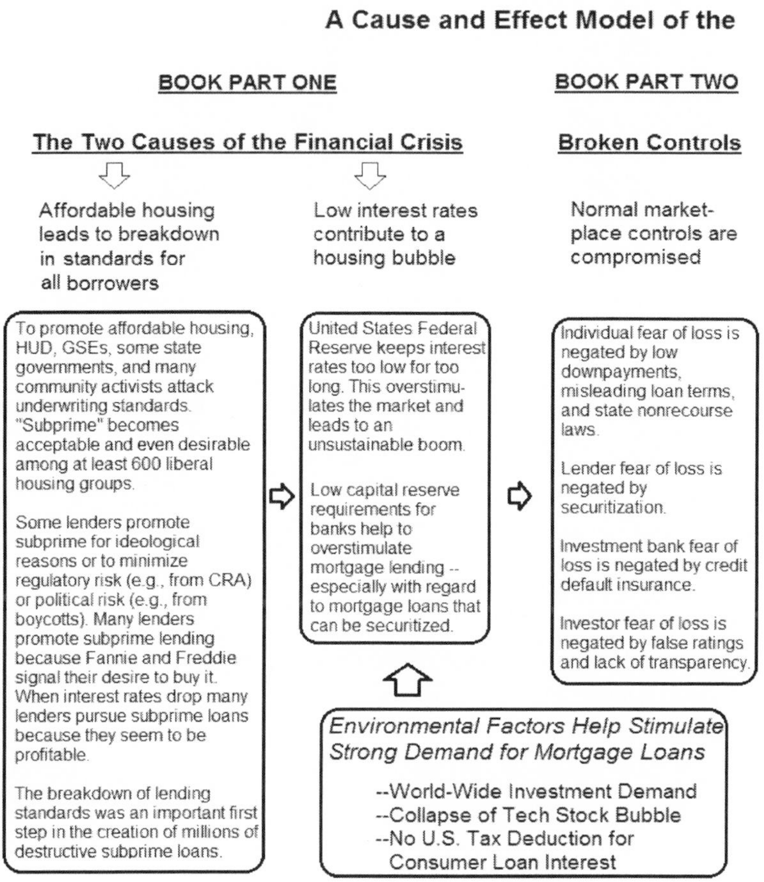

A Cause and Effect Model of the

BOOK PART ONE

The Two Causes of the Financial Crisis

⇩   ⇩

Affordable housing leads to breakdown in standards for all borrowers

Low interest rates contribute to a housing bubble

BOOK PART TWO

Broken Controls

Normal market-place controls are compromised

To promote affordable housing, HUD, GSEs, some state governments, and many community activists attack underwriting standards. "Subprime" becomes acceptable and even desirable among at least 600 liberal housing groups.

Some lenders promote subprime for ideological reasons or to minimize regulatory risk (e.g., from CRA) or political risk (e.g., from boycotts). Many lenders promote subprime lending because Fannie and Freddie signal their desire to buy it. When interest rates drop many lenders pursue subprime loans because they seem to be profitable.

The breakdown of lending standards was an important first step in the creation of millions of destructive subprime loans.

United States Federal Reserve keeps interest rates too low for too long. This overstimulates the market and leads to an unsustainable boom.

Low capital reserve requirements for banks help to overstimulate mortgage lending -- especially with regard to mortgage loans that can be securitized.

⇨

⇨

Individual fear of loss is negated by low downpayments, misleading loan terms, and state nonrecourse laws.

Lender fear of loss is negated by securitization.

Investment bank fear of loss is negated by credit default insurance.

Investor fear of loss is negated by false ratings and lack of transparency.

Environmental Factors Help Stimulate Strong Demand for Mortgage Loans

--World-Wide Investment Demand
--Collapse of Tech Stock Bubble
--No U.S. Tax Deduction for Consumer Loan Interest

Subprime Mortgage Crisis of 2007-2008

BOOK PART THREE   **BOOK PART FOUR**

Sparks   **Boom**   **Aggravating Factors**

These are   Bear Stearns & ML   These factors complicate
just triggers   are sold, Lehman   the crisis aftermath but
                   goes broke, AIG is   do not cause the crisis
                   downgraded, and
                   Feds take over
                   Fannie and Freddie

Mark-to-   Financial Crisis   Banks & borrowers
market   are hurt because of
accounting   documentation
                                                  defects.
Naked short
selling   Taxpayers are hurt
                                                  because bank capital
Sudden   reserves are
downgrades   deficient.
by rating
agencies   Homeowners are hurt
                                                  by nearby
                                                  foreclosures, which
                                                  are aggravated by
                                                  nonrecourse lending
                                                  rules.

CHAPTER 16: THE FRAUDULENT FORECLOSURE BALONEY SANDWICH

> Talk about a financial scandal. A consumer borrows money to buy a house, doesn't make the mortgage payments, and then loses the house in foreclosure — only to learn that the wrong guy at the bank signed the foreclosure paperwork. Can you imagine? The affidavit was supposed to be signed by the nameless, faceless employee in the back office who reviewed the file, not the other nameless, faceless employee who sits in the front.
>
> The result is the same, but politicians understand the pain that results when the anonymous paper pusher who kicks you out of your home is not the anonymous paper pusher who is supposed to kick you out of your home.
>
> – The Wall Street Journal, Review & Outlook, October 9, 2010

By now you have probably heard about "banksters" (banks) who used robo-signers to create thousands of "fraudulent" documents. Generally, these documents were reconstructions of loan notes or assignment papers that had been lost or destroyed when the loans were bundled together as part of the loan securitization process. An outcry of indignation and disgust was produced when the banksters tried to use those reconstructed documents to foreclose against "innocent," "confused," "frustrated," and/or "defenseless" borrowers.

In April 2011 the TV show "60 Minutes" had a segment on the robo-signing scandal, featuring a company called Docx ..."a sweatshop for forged mortgage documents." The daily routine of the business was described by an attorney who was, herself, in the process of fighting foreclosure:

> They [Docx employees] were sitting in a room signing their names as fast as they possibly could to any kind of nonsense document that was put in front of them.[1]

Docx employees were paid $10 per hour to sign as many documents as they could. None of these low-paid employees read the documents or understood them. "60 Minutes" had another good show but, as is often the case with this weekly news "magazine," part of the story was missing. Scott Pelley, who narrated the segment, did not ask the attorney (or anyone else) if she was, in fact, in arrears on her house payments, or whether there was any doubt in the world — in the universe — that money was owed. If he asked those questions, the show did not air them, or the responses.

The truth is that there have been tens of thousands of lawsuits initiated against banks by angry defaulting borrowers, but have you heard of any borrowers who were, morally speaking, wronged? Probably not. Economist Arnold Kling has not seen them:

> If mortgage servicers were foreclosing on the wrong borrowers, that would be a scandal. That would be if they send the foreclosure notice to an incorrect address, or if they foreclose on a borrower who has actually made payments. Maybe there are stories like that, but I have not seen any.[2]

Indeed, one could even argue (morally if not legally) that the homeowners in these cases have no standing, whatever. It is the final owner of the note (a bank or investment trust) that should have to be satisfied with the loan paperwork — not the homeowner who has been skipping his payments. But, there are probably a million or so attorneys who would disagree with me (and would be happy to represent a defaulting homeowner for a modest percentage). Lawyers, politicians, and even the judges (especially those up for re-election) are only too glad to take a swing at the "irresponsible" banks — America's villains de jour.

MERS — the system designed to track loan ownership interests

"60 Minutes" omitted another important aspect of the story: the moronic and sometimes politically-oriented decisions that have led some

---

1   "Mortgage Paperwork Mess: Next Housing Shock?," CBSNEWS (April 1, 2011), http://www.cbsnews.com/2100-18560_162-20086862.html.

2   Arnold Kling, "The Real Foreclosure Scandal," Library of Economics and Liberty (October 8, 2010), http://econlog.econlib.org/archives/2010/10/the_real_forecl.html.

banks to use robo-signers. In the 1990s, a new, streamlined and modern method of tracking mortgage loans was formed by members of the Mortgage Bankers Association and Fannie Mae and Freddie Mac. The system, called MERS (Mortgage Electronic Registration System) was formed without controversy. In an article from the May 2000 issue of Mortgage Banking the motivation behind the creation of MERS was described:

> The rising tide of paper that was choking mortgage loan productivity in the early 1990s provided the impetus for an industry task force to recommend the establishment of MERS in an effort to eliminate the need to prepare and record assignments. MERS would allow mortgage lenders and servicers to cooperate to reduce or eliminate their paperwork burdens and bring a higher level of efficiency to secondary market sales and trades.... MERS took up the task of providing an alternative to using paper for tracking these transfers between trading partners.[1]

In other words, MERS was created to modernize the cumbersome, expensive, and obsolete paper document system and replace it with an efficient electronic system that could more easily and efficiently track loans. This modernization was essential as the mortgage loan business became more national and more securitized. MERS was not just good for banks and investors: It saved document costs for homeowners and gave them valuable information about their loans. With MERS a homeowner could, for example, quickly determine the identity of his loan servicer.

By the year 2000, more than 100 companies were already using MERS for almost 1.5 million loans. Six of the top 10 mortgage originators were using the system. In addition to Fannie and Freddie, the system was accepted by Ginnie Mae, Federal Home Loan Bank, VA, FHA and major Wall Street rating agencies...."[2] MERS was not a fleeting fad, nor was it an after-the-fact defense strategy.

MERS was designed to do more than merely track loans: It was intended to eliminate the need for the formality of endorsing and transferring original promissory notes. To do this the holder of a promissory note would make MERS its "nominee." This aspect of its function is acknowledged by Attorney Wendy Alison Nora, even though she is a bank critic:

> The MERS nomination was intended ... to be the means of transferring assignment of mortgage and promissory note to an investment trust without the formality of actually endorsing the promissory notes and properly

---

1   Carson Mullen, "Mers: Tracking Loans Electronically," *Mortgage Banking* (May 2000).
2   Ibid.

assigning the mortgages to the investment trusts. The original promissory notes usually were destroyed.[1]

Let me reiterate because this is important. When mortgage loans were transferred between mortgage brokers, banks and trusts, they used to be accompanied by a short little assignment document, signed by the seller and buyer. As mortgage lending became securitized, electronic and national, the assignments were not necessarily put onto paper. Instead, they were recorded electronically with MERS. This fact, which was not initially controversial, set the table for many of the "fraud" charges that arose after the financial crisis of 2007/08. At that point, MERS was used for the majority of loans. Suddenly, there were assertions that MERS lacked the legal standing necessary to initiate a foreclosure. What's more, this alleged lack of standing would cause subsequent loan holders to lose standing. Lots of deadbeats were about to get free houses.

Lawyers and even judges engaged in laughable linguistics as they parsed the word, "nominee." In their view, the fact that a note holder appointed MERS to serve as its nominee was no longer significant. A nominee, by their standards, lacked legal standing, and could do little more than fetch a cup of coffee.

This was not always the case. In earlier rulings, several judges used common sense. For example, in reversing a lower court's ruling that MERS lacked the standing needed to initiate foreclosure, the Third District Court of Appeal (Florida) made this very reasonable statement in 2007:

> To the extent that courts have encountered difficulties with the question, and have even ruled to the contrary of our conclusion, the problem arises from the difficulty of attempting to shoehorn a modern innovative instrument of commerce into nomenclature and legal categories which stem essentially from the medieval English land law. ... Because, however, it is apparent — and we so hold — that no substantive rights, obligations or defenses are affected by the use of the MERS device, there is no reason why mere form should overcome the salutary substance of permitting the use of this commercially effective means of business.[2]

Yes, of course. One does not get a free house merely because of post-foreclosure doubts over the word, "nominee." Unfortunately, that is exactly what many of the subsequent court rulings would do. For example,

---

1 Wendy Alison Nora, "Beyond Robo-Signing: Mortgage Foreclosure Defense Basics," Wisconsin Lawyer 84, no. 4 (2011).

2 "Mortgage Electronic Registration Systems, Inc., Appellant vs. Oscar Revoredo, Et Al., Appellees," (State of Florida: Third District Court of Appeal, March 14, 2007).

the U.S. Bankruptcy Court in the Eastern District of New York reached this conclusion in a 2011 ruling. It must have brightened the hearts of defaulters across America:

> The Court recognizes that an adverse ruling regarding MERS's authority to assign mortgages or act on behalf of its member/lenders could have a significant impact on MERS and upon the lenders which do business with MERS throughout the United States. ... MERS and its partners made the decision to create and operate under a business model that was designed in large part to avoid the requirements of the traditional mortgage recording process. This Court does not accept the argument that because MERS may be involved with 50% of all residential mortgages in the country, that is reason enough for this Court to turn a blind eye to the fact that this process does not comply with the law.[1]

The judicial cases involving MERS were both troubling and ridiculous. After a landmark California bankruptcy court case (the Rickie Walker case, discussed below), banks were basically told they would lose hundreds of billions of dollars due to their use of MERS. One civil litigation attorney summed up the situation this way:

> Over 62 million mortgages are now held in the name of MERS, an electronic recording system devised by and for the convenience of the mortgage industry. A California bankruptcy court, following landmark cases in other jurisdictions, recently held that this electronic shortcut makes it impossible for banks to establish their ownership of property titles — and therefore to foreclose on mortgaged properties. The logical result could be *62 million homes that are foreclosure-proof* (emphasis added).[2]

Reliance on MERS is the major reason banks are having trouble foreclosing; however, it is not the only reason. Banks have been challenged for these reasons as well:

- The bank had a copy of the promissory note instead of the original.
- The promissory note was "endorsed in blank" (similar to signing a check without writing in the name of the payee).[3]

---

1 "In Re: Ferrel L. Agard, Debtor," (Eastern District of New York: United States Bankruptcy Court, February 10, 2011).

2 Ellen Brown, "Could a Legal Technicality Prevent Banks from Having the Right to Foreclose on 62 Million Homes?," AlterNet (August 20, 2010), http://www.alternet.org/module/printversion/147901.

3 Previously, this was considered perfectly acceptable. In Mortgage Electronic Registration Systems v. Ventura, No. CV 054003168S, 2006 WL 1230265, Connecticut judges observed that the note held by MERS was endorsed in blank, and was therefore bearer paper that supported its right to bring foreclosure action.

- The note assignment form had one or more blanks on it.
- The mortgage (the part that creates the lien) was not separately assigned to the new note holder.
- The foreclosure process began before the bank established that it was the note holder.
- The employee signing the document acknowledged that he didn't review it first.
- The borrower was considering a restructuring of the loan. (Some courts, such as the Supreme Court of South Carolina, will not proceed with foreclosure while a loan modification is pending. The legal basis for such rulings is unclear.)
- The bank servicer did not properly part his hair.

Just as "60 Minutes" failed to mention the bonafides of the bank loans or MERS, the show failed to mention the other brickbats hurled at banks, itemized above. Instead, Pelley used one loaded statement to make certain the audience knew who was wearing the black hat:

> ...it appears they [the banks] didn't want old fashioned paperwork slowing down the profits.

Banks should not keep sloppy records, and they should not hire teenagers to robo-sign documents retroactively on behalf of bank officers. That is wrong, just as it is technically wrong for my wife to endorse checks I receive so that she can deposit them in our joint bank account (something she does routinely). However, with voluminous documents that are transferred in bulk between many parties it is easy to find a documentation defect. As an auditor who has reviewed many mortgage company loan files I can't recall seeing one that did not have some defects. However, there are always alternative forms of evidence that make it crystal clear if the debtor is behind in his payments and whether the party initiating the foreclosure has economic (and therefore legal) standing. Any court interested in justice would look to these alternative sources.

Real cases that will break your heart

Poor Barry Weisband. He borrowed a small amount ($540,000) from GMAC and, just because he stopped making payments, the lender tried to take his house away. Fortunately, a court blocked this foreclosure because GMAC couldn't prove that the undated "allonge," a sheet of paper showing the assignment of the promissory note from the original lender

(Greenpoint) to GMAC, had been stapled to the note at the time the note was executed. Whew! Barry was almost eaten by a bank shark![1]

Sandra Ford also had a close call. Wells Fargo expected her to make payments on a $403,750 mortgage loan. When she stopped making payments, it tried to foreclose. The bank had plenty of documents in support of its case, including a promissory note and a mortgage, and the trial court found these documents sufficient to support the bank's foreclosure case. Sandra was in trouble. Fortunately, a New Jersey appeals court reversed the lower court's decision because the promissory note did not include an endorsement stamp from the original lender (the now-defunct Argent Mortgage Company), and the assignment of mortgage document was not verified by someone with "personal knowledge" as to its authenticity. The New Jersey appeals court is not stupid. It realized that the loan may, in fact, be owed to an entirely different bank that has yet to step forward. Until that happens, Sandra doesn't owe anything. Wells Fargo tried to pull one, but alert judges stopped it.[2]

Perhaps the best example of a bank-gone-wild is the case of Rickie Walker, a homeowner who was harassed in Bankruptcy Court (Eastern District of California) because of a $1,320,650 home loan. Originally, Rickie borrowed the money from Bayrock Mortgage, which transferred the note and the related mortgage to MERS, the electronic registration system described earlier in this chapter. MERS then transferred the note and mortgage to Citibank, which filed a claim against Rickie. But, not so fast! The judge ruled that the middle step, involving MERS, invalidated the entire assignment process. Since MERS was only a "nominee" of Bayrock, it could not act on its behalf — even though that is precisely what Bayrock intended, and the definition of "nominee" is "a person or entity who is requested or named to act for another...."[3] Since Bayrock no longer exists, the debt is gone, and another bankster is thwarted.[4] Whew!

> I have to tell you ... I hate these guys [MERS] already.
> Their attitude alone bothers me. I looked at pictures of their

---

1   "In Re: Barry Weisband, Debtor," (Arizona District: United States Bankruptcy Court, March 29, 2011).

2   "Wells Fargo Bank, N.A., as Trustee, Plaintiff-Respondent V. Sandra A. Ford, Defendant-Appellant," (State of New Jersey: Superior Court, January 28, 2011).

3   "Definition of "Nominee"," Law.com, 2012, http://dictionary.law.com/Default.aspx?selected=1334.

4   "Rickie Walker, Debtor," (Eastern District of California: United States Bankruptcy Court, May 10, 2010).

three top executives on their Website and thought to myself ... "No way I'd be friends with these guys."

> – Martin Adelman, writing on his blog at <u>www.mandelman.ml-implode.com</u>

Common-sense solutions

This first solution is going to sound very naive. In past years banks would occasionally lose the promissory note related to a mortgage loan. How would this be remedied? The bank would contact the borrower and ask him or her to sign another note, clearly marked as "replacement" or "duplicate." An indemnification clause was often added so that the borrower would not have to worry about paying on the original note and the duplicate.

Of course, such a reasonable and moral course of action doesn't exactly jibe with a new culture that believes, "If they lost the original promissory note, I don't owe anything anymore. Hurray! Let's have a party in my new house." Perhaps, however, with some real political leadership, morality could work in some of these situations. United States senators, congress people, and/or the President might publicly state something like this:

> If you are behind in your mortgage payments, don't claim that you are not. If you know who you were making payments to, don't pretend that you don't know who it is. And, don't tie up the judiciary system with lies. If you can't make your payments, the government has people and programs to help you negotiate with the lender, and to help you financially. If that doesn't work, turn the house over to the lender, who rightfully is claiming it. We'll help you find an apartment.

OK. That's probably not going to work, so here is another way to stop the need for robo-signing. As stated by a *reasonable* judge in his ruling, Congress could pass legislation to "amend the current statutes to confer upon MERS the requisite authority to assign mortgages under its current business practices."[1] That should have been done years ago. Instead, however, the legislators in most states have passed legislation focused on the use of robo-signers. Apparently, these legislators, who routinely vote for bills they never read, are offended that bank employees were signing things they had not read.

Finally, some of these problems could have been resolved if President Obama had simply signed legislation (the Interstate Recognition of Notarizations Act) put on his desk in October 2010. The bill, which

---

1   "In Re: Ferrel L. Agard, Debtor."

was passed by Congress without opposition, would have required the acceptance of out-of-state notarizations of documents used by banks in foreclosures. This was sensible legislation, given that mortgage lending is no longer an intra-state affair, and given the pressing national need to expedite the foreclosure process. Obama vetoed the bill, and "sent the bill back to the House of Representative for further discussion on how it would affect the foreclosure crisis...."[1]

The $25 billion solution

What do politicians do when the Occupy-Wall-Street crowd demands that bankers be thrown in jail for fraud, but it isn't possible because a criminal case does not exist? If it is an election year the politicians squeeze the banks for lots of money. That's the best alternative.

In February 2012 President Obama announced a $25 billion settlement between the federal government, 49 states, and the five biggest banks — Bank of America, Wells Fargo, JP Morgan Chase, Citigroup, and Ali Financial. The funds are to be used to compensate for alleged home mortgage documentation defects and the injury to homeowners caused by those defects. The banks agreed to the settlement in exchange for a pledge by federal and state governments that they will not sue the banks for civil damages related to foreclosure and related matters. Individuals can still sue the banks. Here are a few offhand observations about this bi-partisan deal.

- The $25 billion is not really $25 billion. That sounds impressive, but the banks actually agreed to pay out about 1.5 billion in the form of $2,000 payments to each homeowner who was foreclosed upon between January 1, 2008 and the end of 2011. This is utter foolishness. If someone actually lost his home despite the fact that he properly paid his loan, he is owed a new house — not just $2,000. As for the other 99.9 percent, they deserve nothing.

- Most of the $25 billion settlement is in the form of loan modifications for home owners in default or on the verge of it. This is something the banks would gladly do anyway, and it amounts to political padding. ($25 billion sounds much better than $1.5 billion.)

---

1   Caren Bohan and Scot Paltrow, "Obama Kills Foreclosure Bill as Fury Mounts," Reuters.com (October 7, 2010), http://www.reuters.com/article/2010/10/07/us-usa-housing-whitehouse-idUSTRE6963DJ20101007.

- About $5 billion of the $25 billion goes directly to the federal government ($750 million) and to the states ($4.25 billion). Only the Lord knows how these funds will ultimately be distributed.
- The banks have admitted no wrong-doing. Why should they? In all likelihood they settled to avoid years of costly litigation and the adverse publicity related to it.
- The settlement does not apply to the vast numbers of loans that were sold to Fannie and Freddie. The Neighborhood Assistance Corporation of America believes that these omitted loans "will continue to devastate the mortgage industry."[1]

With this settlement taking place months before an election, the real winners are the politicians who get to beat their chests and tell constituents that they humbled the banksters. But, even here, the victory is incomplete because the bank-hating crazies are still not happy — and never will be. Some of them even see it as a sellout:

> How can our government let these fat cats get away with it? The 99% is disgusted and finds the foreclosure abuse settlement unacceptable. We demand accountability and justice for the criminals involved, not a robo-settlement.
>
> – The Occupy Sacramento Foreclosure Action Team, http://occupysac.com, February 14, 2012

That's not my view. I see the foreclosure scandal in the same way that economist Arnold Kling does:

> If there were any justice, this "scandal" would be regarded as nothing but [a] baloney sandwich.[2]

1 Susanna Kim, "Feds Announce $25b Foreclosure Abuse Deal," ABC News (September 1, 2003), http://abcnews.go.com/Business/feds-announce-25b-foreclosure-deal/story?id=15545458.

2 Arnold Kling, "A Few More Thoughts on the Foreclosure Scandal," Library of Economics and Liberty (October 13, 2010), http://econlog.econlib.org/archives/2010/10/the_real_forecl.html.

CHAPTER 17: THE TRUTH ABOUT BANK LEVERAGE RATIOS

> Since August 2008, commenters in the press and elsewhere have suggested that the 2004 amendments … allowed these firms to increase their debt-to-capital ratios to unsafe levels well-above 12-to1, indeed to 33-to-1…. While this theme has been repeated often in the press and elsewhere, it lacks foundation in fact.
>
> – Erik R. Sirri, former Director, Division of Trading and Markets, SEC[1]

Everything you probably heard about Bush, the SEC and 2004 deregulation of the Wall Street banks is false. Once the Bush critics realized that Gramm-Leach-Bliley and the Commodity Futures Modernization Act could not be sold as creations of his Administration (because Clinton signed them!), the new line of attack became the 2004 changes to bank capital reserve requirements, made by the Security Exchange Commission. However, this canard would also prove to be a tough sell, for these reasons:

- The changes were made with the unanimous approval of SEC commissioners, including Democrat Annette Nazareth
- The changes were never meant to be deregulatory
- The changes were not, in fact, deregulatory

Before 2004, the SEC required "broker dealers" (firms that trade securities) to meet certain net capital reserve standards; however, the par-

---

1   Erik R. Sirri, "Speech on Securities Markets and Regulatory Reform," in National Economists Club (Washington, DC: SEC, April 9, 2009).

ent companies of such broker-dealers were not regulated.[1] Things began to change in 2002. The European Union (EU) adopted a directive, the thrust of which was to require regulation of the parent companies of broker dealers. It was felt by the EU that actions and decisions of the parent companies could affect the financial health of their subsidiaries. U.S. firms doing business in Europe were subject to these new EU rules, unless they could show that they received "equivalent" supervision by U.S. bank regulators. There was no such equivalent supervision of investment banks by U.S. regulators, and that became the impetus for the 2004 SEC changes.

The Consolidated Supervised Entity program

The SEC, led by its chairman, William Donaldson, created a Consolidated Supervised Entity (CSE) program, which "effectively added an additional layer of supervision for the holding company where none had existed previously."[2] Basically, these changes gave the SEC the right to examine, for the first time, holding company activities outside of the U.S. broker-dealer subsidiary. This was no small achievement, although it has been ignored or downplayed by the media.

The SEC made certain calculation changes for the broker-dealer subsidiaries so that their net capital reserve calculations (which are closely related to leverage ratios) would be compatible with those of the parents (i.e., with those of the holding companies).[3] Many analysts claimed that these changes stimulated Wall Street banks to create mortgage-backed securities and other forms of asset-backed securities. However, a former SEC official, Erik R. Sirri, notes that "[t]he Commission did not undo any leverage restrictions in 2004," nor did it intend to make a substantial reduction. Indeed, the historical record shows no significant change in the capital levels of the broker-dealers after 2004. The Government Accountability Office (GAO) subsequently found this to be the case, based on interviews with SEC staff and based on its own financial research:

> ...SEC staff told us that the broker-dealers generally did not [increase their leverage] after joining the CSE program. The staff said that the primary sources of leverage for the broker-dealers were customer margin loans,

---

1 The ratio was nominally 15-to-1, but an "early warning" provision made it, effectively, 12-to-1.

2 Sirri, "Speech on Securities Markets and Regulatory Reform."

3 Capital reserves are based on the net worth of the company. Higher reserves generally minimize the risk that a company will fail. Leverage is based on the ratio of debt to adjusted net worth. More leverage generally increases risk.

repurchase agreements, and stock lending. According to the staff, these transactions were driven by customers and counterparties, marked daily, and secured by collateral — exposing the broker-dealers to little, if any, market risk.[1]

The GAO said that its own studies did not show a remarkable increase in leverage after the CSE program began. In fact, it found that a majority of the 5 CSE firms had asset-to-equity ratios (a variation of leverage ratios) that had been higher in 1998 than in 2006.

> In our prior work on Long-Term Capital Management (a hedge fund), we analyzed the assets-to-equity ratios of four of the five broker-dealer holding companies that later became CSEs and found that three had ratios equal to or greater than 28-to-1 at fiscal year-end 1998, which was higher than their ratios at fiscal year-end 2006 before the crisis began.[2]

Indeed, it was never clear that the CSE program would lead to net capital reductions. While the SEC expected its *preliminary* computational changes to result in a significant reduction in capital, it had added a second requirement: a huge "safety net" of sorts, in the form of a $5 billion "early warning" capital floor. Any company with tentative net capital below that floor had to report to the SEC. Prior to the CSE program the early warning floor was a paltry $250,000 –1/20,000[th] as much!

Of course, these facts did not stop critics from making wild claims about Bush's SEC and its dismantling of leverage limits — specifically the 12-to-1 leverage ratio limit. However, that ratio was not even being used by the large banks — before or after CSE. Since the late 1970s, broker-dealers had been allowed alternative calculations for net capital: the 12-to-1 leverage ratio or a 5-percent-of-accounts receivable standard[3] Each and every one of the Consolidated Supervised Entity (CSE) banks had opted for the 5-percent-of-accounts receivable standard.

By design, the 5-percent-of-receivables measure was intended to put the focus on customer safety rather than firm fiscal safety. SEC's Erik Sirri (now a college professor of finance) emphasized this point, stating that the net capital regulatory regime was never directly intended "to insure the safety or soundness of the broker-dealer. Rather, it focuses on

---

1   "Financial Crisis Highlights Need to Improve Oversight of Leverage at Financial Institutions and across System," ed. GAO (U.S. Government, July 2009), 40.

2   Ibid.

3   Nominally, it was a 2 percent standard, but effectively, it was a 5-percent-of-accounts-receivable standard because of a "early warning" rule.

the return of customer property."[1] And, Sirri noted that the 12-to-1 rule would have never been "absolute," even if firms had chosen to use it. In defining indebtedness it specifically excluded obligations that are "fully collateralized by a liquid proprietary security," and the broker-dealers held substantial amounts of such debt.[2]

Figure 16 – Flowchart showing calculations made to determine compliance with net capital rule

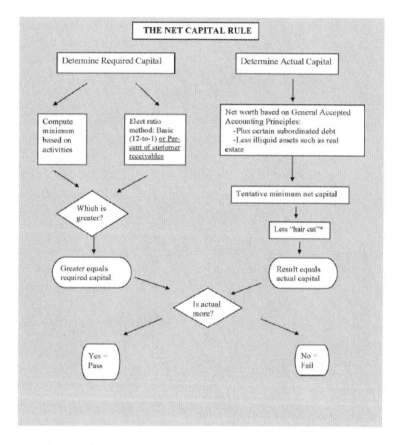

*The calculation of the "hair cut" was changed in 2004, when broker-dealers were allowed to use statistical value-at-risk (VaR) models instead of set percentages. However, to keep the new hair cuts at levels similar to previous levels a huge "early warning" minimum was established. This minimum was set at $5 billion, which was 20 thousand times the previous minimum of $250,000.

---

1   Financial Crisis Inquiry Commission, Testimony of Erik R. Sirri, Professor of Finance, May 5, 2010.
2   Sirri, "Speech on Securities Markets and Regulatory Reform."

All of this is, of course, kind of confusing, so I have graphically depict-ed the key parts of the net capital calculation in Figure 16, above. The two aspects of the calculation that are usually ignored by critics and analysts are found in the underlined words (describing the optional percent-of-receivables ratio used by the big banks) and in the flowchart footnote (describing the $5 billion "early warning" floor on net capital).

The changes to net capital made by SEC in 2004 can be found in just one box within Figure 16 — the box labeled "hair cut" (third from bot-tom on the right side). To calculate the amount of its net capital a bank would first determine net worth using Generally Accepted Accounting Principles (the principles developed by the green eyeshade guys). To that figure they would add back certain subordinated debt that was similar to equity, and from the net worth they would subtract illiquid and risky assets such as fixed assets, goodwill, real estate and unsecured accounts receivables. The result would be tentative net capital, and it would most-ly comprise liquid assets.

The next and final step would be to give the tentative net capital a "hair cut." Prior to 2004 this hair cut consisted of fixed percentage re-ductions, based on the estimated riskiness of each type of asset. These were somewhat crude, but reliable measures. Not satisfied, SEC and the investment banks wanted a more sophisticated haircut, based on statis-tical value-at-risk (VaR) models. These more sophisticated models could be manipulated to produce smaller haircuts, a point made frequently, and correctly, by SEC critics. But, that is why SEC added the $5 billion early warning floor — a point never noted by those same critics.

The drive-by professors

The conservative radio host Rush Limbaugh makes reference to the "drive-by" media, and I assume he means journalists who make slanted or inaccurate reports, and never go back to update or correct them. If that is the case, I'd like to coin a new phrase: "the drive-by professors."

In the early days of the crisis, several members of academia or "think tanks" made false and/or simplistic statements that have become an-chored within the historical record. In many cases those false or mislead-ing statements remain uncorrected, and the public remains misled. An MIT professor of finance and an ex-MIT physicist wrote a great sum-mary of this phenomenon. Andrew Lo and Mark Mueller noted that, in 2008, several newspapers, including the New York Times, had reports of "sudden increases in leverage from 12-to-1 to 33-to-1" at the big in-vestment banks. These increases were supposedly due to the 2004 SEC amendments to Rule 15c3-1 (i.e., the "net capital rule"), and they seemed to constitute a "smoking gun" cause of the financial crisis. But, as noted by Lo and Mueller, "it turns out that the 2004 SEC amendment to Rule 15c3-1 did nothing to change the leverage restrictions of these financial institutions."

Nevertheless, many learned scholars and policy makers parroted the early news reports — with no further investigation. By so doing, those scholars became mere propagandists (wittingly or unwittingly). The guilty include former chief economist Susan Woodward, Columbia University Law Professor John Coffee, Nobel laureate Joseph Stiglitz, and Alan Blinder, a Princeton University professor and former vice-chairman of the U.S. Federal Reserve. Those are just the perps identified by Lo and Mueller, who question how "sophisticated and informed individuals can be so easily misled on a simple and empirically verifiable issue."[1]

The most disturbing finding by Lo and Mueller was that, as of March 12, 2010, the New York Times had not corrected its original misguided report (the one reporting "sudden increases in leverage"). Drive-by media: Meet your new colleagues, the drive-by professors.

Before we leave the subject of the 2004 SEC capital reserve adjustments, it is appropriate to remember that all capital reserve standards were dramatically lower for assets of any type held by Fannie and Freddie (F&F) versus private banks. This is why the required bailout of those two government sponsored enterprises exceeds the bailout of other entities. Efforts to improve capital reserve standards for F&F were made in 2003, but thwarted by Congressional opposition. The people who opposed the increase in required capital reserves for F&F are, in many cases, the same people critical of the 2004 SEC changes for private banks. See page 294 for more information.

Did the SEC fail? If so, why?

> ...then-SEC chairman William Donaldson's reform was anything but deregulation. A regulatory failure, yes, and a cautionary tale for those who think new regulation will solve everything.
>
> – Charles Calomiris, American Enterprise Institute

---

1   Andrew W. Lo and Mark T. Mueller, "Warning: Physics Envy May Be Hazardous to Your Wealth!," (New York: Social Science Research Network, March 12, 2010), http://ssrn.com/abstract=1563882. (The correct leverage numbers are easily found in publicly-available annual reports and SEC filings.)

If the 2004 SEC amendments were not deregulatory, why did the big investment banks fail? The problem precedes the 2004 amendments. First, the SEC (and, indeed, the entire U.S. government) never concerned itself too much with the financial security of the big investment banks. As discussed, capital reserve standards were focused on *customer* security. Second, the Basel I capital standards used by the SEC were counterproductive and obsolete. They did not contemplate the break down of underwriting standards and the eventual securitization of millions of substandard loans. As noted in the first 8 chapters of this book, every policy of the federal government, and many state and local governments, seemed to increase — not decrease — systemic risk. The emphasis was on spreading the American Dream — not on fiscal prudence or financial institution safety. Why else would our government(s) encourage the wide-spread use of low down payments, low FICO (credit) scores, and Nintendo-type property appraisals?

The Basel I risk-based capital reserve standards, used for many years by U.S. government regulators, were almost worse than nothing because they unnecessarily encouraged the widespread creation of securitized investments. Under those standards, capital was adjusted upwards to give the bank credit, so to speak, for having assets perceived to be less risky than average. The formula was a ratio equal to the bank's capital divided by its risk-adjusted assets. Loans secured by residences were considered to be safe, but the AAA tranches of mortgage-backed securities were considered to be even safer. These different perceptions of relative risk translated into significant quantitative differences in the calculation of capital: The AAA tranches of mortgage-backed securities (MBS) were assigned a risk factor of just 0.2 — even if the MBS was comprised entirely of junk. On the other hand, the mortgage loans were given a risk factor of 0.5, even if they were of the highest quality. The impact on capital reserves could be very large.

Figure 17 depicts risk-based capital under two simple scenarios for a company that has, before adjustment, capital of 2 percent of total assets. The column on the left shows the risk-based capital for a bank with assets comprising only the AAA tranches of mortgage-backed securities. The risk-based capital, computed as prescribed in regulations, is 10 percent [2/(.2 times 100)], and that is the case even if the mortgage-backed securities comprise all junk loans. The right-side column depicts the risk-based capital for a bank with assets entirely comprising separate residential mortgage loans of the highest quality. That amount is only 4 percent [2/(.5 times 100)], and this would be the case even if the loans were made to borrowers with excellent FICO scores, and who made large 40 percent down payments.

Blame the banks for using every scheme they could imagine to put their resources into the AAA tranches of MBS, but blame the government regulators for setting up such a naive and simplistic capital scheme, and blame them for not updating that scheme when underwriting standards went into free-fall.

Figure 17 – The risk-based capital standards rewarded banks for securitizing loans

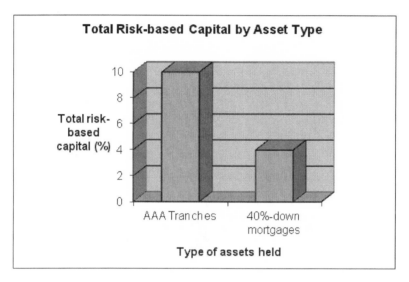

It is clear that inadequately-structured capital reserve standards significantly impacted the crisis: Those standards motivated banks to increase investment in risky mortgage-backed securities. In addition, the deficient level of bank capital reserves increased the size of the bank "bail-out," paid for by the taxpayers. The more rigorous capital reserve standards of the Basel II Accords, the soon-to-be-implemented Basel III Accords, and the new Dodd-Frank legislation may minimize taxpayer risk, but capital reserve standards can't fully solve a problem they did not cause.[1] If a guy has a gambling addiction, telling him to take more

---

1   Basel III standards will be phased in starting on January 1, 2013. They call for minimum common equity of 4.5 percent of risk-weighted assets, an additional equity "buffer," and a countercyclical buffer that increases capital requirements when credit is growing fast. (The goal is to slow down housing bubble growth.) Basel III still relies upon credit rating agencies for determining the risk-weighting of assets. Dodd-Frank imposes similar capital

capital next time he visits Las Vegas won't necessarily help. The real solution lies in stopping the risky behavior. In the case at hand, that risky behavior was subprime lending.

The CSE program was terminated in September, 2008.

---

requirements; however, it differs sharply with regard to rating agencies. It requires regulators to seek alternatives to the use of rating agencies for the risk-assessment of assets. At the time of this writing such alternatives have not been established.

CHAPTER 18: PEOPLE WHO WALK AWAY FROM THEIR DEBTS

> "What if you could live payment free for up to 8 months or more and walk away without owing a penny? Unshackle yourself today from a losing investment and use our proven method to Walk Away."

> – Advertisement on Youwalkaway.com

The hallmark of the financial crisis of 2007/08 was the homeowner's default on his bank loan. However, not all defaults were due to an inability to pay. A survey conducted by Chicago-area university professors revealed that about 3 of every 10 mortgage loan defaults in 2010 were by people who could afford to make the payments.[1] This growing trend is called voluntary foreclosure, the "walk-away strategy," or "strategic default," and it is available only in situations where the bank has no effective recourse against the borrower, other than foreclosing to get the collateral (i.e., the house). In other words, the strategy works when the bank is engaged in nonrecourse lending.

Was nonrecourse lending a cause the financial crisis of 2007/08? Is it good public policy? Is the strategic default appropriate and ethical behavior? Who is most likely to use the tactic? These and other questions are addressed in this chapter.

Nonrecourse lending pertains to two categories of mortgagors: those who have few assets aside from the home, and those who live in states

---

1   As reported by John W. Schoen, "As Home Prices Fall, More Borrowers Walk Away," (January 9, 2012), http://bottomline.msnbc.msn.com/_news/2011/12/21/9614305-as-home-prices-fall-more-borrowers-walk-away.

with "anti-deficiency" or "nonrecourse" laws. Unfortunately, these two types of borrowers comprise the majority of all homeowners in the United States.

The first category of nonrecourse lending includes the borrower who has enough income to pay his mortgage, but little in the way of cash, investments, and other real estate. The lender won't waste its money suing this sort of borrower in court. If the borrower walks, the lender will simply foreclose on the house and hope that the proceeds from its sale are sizeable. Many or most United States homeowners fall into this category. Nonrecourse lending can also apply to the borrower with substantial assets (in addition to the home) if he lives in a state with nonrecourse (or anti-deficiency) lending laws.

The nonrecourse statutes are primarily a United States phenomenon that, for the most part, originated in the aftermath of the Great Depression. They are found in a limited number of states — about 10 to 20. The reason for the wide range (10 to 20) is that there are different types of anti-deficiency laws, and some are more restrictive than others. Many analysts believe that only 10 or 11 states have meaningful anti-deficiency statutes, while others expand the list to include those states that give the borrower limited protections.

Two university law professors, Dov Solomon and Odelia Minnes, offer the following concise description of the various types of nonrecourse protections offered by the states:

> Most state anti-deficiency laws fall into one or more of the following categories: (1) laws that prohibit the recovery of any deficiency under a loan secured by residential real estate; (2) laws that prohibit any deficiency when the mortgage or deed of trust is "purchase money" [used to buy the house]; (3) laws that prohibit the recovery of any deficiency following a non-judicial foreclosure by power of sale [that is, if the bank opts for a fast non-judicial foreclosure sale it can't go after additional amounts]; and (4) laws that limit the deficiency to the difference between the loan balance owing and the greater of the foreclosure sale price or the fair market value of the property.[1]

There are 11 states that are on most short lists of nonrecourse states: Alaska, Arizona, California, Iowa, Minnesota, Montana, North Carolina, North Dakota, Oregon, Washington, and Wisconsin. Note that 2 of

---

1   Dov Solomon and Odelia Minnes, "Non-Recourse, No Down Payment and the Mortgage Meltdown: Lessons from Undercapitalization," (Social Science Electronic Publishing, Inc., 2011), 7, http://papers.ssrn.com/sol3/papers.cfm?abstract_id=1894029.

those states, California and Arizona, had high rates of foreclosure during the financial crisis.

Was the nonrecourse lending a cause of the crisis?

Although nonrecourse lending was not a cause of the crisis of 2007/08, it affected it in two ways. First, it was one of the factors that weakened individual resistance to the risks of acquiring large mortgage debt. (The other two factors weakening borrower resistance were the low down payment requirements and the predatory loan tactics.) Solomon and Minnes, the law professors mentioned earlier, believe that nonrecourse lending was a significant factor in creating the housing bubble leading to the crisis:

> Financing home purchases through non-recourse mortgages, combined with the practice of not requiring an initial down payment, insufficiently deterred borrowers from taking loans despite knowing that they would not be able to fulfill their terms.[1]

I disagree with Solomon and Minnes regarding the importance of nonrecourse lending laws. I suspect those laws were a very small factor in motivating people to buy because most people do not purchase a home with the idea that the market will go bust and they will need to "walk away" from their debt. However, for the purchasers who entered the market as investors rather than homeowners (the flip-this-house crowd) the limit on liability afforded by nonrecourse lending laws might have been important. On the graphic model of the crisis (starting on page 244) you will see nonrecourse laws listed in the third box from the left, under "Broken Controls."

Nonrecourse lending affected the financial crisis in a second way. It aggravated and complicated the crisis by enabling hundreds of thousands of relatively affluent borrowers to strategically default. This hurt the banks, financially, and helped to depress home prices. For this reason, on the graphic model of the crisis (starting on page 244) you will also see nonrecourse laws listed in the box on the far right side (under "Aggravating Factors").

A study prepared for the Federal Reserve Bank of Richmond (but not necessarily reflecting views of the Fed) quantified the effect of recourse on default rates. These were the conclusions of the study:

> The deterrent effect [of recourse debt] on default is significant only for borrowers with appraised property values of $200,000 or more at time

---

1   Ibid., 18.

of origination. At the mean value of the default option at the time of default and for homes appraised at $300,000 to $500,000, borrowers in non-recourse states are 81% more likely to default than borrowers in recourse states. For homes appraised at $500,000 to $750,000, borrowers in non-recourse states are more than twice as likely to default as borrowers in recourse states. For homes appraised at $750,000 to $1 million, borrowers in non-recourse states are 60% more likely to default.[1]

In other words, the researchers found that, when home loan borrowers are "underwater," they can be 60 to 100 percent more likely to default in nonrecourse states. Interestingly, these statistics apply to people in the nice, big houses. The researchers found no impact from nonrecourse laws for those buying homes appraised below $200,000 (at origination time, in 2005 dollars). Perhaps the borrowers in this category are indifferent to the protection afforded by nonrecourse laws because they have few assets at risk.

The ethics and psychology of the strategic default

> Sometimes, borrowers have to acquire that ruthlessness. Helen Sheridan purchased a townhouse condo in 2006 at the height of the boom in San Diego. She paid $630,000 for a place worth $450,000 today. ... She had to overcome some conventional thinking about the sanctity of debt repayment to make what she realizes in the correct financial choice. "I still feel guilty," Sheridan said, "I break out in tears, but I have a family to support."[2]

After the crisis, the use of strategic defaults grew as house values continued to descend. However, many people have difficulty, socially and psychologically, with the idea of walking away from their debts. They feel guilty about leaving a major debt unpaid, and worry about what their friends, co-workers, and neighbors might think. Defaulting is sometimes perceived as an antisocial act.

---

1   Andra C. Ghent and Marianna Kudlyak, "Recourse and Residential Mortgage Default: Evidence from U.S. States," (Social Science Electronic Publishing, Inc., February 25, 2011), 28, http://papers.ssrn.com/sol3/papers.cfm?abstract_id=1432437.

2   Les Christie, "Walk Away from Your Mortgage? Time to Get 'Ruthless'," CNNMoney.com, June 7, 2011, http://money.cnn.com/2011/06/07/real_estate/walk_away_mortgage/index.htm.

John Courson, CEO of the Mortgage Bankers Association, and a critic of the technique, warns borrowers about the "message" they will give "their family and their kids and their friends."[1]

Roger Lowenstein of the New York Times cites two reasons strategic defaults have been considered antisocial:

> One is that foreclosures depress the neighborhood and drive down prices. ... The other reason is that default (supposedly) debases the character of the borrower.[2]

Lowenstein feels that guilt should not prevent someone from using the strategic default option. His primary argument is that businesses have no compunction about defaulting on a loan, when it makes good business sense. So, why should an individual? I understand Lowenstein's logic, but it is an oversimplification. First, most of the larger loans owed by businesses are, in fact, secured by business assets, such as cash, accounts receivable, and inventory. Second, when a business loan is not secured by those assets, it is due to a negotiation process between the lender and the business, and not because of a state law preventing the lender from pursuing full restitution.

A borrower who wants to employ the strategic default technique will often justify the decision by attacking the character of his bank. One finance professor put it this way:

> We're finding that people are much more willing to walk away when the other party is unknown or what you might call a "bad bank." Those are the ones that received a lot of bailout funds or were active in the subprime market, giving loans to people who couldn't afford them and they knew that.[3]

Sometimes the borrower justifies the walk-away decision on the basis of the bank's unwillingness to modify the loan. The *60 Minutes* TV program featured such a borrower on a show pertaining to strategic defaults.

> [Chris Deaner] says he tried to talk his bank into renegotiating his mortgage, but because he earns enough to keep paying, the bank said no deal. ... Asked if he doesn't feel a twinge of guilt, Deaner told Safer, "No, especially after dealing with my lender, trying to contact them. None at all."[4]

---

1   Roger Lowenstein, "Walk Away from Your Mortgage!," The New York Times (January 7, 2010), http://www.nytimes.com/2010/01/10/magazine/10FOB-wwln-t.html.
2   Ibid.
3   Schoen, "As Home Prices Fall, More Borrowers Walk Away."
4   "Strategic Default: Walking Away from Mortgages," CBSNEWS (May 9, 2009), http://www.cbsnews.com/2100-18560_162-6466484.html.

There are other ways to justify the walk-away act. Jane Bryant Quinn, the financial advisor, says a person "should feel free to use it, if that makes sense for your family and your future. It was part of the deal. The bank agreed."[1] Others have justified the action on the basis of the government's ineffectiveness in dealing with the housing crisis and the economy.

I don't admire people who can afford to pay their loans and choose not to. However, they shouldn't be condemned because the problem really lies in public policy.

Nonrecourse lending — bad public policy

Nonrecourse laws do not protect people with few assets because banks never sue such people in any event. It would not be worth the legal expense. In such cases the banks simply foreclose on the properties and take the net sales proceeds. This seems to be the finding of the research of Ghent and Kudlyak, cited earlier. They noted no difference in the rate of default (between recourse and nonrecourse states) for homes valued at $200,000 or less. Presumably, such homes are owned by people with fewer other assets.

On the other hand, nonrecourse laws do protect wealthier home owners with substantial assets at risk. The Ghent/Kudlyak research showed that defaults rates could be as much as 100 percent higher for people owning higher-priced homes. Those people probably have other assets to protect and are, therefore, less likely to default in a state where banks can go after those extra assets.

Nonrecourse lending laws encourage borrowers to strategically default, and that is bad for the economy. They weaken financial institutions and depress home values. It is time to eliminate, or at least modify, these state laws.

There would probably be much opposition to a full repeal of the nonrecourse lending laws, which are seen by some as essential protection against ruthless lenders. If a full repeal is not politically possible, a proposal by Solomon and Minnes might be better than nothing. They propose that a borrower's liability be tied to the size of his original down payment. If the borrower gave a full down payment — say, 20 percent — the lender would have no recourse against the borrower's personal assets in the event of a default. However, if the borrower put down only 3

---

1   Jane Bryant Quinn, "What Happens When You Walk Away from a Mortgage Loan?," CBSNEWS.com, June 16, 2010, http://www.cbsnews.com/8301-505123_162-41240261/what-happens-when-you-walk-away-from-a-mortgage-loan/.

percent, the lender would have recourse against a certain percentage of the borrower's assets.[1]

The problem with this proposal is that a person who can't make the whole down payment will probably not accumulate any assets to give the bank at a later time. A wiser course of action is to always require meaningful down payments — period. Those who don't have them should wait — just like grandma and grandpa used to do.

---

1   Solomon and Odelia Minnes, "Non-Recourse, No Down Payment and the Mortgage Meltdown: Lessons from Undercapitalization," 37.

PART FIVE: SCAPEGOAT POLITICS

It's understandable that people are angry about the financial crisis, the stagnant economy, and the taxpayer bailouts. Many people and many sectors of the economy took irresponsible actions that helped lead us to the calamity. However, government affordable housing and interest-rate policies were primarily responsible. Politicians behave reprehensibly when they try to deflect the blame to other government policies and other sectors of the economy.

CHAPTER 19: "EIGHT YEARS OF BLAH, BLAH, BLAH"

> This is a final verdict on 8 years of failed economic policies
> — a theory that says we can shred regulations & consumer
> protections and give more to the most [prosperous], and
> somehow prosperity will trickle down. It hasn't worked.
>
> – President Barack Obama in the first presidential debate
> on September 26, 2008

In September 2008, presidential candidate Barack Obama was given a political goldmine: a financial debacle he could hang around the necks of Republicans. Lehman was failing, Merrill Lynch was desperately seeking salvation from a corporate suitor, and AIG was begging for a federal bailout. Bank lending virtually stopped and the U.S. economy was in a tailspin.

Candidate Obama charged that the financial crisis was the result of Republican tax cuts for millionaires, cutting "rules for corporations," and shredding regulations. He also complained that President Bush was leaving office with "projected deficits of $8 trillion."[1]

Obama's claims were questionable but it did not matter. His opponent, John McCain, was going down. To be fair, blaming the opposing political party is automatic in a presidential campaign. A Republican in his position would have done the same.

This is a book about the causes and other factors that led to the financial crisis, so it is appropriate to examine the accuracy of the President's assertions. In addition, we need to consider the fairness and appropri-

---

1   President Obama in the January 27, 2010 State of the Union Speech

ateness of the President's on-going rhetoric about "the rich" and "the wealthy,' and the unique advantages that they (supposedly) have been given. Are these legitimate, constructive issues, or has the President used the crisis as an excuse to engage in class warfare?

To begin, here are the key questions we must answer:

- What deregulations were shredded, by whom, and when?
- How do deficits relate to the crisis (and was there really an $8 trillion projected accumulated deficit when Obama took office)?
- In what way did "tax cuts for the rich" cause the financial crisis and were there, in fact, special tax cuts for the wealthy?

Did broccoli cause the mortgage meltdown?

Let's start with the easiest part: tax cuts for the rich. Regarding the alleged connection between "tax cuts for the rich" and the subprime mortgage crisis, there is not much to say. It is like arguing against the notion that the mortgage crisis was caused by the amount of broccoli the nation consumes. If there is a connection, someone in the Administration should explain it to us. However, for those who think that tax cuts were a cause of the crisis, here are some important characteristics of the federal income tax legislation signed by George W. Bush during his first year in office.

First, President G.W. Bush did not cut taxes, he cut the *rate* of taxes, which is entirely different. Analogy: If I open a pizza shop and charge $50 per pizza, I'll be lucky to sell 2 pizzas (to my wife and to my mother). So, my total revenue will be $100, at most. On the other hand, if I cut the rate I charge for pizzas — say, to $20 each — I'll probably sell lots of pizzas, and collect much more than $100. Thus, by cutting my rate I will increase my total revenue. Although Dubya cut the rate of individual income tax, taxes as a whole were not cut — they increased, both in absolute dollars and in inflation-adjusted dollars (as compared to the 8 years under President Clinton). This is evident in Table 8, below, which is based on Congressional Budget Office (CBO) amounts. In absolute terms, Bush brought in an average of $967 billion per year versus about $719 billion per Clinton. This is shown on the left side of the table. In inflation-adjusted terms (with all amounts stated in 2001 dollars) Bush brought in $882 billion compared with an average of $798 billion per Clinton (10.5 percent more). These amounts are shown in the shaded area on the right side of the table.

Some analysts perform a little Houdini act with these numbers. They express revenues as a percentage of Gross Domestic Product (GDP), and by so doing, they make it appear that tax collections sagged. However, they are employing circular reasoning because the essential conservative hypothesis is that GDP will increase — precisely because of the cuts in the tax rate. If we divide tax revenues by an increasingly large GDP, tax collections will, of course, appear to be smaller. That is exactly what supply-side economists predict.

Table 8 – Individual income tax revenues, in billions of dollars, based on Congressional Budget Office Table E-3 dated January 2011, and adjusted for the Consumer Price Index per the Bureau of Labor Statistics

Bill Clinton's Eight Years		George Bush's Eight Years		Bill Clinton's Eight Years	George Bush's Eight Years
Year	Nominal Dollars	Year	Nominal Dollars	2001 Dollars	2001 Dollars
1993	509.7	2001	994.3	624.7	994.3
1994	543.1	2002	858.3	649.0	844.9
1995	590.2	2003	793.7	685.9	763.9
1996	656.4	2004	809.0	740.9	758.5
1997	737.5	2005	927.2	813.8	840.8
1998	828.6	2006	1043.9	900.3	917.0
1999	879.5	2007	1163.5	934.9	993.8
2000	1004.5	2008	1145.7	1033.1	942.4
Ave.	718.7	Ave.	967.0	797.8	882.0

The absurdity of the "tax fairness" complaint

We also need to discuss the charge that Bush gave special tax breaks to the rich. Yes, their tax rates were cut; however, it was by a much smaller percentage than the tax rate cuts that went to everyone else.[1] As a result, the total share of federal income taxes (and, for that matter, total taxes) paid by wealthy Americans increased during the Bush years. In Figure 18 we see the shares of federal income taxes and federal total taxes paid by the highest quintile of earners in years 2000 through 2007, which was the last year presented by the Congressional Budget Office as of March, 2012. Note: These are actual tax collections after any and all tax deductions, credits, the special low rates for qualified dividends and capital gains, and "loopholes." As can be seen, the share of total taxes

---

1   During the G.W. Bush Administration there were two major tax acts: the Economic Growth and Tax Relief Reconciliation Act of 2001 and the Jobs and Growth Tax Relief Reconciliation Act of 2003.

went from 66.6 percent in 2000 to 68.9 percent in 2007, and the share of income taxes climbed from 81.2 percent in 2000 to 86.0 percent in 2007.

Figure 18 – According to the Congressional Budget Office, these are the percentages of taxes paid by the wealthiest twenty percent of Americans (based on household income).

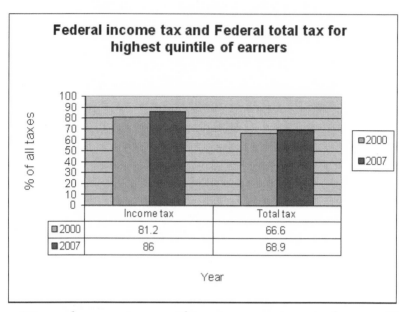

We see the same pattern with respect to taxpayers in the upper 10 percent, 5 percent, and in the much-maligned 1 percent. The total percentage of individual income taxes paid by people within each of these 3 categories is presented in Figure 19, below.

Figure 19 – The change in the total percentage of income taxes paid by individuals during the first 7 Bush years (based on household income)

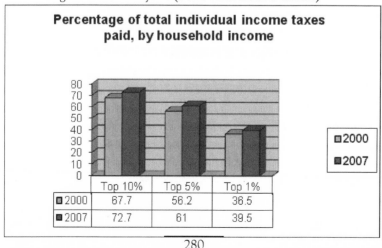

There is a tax fairness argument to be made, but it is not the one President Obama has offered. It is shocking to consider how many Americans (with income) pay zero federal income tax. According to the conservative Heritage Foundation, which analyzed IRS data, 12 percent did not pay federal income tax in 1970; however, by 2009 the percentage was 49.5 percent. These amounts are depicted in Figure 20.

Figure 20 – The percentage of people not paying income tax has quadrupled

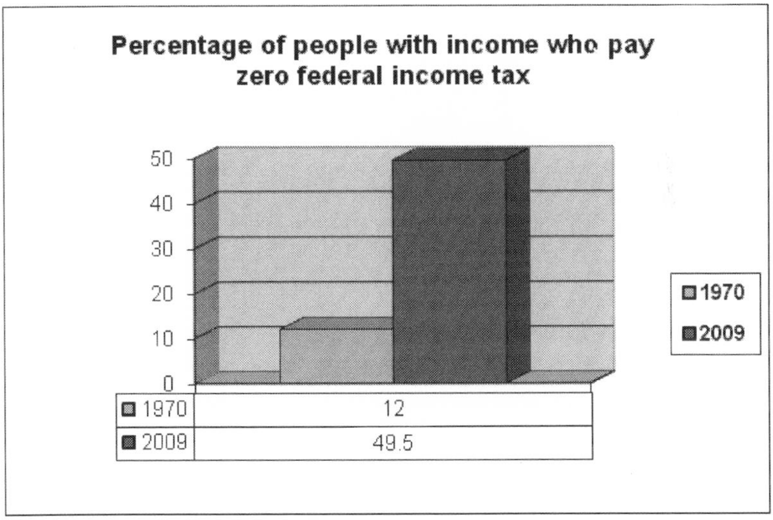

Percentage of people with income who pay zero federal income tax

☐ 1970	12
■ 2009	49.5

What about tax rates? Do the wealthy pay at a higher or lower rate? The Treasury Department's Web site has the answer, and it is summarized in Figure 21, below.

People in the top 1 percent pay an average federal income tax rate of 24 percent, while half of our income-reporting population pays only 1.85 percent. Expressed another way, the despised "one percent" pay at a rate that is nearly 13 times that of the rate paid by half of the population. If there is a fairness issue, it has to do with the fact that half of the population has income, yet pays virtually no income tax.

Thus, it is clear that wealthy Americans, as a group, did not receive a special tax break, as implied by President Barack Obama repeatedly. Further, Bush did not cut taxes. He cut rates, but overall tax collections increased. Even if he had done these things, however, President Obama and his supporters have never shown the connection between tax policy and the financial crisis.

Figure 21 – Per Treasury Department: Tax rates by income category. Note: Treasury states that "The average tax rate was computed by dividing total income tax ... by (positive) adjusted gross income." The chart only includes people who have income to report.

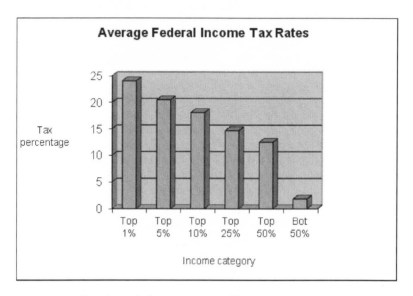

What about the low tax rate paid by Mitt Romney?

The discussion, above, concerns taxes paid by the *average* wealthy person. However, there are some wealthy people, like Warren Buffet and Mitt Romney, who pay at a lower rate. Why is that? The primary reason has to do with the nature of their taxable income. Most of that income is in the form of dividends and long-term capital gains, and they pay a rate of about 15 percent on that income. We can debate what, precisely, the rate of tax should be on these forms of income, but it should be lower than ordinary income.

In the United States, dividend income is double-taxed. The corporation pays tax on its income — usually at a 35 percent federal rate (plus state and local taxes). When the income is distributed to the shareholders, the very same income is taxed again, at the 15 percent rate. That adds up to 50 percent, before consideration of state and local taxes. (What? The President forgot to explain that to you?) If we tax dividends as ordinary income, and we let the Bush tax decreases expire (as President Obama wants) the federal tax rate on dividends would be an astronomical 75 percent. With state and local corporation and individual taxes added the rate would probably be around 90 percent. That sounds fair ...

Regarding capital gains, the matter is more complicated. First, capital gains are not indexed for inflation, so part or all of the so-called gain is simply inflation, and should not be taxed at all. In addition, capital losses are only partially deductible, while all of the gain is taxable. This adds a special element of tax risk which discourages investment. A lower capital gains rate is needed, in part, to compensate for that tax risk. Finally, a capital gain is often subject to its own form of double taxation. This phenomenon, which is somewhat complicated, is explained by economists Victor Canto and Harvey Hirschorn:

> A government can choose to tax either the value of an asset or its yield, but it should not tax both. Capital gains are literally the appreciation in the value of an existing asset. Any appreciation reflects merely an increase in the after-tax rate of return on the asset. The taxes implicit in the asset's after-tax earnings are already fully reflected in the asset's price or change in price. Any additional tax is strictly double taxation.[1]

Since the value of the asset is tied to expectations of future earnings, taxing the increase in value should preclude taxing the future earnings. (Or, taxing the future earnings should preclude taxing the increase in value.) To tax both is to double tax. The logic offered by Canto and Hirschorn may not hold up with respect to non-productive assets, such as museum art works. However, it makes sense with regard to business capital stock and investment assets, such as machinery, patents, goodwill, etc.

Finally, with regard to capital gains it is good public policy to offer a lower tax rate. Indeed, this is the primary reason we tax capital gains at a lower rate. If the rate is too high, many wealthy people will cling to land, businesses, common stock, and other assets that may be more efficiently utilized by others. For example, a wealthy person may decide to retain vacant land and bequeath it to his heirs, rather than sell it and pay a stiff income tax. Yet, that land might be needed now as a location for residential housing, retail shops, or manufacturing facilities. Taxing capital gains at ordinary rates could lead to excessive asset hoarding.

We can have a legitimate debate regarding the proper capital gains rate. However, the President is not engaging in such a debate. Rather, he is promoting class envy and division. This is regrettable but understandable, as it is an election year.

---

1   Victor Canto and Harvey Hirschorn as cited by Stephen Moore, "Capital Gains Taxes," (Library of Economics and Liberty), http://www.econlib.org/library/Enc/CapitalGainsTaxes.html.

The truth about deficits

The analysis, above, shows that President Obama was misleading when he talked about Bush's tax policies, but let's give him the benefit of the doubt. Perhaps he thought that the Bush tax rate cuts led to tax collection cuts, which led to deficits that caused the financial crisis. If that was his thought process, I still don't get the logic. Deficits can cause the government to borrow more, but increased government borrowing can only contribute to higher interest rates, which dampen home buying. Our problem was that interest rates were too low, and too many houses were being sold. Besides, if deficits caused the crisis, why has the Obama Administration increased deficits so dramatically?

Of course, the Obama Administration has argued that it is in the process of reducing deficits, but that assertion is highly misleading. To see why, consider the issue in three parts: What deficit did Obama inherit, what was the projected accumulated deficit for the next ten years, and what are deficits likely to be during his Administration?

In his January 2010 State of the Union speech Obama charged: "By the time I took office, we had a one-year deficit of over $1 trillion and projected deficits of $8 trillion over the next decade." The one-year deficit the president was referring to was fiscal year 2009, and the amount he cited was fairly close to actual. (It turned out to be $966 billion.) However, 2009 was a year shared by the Bush Administration and Obama's administration. That fiscal year ran from October 1, 2008 through September 30, 2009 (about 4 months of Bush's last year and 8 months of Obama's first year). The last entirely-Bush year was 2008, and in that year the deficit was $455 billion — an amount that is still very high. Nevertheless, it is disingenuous for Obama to state that he inherited a $1 trillion deficit, since it was largely created by his own administration.[1]

Regarding the 10-year projection of accumulated deficits, President Obama simply misstated the facts. According to the Congressional Budget Office, the 10-year projection of accumulated deficits was only $3.1 — not $8 trillion. Of course, that $3.1 trillion amount was the projected deficit when Obama first stepped into the Oval Office. A year or two after he became president the accumulated deficits were estimated to be almost $10 trillion, but by then those were Obama's deficits — not Bush's.

Despite this frightening estimate, President Obama claimed that, with his policies, "the deficit is cut in half" within 5 years. How is that

---

1   In addition, the final Bush deficit was a product of a Democratic House and Senate.

possible? With politicians, all things are possible. Refer to the Congressional Budget Office (CBO) numbers in Figure 22, below. By focusing on the projected amounts (right side of chart) we can see the estimated impact of Obama's budget. It has been crafted in such a way that, in one particular year — 2014 — the deficit should be about half of what it was in 2010. However, annual deficits increase sharply thereafter. Thus, the deficit *for one specific year*, and that year only, is expected to be about half of the deficit in the year with the all-time highest deficit — 2010 (Obama's first full year in office). Let's uncork the champagne!

Summarizing, President Obama was disingenuous in reporting the amount of deficit he inherited, flat-out wrong in is citing the amount of the projected accumulated deficits, and rather sneaky in citing a single, solitary year that was projected to have a relatively low deficit.

Figure 22 – Congressional Budget Office estimates of actual and projected deficits (as of March 2010)

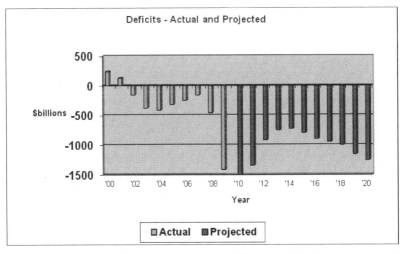

In truth, the President is not cutting deficits at all. He has increased and is increasing them dramatically. It is hard to believe that he would let deficits rise so sharply if he truly felt deficits caused the financial meltdown of 2007/08.

There is even better evidence suggesting that deficits did not cause the financial crisis. Let's concentrate on the years leading up to the financial crisis of 2007/08 (years 2004-2007 in Figure 22). The deficits in those years were large, but only a pittance compared to the projections for the Obama years. Further, the Bush deficits were decreasing steadily from 2004 through 2007. Given this trend, it seems unlikely that deficits caused the financial crisis. (But, if they did, we should expect an even greater housing crisis in the coming years.)

Was the problem deregulation, regulation, or something else?

> Obama nonetheless attacks President Bush's policies to "strip away regulation," without mentioning a single example. ... One alleged perpetrator, the Gramm-Leach-Bliley Act, was released without charges after the record revealed that Senator Joe Biden voted for it and Bill Clinton signed it into law.
>
> – Charles Calomiris, AEI, 2008

We have dismissed tax cuts and deficits as causes of the crisis. What about deregulation? There has been some deregulation, and it was a factor leading to the financial crisis. However, it is important to remember 3 relevant facts:

- Nearly all of the deregulation took place before the "last 8 years."
- All of it involved a bipartisan effort.
- The most egregious deregulation was — guess what? Another attempt to promote affordable housing.

The Merriam-Webster Online Dictionary defines "deregulation" as "the act or process of removing restrictions and regulations." About 30 years ago there were two major acts involving bank lending standards, and each met that definition of deregulation. The first was the Depository Institutions Deregulation and Monetary Control Act (DIDMCA).

DIDMCA was bipartisan legislation, signed by President Jimmy Carter in 1980, and was primarily an attempt to help the thrift industry (savings banks) by authorizing thrifts to offer checking accounts and other products previously reserved for commercial banks. The Act preempted state interest rate caps for loans (purchase or home equity) secured with the borrower's house, although states could overtly opt out of the federal guidelines. No federal interest rate limit was established, and this enabled lenders to set rates high enough to price the risk associated with borrowers with impaired credit. For this reason, DIDMCA could be considered the first major deregulation that opened the door to subprime lending. That said, I think it is sensible to allow lenders to adjust rates *to a degree* for risk. Otherwise, a person with low income and few assets (yet good credit history) would never get a loan.

AMTPA: Deregulation to promote affordable housing

A far more questionable piece of legislation was the Alternative Mort-gage Transaction Parity Act (AMTPA), which was part of the Garn-St. Germain Depository Institutions Act of 1982. Although AMTPA was signed by a Republican president (Reagan), it was a bi-partisan piece of legislation with broad support (272 in favor and 91 opposed in the House). It preempted sensible state restrictions on variable interest rates, balloon payments, and negative amortization (where the borrower pays no principal and does not even pay the full interest on the loan). The liberal loan features of AMTPA are those generally associated with sub-prime borrowers who don't have the financial capacity to meet regular (30-year, fixed rate) terms.

AMTPA was a mistake. As a CPA I have seen the way people can get confused by financial matters, and this is true whether we are talking about investments, auto leases, home mortgage loans, whatever. Further, people sometimes need to be protected from themselves. (I am proudly not a libertarian.) Our government should not be encouraging people to get into untenable financial arrangements.

The most interesting aspect of AMTPA is the motivation behind it. Why was it enacted and how was the legislation justified? It is hard to get a candid assessment now (post-crisis), but according to a HUD analysis prepared before the crisis (in 2002) by the center-left Urban Institute:

> [AMTPA's] intent was to increase the volume of loan products that re-duced the up-front costs to borrowers in order *to make homeownership more affordable* (emphasis added).[1]

Bingo! We have just learned an important lesson: Deregulation was used to promote affordable housing, just as regulation was used for the same purpose. Don't get hung up on whether there was regulation or deregulation: The issue is whether the government uses its resources and power to promote so-called "affordable housing" or to promote the soundness and fiscal integrity of financial institutions.

It sounds so noble to use government authority (regulation or deregu-lation) to increase access to housing, or for that matter education, jobs, etc., but such policies can have disastrous side effects. There are many in government and advocacy groups who are eager to take short-cuts to a solution, but those shortcuts usually involve a lowering of standards that leads to long-term problems. If there are too few women in college math

---

1   Temkin and Jennifer Johnson and Diane Levy, "Subprime Markets, the Role of GSEs and Risk-Based Pricing," 8.

programs, modify the math SAT tests until the right result is reached. If there are too few minorities on a police force, make police departments to change the minimum qualifications. And, if low-income people can't afford homes, have banks lower the underwriting standards. You get the picture.

Some might argue that the motivation for the Alternative Mortgage Transaction Parity Act (AMTPA) was not just affordable housing: It was also the promotion of the lending industry. Those critics would be absolutely correct. Most governmental programs have numerous corporate supporters because, in most cases, the United States government implements its programs via private businesses. Unfortunately, the involvement of private business makes it very easy for people to delude themselves regarding the ultimate, strategic responsibility for a government program. They might conclude that business is responsible because it received the related profits. However, if the government decides, for example, that we must send a man to Venus, and the project turns into a costly disaster, the blame goes to government — no matter how many private businesses made billions from the failed venture. Likewise, if pushing millions of unqualified borrowers into home loans was stupid, prime responsibility has to go to the government architects who encouraged that idea, even though many banks eagerly profited.

Possibly, AMTPA was the first major effort to promote affordable housing, but it did not push lenders into subprime lending; it merely made it possible. In 1992, ten years after AMTPA's enactment, the new Clinton Administration was not content to merely let subprime be possible: It drew up plans to persuade and, in some cases, compel lenders to give subprime loans. Those destructive efforts are thoroughly reviewed in Part One of this book.

It is interesting that many of the same analysts who blame AMTPA for permitting the use of more relaxed standards are totally silent with regard to the 1990s legislation and regulations that encouraged and even (in some cases) required the use of relaxed standards. Perhaps, these analysts are simply more ideologically opposed to deregulation than regulation. Or, perhaps, they prefer to ignore the possible transgressions of President Bill Clinton. Columnist Paul Krugman epitomizes the lack of objectivity that exists. In a piece called, "Reagan Did It," Krugman rails against the AMTPA, blaming it and Reagan for the financial debacle that ensued 25 years later. Krugman forgets the large number of Democrats who supported the legislation, and ignores the fact that a President can sign legislation but can't vote for it. He also overlooks the fact that, 10 years later, fellow Democrat Bill Clinton pressured banks to use the "flexible" AMTPA standards.

Financial Services Modernization Act (Gramm-Leach-Bliley)

> A MoveOn.org Political Action ad plays the partisan blame game with the economic crisis, charging that John McCain's friend and former economic adviser Phil Gramm "stripped safeguards that would have protected us." The claim is bogus. Gramm's legislation had broad bipartisan support and was signed into law by President Clinton. Moreover, the bill had nothing to do with causing the crisis, and economists — not to mention President Clinton — praise it for having softened the crisis.
>
> – FactCheck.org, October 1, 2008

The Financial Services Modernization Act of 1999, a.k.a. Gramm-Leach-Bliley (GLB), was enacted a year or two before Bush became President, was supported enthusiastically by President Bill Clinton, and had zero to do with the financial crisis. However, the lead sponsor was Phil Gramm, and he had served as a top economic advisor to Obama's rival, John McCain. For this reason (apparently), the Obama campaign made two deceptive claims regarding GLB: The legislation led to the financial crisis, and it was tied to the competing Presidential candidate, John McCain. Let's consider these two issues in order.

You have probably heard, many times, how GLB repealed the Depression-era Glass-Steagall Act and its requirement that commercial and investment banking be separated. Obama and his media supporters tried to make a case that, somehow, repeal of Glass-Steagall led to the subprime lending crisis. How it led to the crisis is never explained.

The allegations raised by Obama and Co. were logically problematic and, ultimately, repudiated. As noted in the dissenting opinion to the Congressional Oversight Panel for TARP, "a wide variety of experts across the political spectrum have dismissed that claim as 'a handy scapegoat' at best."[1] Alice M. Rivlin, who served as a deputy director of the Office of Management and Budget under Bill Clinton, said that GLB was a necessary piece of legislation because the separation of investment and commercial banking "...wasn't working very well."[2] Even Bill Clinton stated (in 2008): "I don't see that signing that bill had anything

---

1   Congressman Jeb Hensarling and Congressman John Sununu, "Joint Dissenting Views," ed. The Congressional Oversight Panel for the Troubled Asset Relief Program (United States of America, January 29, 2009), 58.
2   Ibid.

to do with the current crisis."[1] Some economists go further, stating that GLB attenuated the severity of the crisis by allowing healthy commercial banks (such as Bank of America) to merge with the less healthy investment banks (such as Merrill Lynch). Without GLB, a greater burden would have been placed on taxpayers.

As noted, Phil Gramm was an economic advisor to John McCain, so he was the key to the second Obama claim: GLB was partisan, Republican legislation. However, even the President's supporters were hesitant to go that far. The Washington Post stated:

> Mr. Obama said yesterday, "Phil Gramm, one of the architects of the deregulation in Washington that led directly to this mess on Wall Street, is also the architect of John McCain's economic plan." Would it be churlish to point out that another author of the Gramm-Leach-Bliley law is former congressman Jim Leach, a founder of Republicans for Obama? Or that Obama advisers Lawrence H. Summers and Robert E. Rubin supported the repeal, which was signed by President Bill Clinton?

Fair or not, the attack used by Obama was extremely successful in the weeks leading up to the 2008 election. Will historians stand in awe of Obama's political chutzpah, or will they laugh at it? I don't know. On the substance of the issue, however, the jury has already rendered its verdict: Gramm-Leach-Bliley was not a significant cause of the financial crisis. In a Wall Street Journal OP-Ed, two economists summarized the controversy this way:

> There has indeed been deregulation in our economy — in long-distance telephone rates, airline fares, securities brokerage and trucking, to name just a few — and this has produced much innovation and lower consumer prices. But the primary "deregulation" in the financial world in the last 30 years permitted banks to diversify their risks geographically and across different products, which is one of the things that has kept banks relatively stable in this storm.[2]

The Commodity Futures Modernization Act (CFMA)

As noted in Chapter 13, the CFMA was enacted with bipartisan support and little controversy. Prominent Democrats praised the legislation as well as its sponsors. President Clinton's Working Group on Financial Markets even wrote a letter stating that its members "strongly support ...

---

1   Ibid.
2   Calomiris, "Blame Fannie Mae and Congress for the Credit Mess."

this important legislation...."[1] President Clinton promptly signed the legislation without reservations.

After the financial crisis began, things changed. Democrats asserted that the CFMA deregulated credit default Swaps (CDSs), and blocked states from regulating CDSs. Specifically, the critics blamed CFMA for the failure of the SEC to regulate the London subsidiary of AIG, which sold credit default swaps on a massive scale, and created huge losses that led to a taxpayer bailout. For these reasons, however, the facts do not support the Democratic claims:

- The legislation did not change the regulation of CDSs: It merely created a legal "safe harbor" for the treatment already in effect.

- It is doubtful that the states would have had jurisdiction over the London subsidiary, and it is clear that they had no intention of applying antiquated "gambling and bucket shop" laws. Likewise, there is no indication that any state planned to subject AIG's CDS operations to regulation as insurance.

- AIG's London subsidiary was, in fact, regulated by the Office of Thrift Supervision (OTS) as a part of the larger AIG holding company. Testimony of the OTS Acting Director, Scott Polakoff, established that OTS had the authority and felt it had the resources to regulate the London enterprise. Like everyone else, however, these regulators simply did not discern the dangerous systemic risks.

Thus, it is hard to credibly assert that the CFMA was a cause of the financial crisis of 2007/08. I do believe, however, that it aggravated the situation by providing the legal clarification that accelerated the growth of the credit default swap industry.

The 2004 SEC amendments to the net capital rule

We put this one to bed in Chapter 17. There was no deregulation of the big 5 investment banks, and no substantive change in leverage restrictions. That was the early spin put out by many "learned" people who simply parroted untruths without checking the facts. For the most part, the mainstream press has allowed those misstatements to stay unchallenged and uncorrected in the historical record.

---

1   Sarbanes, "Submission of Letter from the President's Working Group," S11946.

Here is a summary of key points related to the 2004 amendments, quoting the exact words of Erik R. Sirri, a former official with the Securities and Exchange Commission (SEC):

> First, and most importantly, the Commission did not undo any leverage restrictions in 2004. ...
>
> [T]he Commission effectively added an additional layer of supervision at the holding company where none had existed previously. ...
>
> The $5 billion minimum amount was comparative to the amount of tentative net capital they maintained prior to the 2004 amendments. It was designed to ensure that the use of models to compute haircuts would not substantially change the amount of capital maintained by the broker-dealers. ...
>
> [T]he "12-to-1" restriction was not even affected by the 2004 amendments. Moreover, even if it had been eliminated, the CSE broker-dealers would not have been impacted because they had been using a different financial ratio since the late 1970s.[1]

Sirri's views are shared by Andrew Lo and Mark Mueller. The MIT professors studied the issue and reported on its misreporting by various scholars:

> [I]t turns out that the 2004 SEC amendment to Rule 15c3-1 did nothing to change the leverage restrictions of these financial institutions.[2]

The relationship between the 2004 SEC amendments and the financial crisis has been grossly distorted. Rest assured, however, that the historical record will soon be corrected — when Michael Moore produces his next "documentary."

The mixed record of the Bush Administration

> [W]e have a problem here in America because fewer than half of the Hispanics and half the African Americans own [a] home. ... I set an ambitious goal. It's one that I believe we can achieve. It's a clear goal, that by the end of this decade we'll increase the number of minority homeowners by at least 5.5 million families.
>
> – President George W. Bush, courting minority voters in 2002

There is nothing in the historical record to indicate that Bush deregulated anything related to the crisis. That said, his Administration is not

---

1 Sirri, "Speech on Securities Markets and Regulatory Reform."
2 Lo and Mark T. Mueller, "Warning: Physics Envy May Be Hazardous to Your Wealth!."

without blame. The Bush Administration has culpability with respect to the financial crisis because it continued and substantially expanded the destructive affordable housing policies initiated during the Clinton years. Under Bush, HUD pressured Fannie and Freddie with unreasonably high affordable housing lending targets. In response, Fannie and Freddie lowered the standards for the loans and securities they bought, and this encouraged lenders to make subprime loans.

In the Bush years the subprime loan frenzy reached its zenith. It seems that the Administration was blind to the systemic threat, until it was too late. It did little to improve underwriting standards or to curtail subprime lending.

On the other hand, the Bush Administration made some positive efforts that are rarely mentioned. These efforts include a failed attempt to rein in the excesses of Fannie and Freddie. Here are some of the major and minor Bush initiatives (I bet you haven't heard of them):

In 2003, Bush attempted to tackle real estate transaction "markups," which are extra fees tacked onto closing costs by the broker (e.g., credit report costs broker $15 but he charges borrower $65.):

> In a controversial move, the Bush Administration is taking an aggressive, hardball approach to real estate transaction cost "markups" nationwide. Despite appellate court defeats in three federal court districts covering 15 states, the government says it plans to investigate and prosecute real estate-related markups in all 50 states.

– Kenneth Harney, Realty Times, October 20, 2003

The Bush Administration tried to weed out unscrupulous appraisers, as reported in November 2003.

> Despite bitter opposition from appraisers, federal housing officials last week inaugurated a controversial new electronic monitoring system called Appraiser Watch that's designed to spot appraisers who inflate valuations on FHA-insured home mortgages. Appraisers cited by the system face termination from the agency's roster of approved appraisers — effectively putting them out of the FHA loan business — and civil penalties.

– Kenneth Harney, Realty Times, November 3, 2003

In the early years of the Bush Administration, consumers were offered, for the first time, free credit reports and "risk-based pricing" alerts.

> ...under the risk-based pricing reform, every time a home buyer or other credit applicant receives less-than-the-best-available quote on interest rates or terms because of an electronic underwriting system, the lender will need to provide a disclosure.

– Kenneth Harney, Realty Times, December 22, 2003

In 2004, Bush clamped down on mortgage companies that pressured appraisers to inflate values.

> The Bush Administration has sent a shot across the bow of mortgage lenders who attempt to influence or pressure appraisers to inflate home valuations or ignore property defects. ... [H]ousing secretary Alphonso Jackson says the government will now penalize lenders who knew — or should have known — that the appraiser they hired submitted an intentionally inaccurate valuation on a home.

– Kenneth Harney, Realty Times, August 9, 2004

In 2006, Bush signed the Credit Rating Agency Reform Act, which gave the SEC new authority to inspect credit-rating agencies.

> The law is designed to curb alleged abusive practices cited by members of Congress and corporate trade groups, including the practice of sending a company unsolicited ratings with a bill; notching, which occurs when a firm lowers ratings on asset-backed securities unless the firm rates a substantial portion of the underlying assets; and tying ratings to the purchase of additional services.

– Marie Leone, CFO.com[1]

The most important initiative of the Bush Administration concerned Fannie and Freddie — the two entities bailed out with more U.S. taxpayer bucks than anyone else. The plan was described by the New York Times in 2003:

> The Bush administration today recommended the most significant regulatory overhaul in the housing finance industry since the savings and loan crisis a decade ago.

> Under the plan, disclosed at a Congressional hearing today, a new agency would be created within the Treasury Department to assume supervision of Fannie Mae and Freddie Mac, the government sponsored companies that are the two largest players in the mortgage lending industry.

> The new agency would have the authority, which now rests with Congress, to set one of the two capital-reserve requirements for the companies. It would exercise authority over any new lines of business. And it would determine whether the two are adequately managing the risks of their ballooning portfolios.[2]

1   Marie Leone, "Bush Signs Rating Agency Reform Act," CFO.com (October 2, 2006), http://www.cfo.com/article.cfm/7991492.

2   Stephen Labaton, "New Agency Proposed to Oversee Freddie Mac and Fannie Mae," The New York Times (September 1, 2003), http://www.ny-

This plan could have gone a long way towards diminishing the funding of subprime loans that took place after 2003. But, the Bush efforts went nowhere after being blocked by Democratic congressional opposition. The problem? Democrats saw the regulations as a potential constraint on affordable housing. Said Representative Barney Frank:

> These two entities — Fannie Mae and Freddie Mac — are not facing any kind of financial crisis. The more people exaggerate these problems, the more pressure there is on these companies, the less we will see in terms of *affordable housing* (emphasis added).[1, 2]

Another Democratic Congressman, Melvin Watt of North Carolina, opined that the Bush regulations would lead to "weakening the bargaining power of poorer families and their ability to get *affordable housing*" (emphasis added).[3]

This Democratic opposition ended the last best chance to head off the financial crisis that was going to erupt just a few years later. As expected, the opposition to GSE reform by Democrats was criticized by Republicans. However, it was even criticized by President Bill Clinton in an interview with ABC News in 2008:

> I think the responsibility the Democrats have may rest more in resisting any efforts by Republicans in the Congress or by me when I was president to put some standards and tighten up a little on Fannie Mae and Freddie Mac.[4]

Class warfare politics

> To frame the debate as one of rich-and-entitled versus poor-and-dispossessed is to both miss the point and further inflame an already incendiary environment. It is also a naked, political pander to some of the basest human emotions — a

---

times.com/2003/09/11/business/new-agency-proposed-to-oversee-freddie-mac-and-fannie-mae.html?pagewanted=all&src=pm.

1   As cited by Ed Morrissey, "Whose Policies Led to the Credit Crisis?," (September 16, 2008), http://hotair.com/archives/2008/09/16/whose-policies-led-to-the-credit-crisis/.

2   To his credit, Congressman Frank later acknowledged that he had been too trusting with regard to Fannie and Freddie. In 2010 he stated to Lawrence Kudlow, "It was a great mistake to push lower-income people into housing they couldn't afford and couldn't really handle once they had it. I had been too sanguine about Fannie and Freddie."

3   Morrissey, "Whose Policies Led to the Credit Crisis?."

4   "Editorial: In Bed with Fannie and Freddie," The Washington Times (May 10, 2010), http://www.washingtontimes.com/news/2010/may/10/in-bed-with-fannie-and-freddie/.

strategy, as history teaches, that never ends well for anyone but totalitarians and anarchists.

 – Leon Cooperman, CEO of Omega Advisors (hedge fund)[1]

A major thesis of this book is my contention that government policies, originating in the 1990s, were primarily responsible for the financial crisis of 2007/08. That said, there are many analysts who believe the crisis started years later, on Wall Street. I disagree with that viewpoint, but respect the sincerity of those who make the argument. Indeed, it is undeniable that banks, mortgage companies, rating agencies, and other private entities were major factors contributing to the crisis.

During his presidency, and especially in the months preceding the 2012 presidential election, President Obama frequently made references to "the breathtaking greed of a few,"[2] while demanding that "big corporate interests play by the rules."[3] He said that the "rules are rigged" for middle class families and that he wants to "restore balance, restore fairness."[4] I can respect these comments and criticisms — provided they are supported with specifics, tied to facts, and stated unambiguously. For the most part this is not the case.

Are the President's charges supported with facts?

At the beginning of this chapter we addressed some of the factual misstatements made by the President. Those misstatements pertained to the size of deficits and their role in the crisis, the amount of deregulation and when it took place (and by whom), and the size and distribution of "tax cuts" (actually, tax rate cuts).

I could cite additional misstatements, but they are beyond the scope of this book because they relate to other issues. For example, does big oil really receive public "subsidies," or does it simply get the normal de-

1   as cited by Gary Bauer, "Obama's Class Warfare May Backfire as Big Business and Workers Team Up," Human Events.com, http://www.humanevents. com/article.php?id=47936.

2   As cited by Michael Kinsley, "When Obama's Music Stops, Class Warfare Starts," (December 8, 2011), http://www.bloomberg.com/news/2011-12-09/ when-obama-s-music-stops-class-warfare-starts-michael-kinsley.html.

3   "Obama Hits Republicans, Wall Street in Populist Speech," (December 7, 2011), http://us.mobile.reuters.com/article/politicsNews/ idUSTRE7B527620111207?irpc=932.

4   As cited by Karl Rove, "Obama Can't Win with Crude Class Warfare in 2012," (December 22, 2011), http://us.mobile.reuters.com/article/politicsNews/ idUSTRE7B527620111207?irpc=932.

preciation and depletion tax deductions every business gets in order to properly compute net taxable income? Did big health care insurers really drop people simply because they got sick, as claimed by the President, or did they drop a finite and specific group of named individuals who were found to be committing fraud?[1] Does Warren Buffet's secretary earn a typical secretary's salary or something higher than the salary paid to many executives? And, is her tax rate higher than Buffet's due to the inclusion of Social Security and Medicare "taxes"?[2] Without walking into the weeds of each of these issues, let me simply state that the President shoots fast and from the hip.

Yes. He is promoting class warfare.

I can't prove that the President deliberately misstates the facts, but it can be demonstrated that this president, who ran for office as a "uniter," is deliberately promoting dishonest and divisive class warfare. The evidence is in the repeated conflation of high earners with alleged crooks and scoundrels. That is inexcusable, cannot be accidental, and can only lead to class envy and hatred. The tendency of Obama to ambiguously conflate wealthy innocents with the guilty is well-described by Michael Kinsley of Bloomberg:

> My problem with Obama's speech is that the president muddles together a variety of very different categories. There are out-and-out crooks and shysters. There are clever financiers who manipulated the rules and took advantage of loopholes — and ought to be thoroughly ashamed of themselves — but did nothing illegal. There are the very, very rich — the notorious 1 percent, or 1 percent of 1 percent — who have benefited from changes in the economy that they may or may not have had any control over.[3]

Kinsley's point is that it is not a sin to be wealthy, and it is wrong to mix those people with crooks, charlatans, and thieves. Yet, that is what Obama does — often. Interestingly, the President has nothing but praise

---

1 This subject has been grossly distorted in the press. In June, 2009, executives of three large health insurers testified before a House committee, and were asked about customers who were dropped because they had become ill. The insurers agreed that a specific list of about 20,000 customers had been dropped, but only after careful investigation revealed that they had made material and often fraudulent misstatements on their insurance applications.

2 A fair comparison requires the use of net social security and Medicare taxes — taxes paid net of estimated benefits to be received. If taxes were computed using the net amounts it is unlikely that the secretary would be paying a higher tax rate than Buffet.

3 Kinsley, "When Obama's Music Stops, Class Warfare Starts."

for the great middle class, which he seems to define as nearly everyone falling below the top 1 percent. That is an interesting definition of "middle class," and it makes for great politics also.

This country, and most of the world, has suffered greatly from the financial crisis of 2007/08. Let us not compound the suffering by promoting divisiveness and resentment between the classes. Perhaps it is my conservatism speaking, but I find the promotion of class divisions to be just as odious as the promotion of racial divisions, gender divisions, or ethnic divisions. And, when it is done for political purposes, it is particularly egregious.

Conclusion

We can hardly blame Candidate Barack Obama for utilizing the good campaign fodder that was handed to him on a silver platter. Any Republican would have done the same. However, his allegations regarding taxes, deficits, and regulations are not supported by the facts. In addition, his ongoing class warfare rhetoric is beneath the dignity of the presidency.

George W. Bush did not commit the many sins described by his successor; however, he is culpable. Bush bought into and promoted the affordable housing policies started by his predecessor, and he failed to clearly see the growing threat from subprime lending.

On the other hand, the Bush Administration did initiate some positive actions that are rarely reported. These included the investigation of real estate brokers for excessive fees, the initiation of a controversial electronic monitoring program to regulate appraisers, and the signing of the Credit Rating Agency Reform Act of 2006, which gave SEC authority to inspect rating agencies. Bush's most important initiative was a proposal, in 2003, to create a new agency (within Treasury) that would monitor Fannie and Freddie with regard to their capital reserves and new lines of business. If implemented, this plan might have significantly reduced the funding of subprime loans. The effort was blocked in Congress.

Addendum A: Overview

> U.S. housing policies are the root cause of the current
> financial crisis. Other players — "greedy" investment bankers;
> foolish investors; imprudent bankers; incompetent rating
> agencies; irresponsible housing speculators; shortsighted
> homeowners; and predatory mortgage brokers, lenders, and
> borrowers — all played a part, but they were only following
> the economic incentives that government policy laid out for
> them.
>
> – Peter J. Wallison, American Enterprise Institute

In the years preceding the financial crisis of 2007-08, there was "sharp relative growth" in lending to people within subprime zip codes. This was followed by a "sharp relative increase in defaults" in those same zip codes. The researchers who reached these conclusions, Atif Mian and Amir Sufi, found this pattern to be "prevalent in almost every city in the U.S." They added:

> These facts demonstrate that any study seeking to understand the origins
> of the mortgage default crisis must explain the expansion of mortgage
> credit to subprime neighborhoods across the entire county.[1]

I agree. If we are to understand the origins of the financial crisis, the unprecedented expansion of credit to subprime borrowers must be analyzed and understood.

If we could take subprime lending out of the equation, all other factors contributing to the crisis would become relatively unimportant. Se-

---

1   Mian and Amir Sufi, "The Consequences of Mortgage Credit Expansion:
     Evidence from the U.S. Mortgage Default Crisis," 1449-96.

curitization would matter little because securities would not be laced with defaulting loans. Low interest rates would create a housing bubble, but it would be much smaller and more easily resolved. Complex mort-gage-backed securities would make the foreclosure process more diffi-cult, but the number of foreclosures would be relatively few. And, low capital reserves would not matter because investment banks and Fannie and Freddie would have far less need to tap those capital reserves. In short, the influx of subprime homeowner/borrowers caused much of the housing bubble, most of the subsequent defaults, and most of the fore-closure complications.

Many claim that the private banking sector, in and outside of the United States, was primarily responsible for the subprime lending, and it is true that many lenders and investment banks acted recklessly. In the years immediately preceding the crisis, Wall Street firms enthusias-tically bundled risky subprime loans into complex securities. However, the origin of subprime lending can be clearly traced to United States governmental policy. Federal legislation, enacted in 1992, mandated that Fannie Mae and Freddie Mac purchase huge numbers of "afford-able housing" loans, and the legislation put HUD in charge of enforcing those mandates. At first, the required targets (30 percent of Fannie's and Freddie's loan purchases) were reasonably attainable. Before long, how-ever, HUD increased the goals substantially (to as high as 56 percent in 2008). To meet the stringent, HUD-imposed affordable housing goals, the two huge companies began to soften their loan standards dramati-cally. After that, many of the "prime" loans purchased by F&F were actu-ally subprime.

HUD did not limit its affordable housing agenda to Fannie and Fred-die. In 1995 it published a *Strategy* that vigorously promoted affordable housing among governmental entities at the federal, state and local levels. The *Strategy* also included private banks and local housing activists. As a result, all of these groups began a quest to make housing more affordable and accessible. Subprime lending was the primary tool used to do this.

The quest for affordable housing turned into a direct assault on loan underwriting standards — for people at all income levels and in all neighborhoods. This is a key point, and a source of confusion. Some people think it is wrong (even mean-spirited) to blame affordable hous-ing programs because there have been many foreclosures in neighbor-hoods with very expensive homes — not the kind of homes associated with affordable housing programs. However, it was impossible to loosen underwriting standards for people with marginal credit while maintaining rigorous standards for people with good credit histories. Affordable housing policies led to a degrading of underwriting standards for loans of all sizes. Before long, people who could afford $400,000 homes were stretching to buy $700,000 homes. Effectively, these people became subprime borrowers, relative to the size and terms of their mortgage loans.

Affordable housing activists in and out of government weren't trying to destroy sensible banking practices, and they certainly did not want to create a subprime mortgage loan crisis. They just wanted banks and Fannie and Freddie to make some underwriting exceptions for people living in certain neighborhoods, and for those with below-median incomes. They wanted to end discrimination and so-called "red-lining."[1]

People in HUD,[2] in some state and local agencies, and in community groups like ACORN thought lenders should give loans to people with lower-than-normal credit (FICO) scores. They believed bankers should accept smaller down payments and, in some cases, they felt these down payments should be "gifted" to the borrower or take the form of "sweat equity" instead of hard cash.[3] This is not speculation: It was all laid out in a 1995-era HUD "*Strategy*" document (discussed in great detail in Chapter 1).

Lenders were asked, and in some cases warned, to be more flexible with regard to loan applicants. This could be done safely, activists theorized. Of course, if lenders could safely make underwriting exceptions for borrowers who were below-average credit risks, they could surely make those same exceptions — safely — for borrowers who were good credit risks. In other words, the exceptions were not really exceptions at all: They were for everybody.

Fannie and Freddie (F&F) got into the act by creating new, easy-to-qualify automated underwriting (AU) systems that were significantly more likely to give a "thumbs up" to shaky new borrowers (Chapter 2). To make matters worse, they distributed the easy-to-qualify, AU systems to tens of thousands of tiny, inexperienced mortgage brokers, even after they realized that those brokers were associated with predatory prac-

---

1 Redlining is defined by the Merriam-Webster online dictionary as the withholding of "home-loan funds or insurance from neighborhoods considered poor economic risks."
2 The United States Department of Housing and Urban Development
3 A down payment in the form of "Sweat equity" would be a promise by the borrower to make improvements to the home, in lieu of the normal cash down payment he would, otherwise, be required to pay.

tices and high default rates (Chapter 7). If lenders wanted to sell their loans to F&F, they were required to use these easy-approval systems.

The particular underwriting standard most despised by housing activists was the down payment. It was seen as Shylock's tool of discrimination, rather than a prudent requirement. Equity in newly-purchased and refinanced homes became razor-thin as down payments were reduced and eliminated.

Home equity balances were further depleted after F&F rolled out new AVMs — Automated Valuation Models (Chapter 3). The Zillow-like AVMs undermined traditional, onsite home appraisals, and led to unrealistically high valuations. When those inflated valuations were coupled with the tiny down payments, the result was a financial house of cards ready to collapse.

Private lenders got the message. It was now OK — even good — to loosen loan standards. If you have doubts about this, review the words of the trench-level loan officers who worked during the subprime heydays (see Chapter 1). They confirm that subprime originated with do-gooder bureaucrats within the U.S. government and within its progeny — Fannie and Freddie.

Although private lenders were encouraged and sometimes even coerced to issue subprime loans, it is likely that many of them simply used the government's advocacy for affordable housing as a convenient excuse to engage in risky but profitable lending. Those lenders deserve our scorn, but the government did the initiating and encouraging, and gave a bright "green light" (or an excuse, if you prefer) for this risky activity. Instead of regulating against subprime lending, as it should have, the U.S. government advocated for it.

Before long banks were competing with each other in a vicious cycle of lower and lower lending requirements. The result was that millions of people were allowed to buy homes they could not afford. This is not a problem easily undone. Millions of subprime borrowers can't or won't become good credit risks overnight — or ever. And, house values are not going to magically return to those inflated values of yesteryear. In other words, we're screwed.

There is an alternative theory. According to President Obama and many liberals, subprime lending was largely the result of the Bush Administration policies — primarily its alleged deregulation of lenders and investment banks. Initially, Bush was charged with committing two deregulatory sins: the Financial Services Modernization Act of 1999 (a.k.a. "Gramm-Leach-Bliley") and the Commodity Futures Modernization Act of 2000. However, these Acts were signed into law by Bill Clinton (enthusiastically). Another indictment against Bush would be needed.

A new theory asserted that the greedy ways of Wall Street were unleashed in 2004 when Bush's Securities and Exchange Commission (SEC) allowed investment banks to dramatically increase leverage ratios — from as little as 8-to-1 to more than 40-to-1. The New York Times and many others pushed that line of reasoning, but, when the story was debunked, they couldn't find space to print the retractions. You probably haven't heard the whole story, so I present it in Chapter 17.

Although Bush didn't deregulate anything, he deserves no medal for his performance. He did succeed in strengthening a few sensible lending regulations (page 293), but the one Bush initiative that might have curtailed the crisis (his effort to clamp down on Fannie and Freddie) was killed by Democratic opposition — *and Republican lack of resolve.*

When Democrats say that there should have been more regulation of the banks, they usually mean the banks should have been required to keep more of their money on reserve. Perhaps they are right, but the bank regulations most needed were entirely different. Those regulations would have focused on the "capital reserves" of the borrower. What money does she have in the bank? How much cash can he give as a down payment?[1]

The dog who did not bark

The issue of regulation brings us to another, broader point: It is not enough to merely describe loony advocacy that promoted destructive subprime lending (e.g., the NACA protestors throwing trash on the front lawn of a banker's home because his bank did not lend enough to losers). Like Sherlock Holmes and the curious incident of the dog who did not bark, we must also take notice of the things that have *not* been heard, and *not* been done. Namely, Dear Watson, no one, inside or outside of government, advocated the use of regulations to ensure prudent bank underwriting standards. To many people, banks were just a bunch of rich guys who could be used to carry out social engineering and wealth-shifting schemes. Until recently, it was assumed that banks were wealthy enough to handle any type of lending, no matter how imprudent. The near-death of the golden goose was not contemplated.

---

1   To be perfectly accurate, until the crisis occurred, liberals did not advocate regulations of any kind – except those related to so-called predatory lending, which is discussed in Chapter 11. The liberal calls for increased bank capital reserves did not materialize until the financial crisis was underway.

Let's envision what would have happened if the government had actively promoted tough underwriting standards instead of weaker ones. Imagine greeneyeshade regulators, testing bank loans to make sure down payments were actually made by the borrowers — in cash and in amounts equal to no less than 10 percent of the loan balances. Visualize the regulators testing those loans to see if FICO credit scores were at least 660 (the traditional division point between prime and subprime borrowers), and testing loanrelated documents (such as W2 statements) for authenticity. And, what if regulators testchecked loan files to ensure that borrowers could verify income levels sufficient to pay mortgages based on the fullyindexed (vs. "teaser") interest rates? Where were those government regulators?

Let's put some regulatory teeth behind our imaginary tough underwriting standards (as the Community Reinvestment Act did with its looser standards). Assume that lenders found to be deficient in maintaining prudent underwriting standards would be denied the right to add branches or ATM machines, and would be denied the right to expand through merger. Assume that community activists, such as ACORN, could delay or even block expansion plans of banks that didn't maintain the tough lending standards. Further assume that those same activists could threaten lawsuits, boycotts, and protests if prudent bank standards were not maintained. Finally, suppose that our imaginary regulators would not permit Fannie and Freddie, the main purchasers of bank loans, to do business with lenders who didn't maintain prudent lending standards.

What would have happened? Nothing! There would have been no subprime mortgage crisis of 200708 because the frenzy to lower underwriting standards would not have even started. The boom in housing prices would have been a small bump, and there would not be millions of rotten loans entangled within the mortgagebacked securities that have been sold all over the world. Government advocacy does matter, and it is disingenuous to now pretend otherwise.

Terror by (mid) Night

Do you recall the outcry over John Yoo, the White House attorney who gave an opinion to President George W. Bush about the legality of torture? Liberal veins were popping because, supposedly, Yoo's legal opinion directly led to the midnight abuses at Abu Ghraib — even though his opinion was not even known by the Abu Ghraib miscreants (details ... details). Supposedly, Yoo's memo was the equivalent of a "green light" to abuse. But, if the mere expression of a confidential legal opinion is a green light to torture, how would you characterize these statements and their relationship to risky lending among private bankers and brokers?

- In the year 2000, the Boston Federal Reserve reminded lenders that Fannie and Freddie would give borrowers credit for "welfare payments, and unemployment benefits" when estimating their income capacity. In other words, don't turn down these borrowers: Uncle Sam wants them.
- In that same year, the Boston Fed told lenders that "Lack of [borrower] credit history should not be seen as a negative factor." Really?
- Franklin Raines, Fannie's CEO, told mortgage brokers they "need to learn the best from the subprime market...." (San Francisco, 2004)
- Since the 1990s, HUD has repeatedly advocated that low-income families be allowed to substitute "sweat equity" for cash down payments. (Sweat equity is a promise by the borrower to improve or maintain his home, or the home of someone else.)
- HUD had (and has, last time I checked) this question and answer on its Web site:

"Question. Can I become a homebuyer even if I have had bad credit, and don't have much for a down payment?

"Answer. You may be a good candidate for one of the federal mortgage programs...."

"Affordable Gold 100s" — not cigarettes, but nearly as deadly

The growth of subprime lending was encouraged by reckless statements by government officials. Much more damaging, however, was the fact that Fannie and Freddie (government-backed entities) were deliberately and massively buying subprime loans and securities backed by subprime loans. Several erudite economists deny it, but this fact was confirmed by an email produced at hearings before the House Committee on Oversight and Government Reform in 2008. In that email a top deputy of Fannie told Fannie's CEO, Daniel H. Mudd that "banks were modeling their subprime mortgages to what Fannie was *buying*" (emphasis added). How bright is that green light?

We have much more than an email telling us that Fannie and Freddie were buying subprime loans in massive quantities. A quantified analysis has been prepared, and it contains the kind of sourced and reasonable estimates and quantifications that a CPA, such as myself, can respect. The analysis, prepared by Edward Pinto (former Chief Credit Officer for Fannie Mae in 1987-89), shows that, as of June 2008, Fannie and Freddie held about 12 million subprime loans with a dollar value over $1.8 trillion. His definition of "subprime" and his methodology are outlined, starting on page 92. Although the estimates made by Pinto are massive, they are smaller than the estimates subsequently made by the Securities and Exchange Commission (SEC). As part of its securities fraud case against 6 former executives of Fannie and Freddie, the SEC charged that, at June 30, 2008, Fannie and Freddie s held about 13 million subprime (or similar) loans with a face value of over $2 trillion. F&F made sure that lenders knew of their desire to buy subprime loans. Interviews show that lenders were keenly aware of Fannie's and Freddie's preferences, and very much influenced by them (Chapter 1).

As discussed in Chapter 7, Fannie and Freddie promoted subprime lenders over traditional (and responsible) banks, and they even designed many of the subprime loans offered by the banks. The "Freddie Mac 100" mortgage loan was already in place by 2000 (years before the crisis), and it required a down payment of exactly zero. It was designed to alleviate "the largest barrier to homeownership," which was, according to Freddie, a lack of funds for a down payment. Later, Freddie added the "Affordable Gold 100" loan, which created another milestone in the sad saga of subprime lending. The Gold 100 required a down payment of zero — plus closing costs of zero. All you needed was a smile and a warm spot in your heart for the bureaucrats dumb enough to promote this product. But, Freddie didn't stop there. Freddie's 105 percent loan (yes, a loan that was 5 percent larger than the house was worth) took us boldly (and stupidly) where no man had gone before. Fannie Mae designed loan products that were just as irresponsible.

Conservative wisdom from ... Canada??

When evaluating the impact of subprime lending, it is instructive to study the country just north of the United States. Canada fared relatively well in the financial crisis; it largely avoided it until being ensnared in the world-wide recession. Here are a few reasons. Canada had tougher down payment requirements. Writing for the Federal Reserve Bank of Cleveland, James MacGee notes: "the fact that the government mandated mortgage insurance for high LTV loans issued by Canadian banks effectively made it impossible for banks to offer certain subprime products."[1] Such a law would have been contrary to the affordable housing goals promoted in the United States, and would have been opposed by groups such as NACA, the late ACORN, or any of the other 600 housing activist entities, who pushed mightily to reduce or eliminate down payments, or replace them with so-called "sweat equity."

Here is some more conservative common sense from the land of Lorne Greene and Alex Trebek. In Canada, defaulting on a loan is much more difficult than it is in the United States. "You can't just drop off the keys and walk away," according to Michael Gregory, an economist at BMO Nesbitt Burns, and investment company. Because Canada does not have nonrecourse lending rules such as those in the U.S., "Strategic defaulting is not an attractive option." If you have the money you have to make the payments. (The nonrecourse lending problem is discussed in Chapter 18.)

James MacGee (cited above) notes that "The Canadian market lacks a counterpart to Freddie Mac and Fannie Mae, both of which played a significant role in the growth of securitization in the U.S." He might have added that Canada did not have massive organizations like Freddie and Fannie, trolling for subprime loans and over-stimulating the mortgage loan market with reckless purchases and policies. Indeed, there has never been a major push for affordable housing in Canada.

And, here is a good one. "Canadian fixed-rate mortgages generally come with anti-refinancing prepayment penalties to protect lenders from interest rate drops, and the mortgage interest rates on these loans are fixed for a maximum of five years...." In the U.S., this is known as "predatory lending," but in Canada it is called, "common sense." Think about it: T-Mobile, Verizon, et al. will give you a free phone if you sign an extended contract — usually two years. But, what happens if you terminate the contract early? You get a penalty — of course.[2]

---

1 James MacGee, "Why Didn't Canada's Housing Market Go Bust?", Economic Commentary (December 2, 2009), http://www.clevelandfed.org/research/commentary/2009/0909.cfm

2 Perhaps, liberals in the Federal Communications Commission will someday issue regulations forbidding the cell phone companies from issuing those penalties. That way, the U.S. can have a communications crisis to go along with its financial crisis.

The government and its advocacy of affordable housing

Some analysts might argue that I have exaggerated the impact that affordable housing programs had on the crisis. They would probably defend the Community Reinvestment Act (CRA) vigorously, noting that banks were never *required* to give unsafe loans. They might also defend the affordable housing programs of Fannie Mae and Freddie Mac, pointing out that private sector loan securitizations had worse delinquency rates than the securitizations of Fannie and Freddie. These exonerations of affordable housing programs would be misguided. As I describe in detail, the government and its sponsored entities (Fannie and Freddie) did not merely advocate lending to people with moderate and low incomes. Beginning in the 1990s, they directly lobbied for a degradation of underwriting standards in order to ensure that those targeted borrowers got loans.

Later, Fannie and Freddie began to buy subprime loans in massive amounts, and banks that wanted to sell their loans had to deal with them. Fannie and Freddie effectively forced lenders to use their automated underwriting and appraisal systems, which eliminated many time-tested and prudent standards. And, to the dismay of traditional community banks, Fannie and Freddie distributed those automated systems to thousands of tiny, untested mortgage brokers, many of whom had problematic pasts. The support for affordable housing — ostensibly a good thing — became support for sloppy, substandard underwriting methods, and in many cases, this attack on underwriting standards was supported by community activist goon squads and misguided state and local governments (such as California and San Francisco).

Big investment banks were, of course, a large part of the problem, and those "Wall Street" banks bundled up many of the worst subprime loans into the securities that they peddled around the world. But to say Wall Street started the crisis, as many analysts do, is to ignore the guerilla campaign waged during the preceding ten years. Some banks were influenced by the cajoling and noisy threats; others were, no doubt, persuaded by the knowledge that their junky securities could be profitably sold to Fannie, Freddie, or others. Some big-wig lenders, such as Countrywide's Angelo Mozilo, seemed to sincerely believe in the affordable housing doctrine. Whatever the motive, a review of the chronology makes one thing clear: The shift to subprime lending standards was initiated in the early to mid-1990s by governmental agencies and by community activists. To dismiss the importance of those early years of subprime development because worse subprime was later developed would be like calling the U.S. Manhattan Project "insignificant" because much, much larger nuclear bombs were later developed. The 1940s gave birth to the nuclear bomb, and the 1990s gave birth to subprime. The mother of subprime — the attack on underwriting standards — was carried out by leftists in the name of affordable housing.

Finally, is there anyone who seriously doubts that subprime lending — the troubled step child of affordable housing — was the leading factor in causing and perpetuating the financial crisis? If so, he or she should consider the detailed research performed by professors Atif Mian and Amir Sufi. After performing a within-county analysis using zip code-level data they reached the following conclusions:

> The recent sharp increase in mortgage defaults is significantly amplified in subprime zip codes, or zip codes with a disproportionately large share of subprime borrowers as of 1996. *Prior to the default crisis, these subprime zip codes experience[d] an unprecedented relative growth in mortgage credit* (emphasis added).[1]

The authors of the study note that this unprecedented expansion in subprime credit, which took place from 2002 to 2005, occurred "despite sharply declining relative (and in some cases absolute) income growth in these neighborhoods." According to Mian and Sufi, this was "the only period in the last eighteen years when income and mortgage credit growth are negatively correlated."

Many analysts, including some Bush Administration officials, cited the housing boom as a sign of a strong economy. The work of Mian and Sufi shows that opinion to be foolish: The boom was a sign of reckless subprime lending. Something caused that "unprecedented" growth in lending to people with substandard credit, and the root of that something was in the affordable housing programs initiated during the salad days of the Clinton Administration.

---

1   Mian and Amir Sufi, "The Consequences of Mortgage Credit Expansion: Evidence from the U.S. Mortgage Default Crisis," Abstract.Atif</author></authors></contributors><titles><title>The Consequences of Mortgage Credit Expansion: Evidence from the U.S. Mortgage Default Crisis</title><secondary-title>Quarterly Journal of Economics</secondary-title></titles><pages>1449-1496</pages><volume>124(4

They're still pushing deadbeat loans

It is hard to fathom, but well after the crisis Obama's Attorney General, Eric Holder, is pushing banks to loosen lending standards. After reviewing Court documents in July 2011, Investors Business Daily stated:

> In what could be a repeat of the easy-lending cycle that led to the housing crisis, the Justice Department has asked several banks to relax their mortgage underwriting standards and approve loans for minorities with poor credit as part of a new crackdown on alleged discrimination, according to court documents reviewed by IBD.[1]

According to the report, bank defendants must notify minority customers, via notices posted at all branches, that they cannot be denied credit because they receive welfare, unemployment benefits, or food stamps. Remedies include down payment assistance and special low interest rates. Makes you just want to hit your head against the wall.

The complete model

Although the erosion of underwriting standards was the primary cause of the crisis, there were many other contributing factors, including a super-low Federal Reserve lending rate, complex loan securitizations, over-reliance on credit default swaps (an informal type of insurance), inaccurate credit rating agencies, those low capital reserve requirements (for Fannie and Freddie as well as investment banks), mark-to-market accounting, naked short selling, and a world-wide demand for investments with high yield and low risk. In this book, each of the other factors is classified as either a secondary cause, broken control, crisis trigger, aggravating factor, or environmental factor. Most of the factors were, to some degree, international, but they were most prevalent in the United States.

In Figure 23, on page 312 (and in other locations in this book), you will find a flow chart of the various factors affecting the financial crisis. The flow chart is roughly chronological, from left to right, and we will briefly review it in that order.

Model Part One — The two causes of the crisis

The main cause of the crisis is shown in the box on the left side of Figure 23. As noted, this primary cause was government affordable housing policies that led to an attack on all lending standards. The government's

---

1   Paul Sperry, "Holder Launches Witch Hunt against Biased Banks," Investors.com (July 8, 2011), http://www.investors.com/NewsAndAnalysis/Article/577794/201107081851/DOJ-Begins-Bank-Witch-Hunt.aspx.

assault on lending standards is described in the first 8 chapters of Part One.

The secondary cause of the crisis was the Federal Reserve's low-interest rate policies. After the stock market collapse at the end of the Clinton Administration, and after the 911 terrorist attack in the first year of the Bush presidency, the U.S. central bank set rates so low that banks were, essentially, paid to borrow money from the government. The money banks borrowed from the Fed was re-loaned in the form of home mortgages, at ultra-low rates that over-stimulated the housing market. Along with the relaxation of underwriting standards, the Fed's low-rate policy contributed to growth of an unsustainable housing "bubble." This issue is discussed in the last chapter in Part One (Chapter 9), and is represented in Figure 23 by the box which is second from left.

Figure 23 – A model of the subprime mortgage loan crisis of 2007/2008

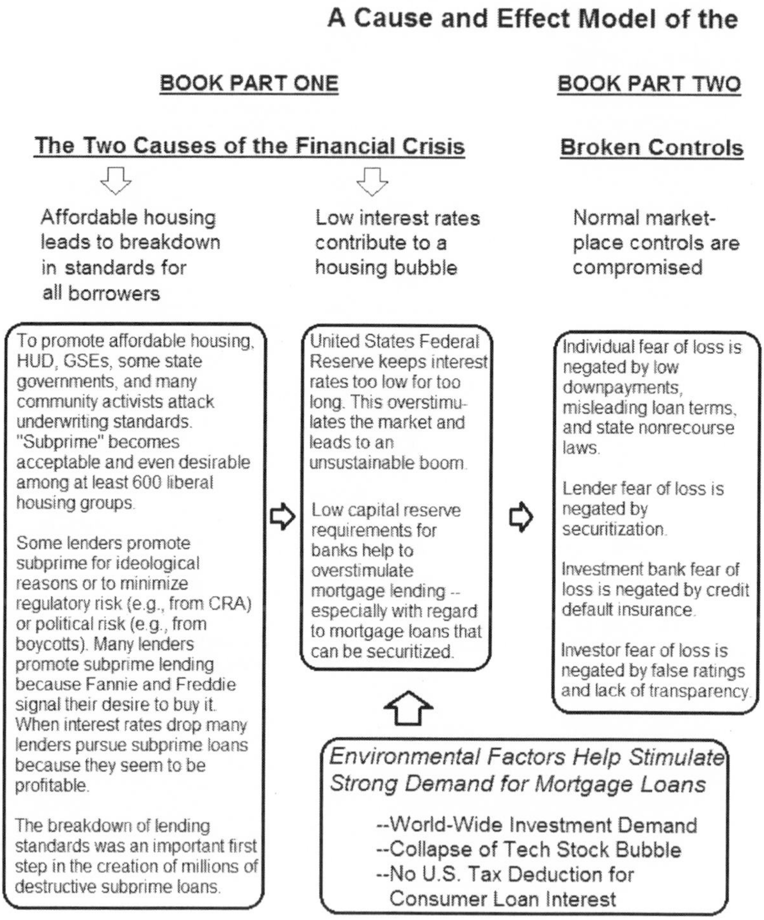

A Cause and Effect Model of the

BOOK PART ONE   **BOOK PART TWO**

The Two Causes of the Financial Crisis   Broken Controls

Affordable housing leads to breakdown in standards for all borrowers

Low interest rates contribute to a housing bubble

Normal market-place controls are compromised

To promote affordable housing, HUD, GSEs, some state governments, and many community activists attack underwriting standards. "Subprime" becomes acceptable and even desirable among at least 600 liberal housing groups.

Some lenders promote subprime for ideological reasons or to minimize regulatory risk (e.g., from CRA) or political risk (e.g., from boycotts). Many lenders promote subprime lending because Fannie and Freddie signal their desire to buy it. When interest rates drop many lenders pursue subprime loans because they seem to be profitable.

The breakdown of lending standards was an important first step in the creation of millions of destructive subprime loans.

United States Federal Reserve keeps interest rates too low for too long. This overstimu-lates the market and leads to an unsustainable boom.

Low capital reserve requirements for banks help to overstimulate mortgage lending -- especially with regard to mortgage loans that can be securitized.

Individual fear of loss is negated by low downpayments, misleading loan terms, and state nonrecourse laws.

Lender fear of loss is negated by securitization.

Investment bank fear of loss is negated by credit default insurance.

Investor fear of loss is negated by false ratings and lack of transparency.

Environmental Factors Help Stimulate Strong Demand for Mortgage Loans

--World-Wide Investment Demand
--Collapse of Tech Stock Bubble
--No U.S. Tax Deduction for Consumer Loan Interest

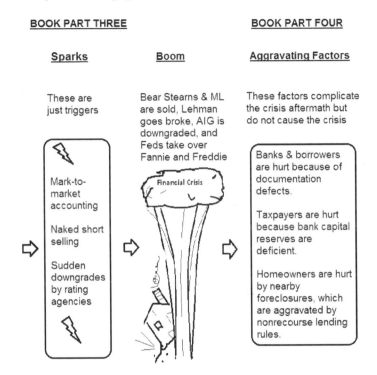

Subprime Mortgage Crisis of 2007-2008

Model Part Two — Broken controls

Part Two, which is depicted by the box in the middle of Figure 23, pertains to broken controls. There should have been four sources of resistance to subprime lending, and that resistance should have acted to brake, or control, subprime lending. It did not. Instead, normal instincts were suppressed by misguided public policy and by numerous errors made in the private sector. Although these broken controls were not crisis causes, per se, they permitted the crisis to grow unchecked until it reached catastrophic dimensions.

- Individuals (borrowers) should have resisted taking on more debt than they could afford, but many did not. Their fears were mollified by extremely low down payments, by misleading loan terms, and (in some cases) state nonrecourse lending laws.
- Lenders should have been terrified to make some of the loans they made. Instead, they were confident that they could peddle their weak loans to Fannie, Freddie, or an investment bank that would securitize them.
- Investment banks should have been fearful of putting crappy loans into their securities. They were not because they didn't comprehend the extent to which loan quality had deteriorated, or because companies like AIG gave them assurances in the form of credit default swaps (a type of insurance).
- Investors should have been reluctant to buy shaky mortgage-backed securities and collateralized debt obligations. They bought them from Fannie and Freddie because they guaranteed them, or they bought them from investment banks on the basis of overly-high ratings given by the rating agencies.

These issues are discussed in Chapters 10 through 13.

Model Part Three — Sparks that ignited the crisis

The financial crisis had three "triggers," and they are shown in the box just to the right of center in Figure 23. One of them, the sudden downgrade of credit ratings, also relates to Part Two of this book, where it is found in Chapter 12. The other two triggers, mark-to-market accounting and "naked short" selling, are the topics of Chapters 14 and 15, respectively.

Mark-to-market accounting, a.k.a. fair value accounting, has been evolving within the accounting profession since the early 1990s. These developing rules were further modified by a ruling of the Financial Accounting Standards Board (FAS 157) that took effect for fiscal years commencing after November 15, 2007 — as the crisis erupted.

Under FAS 157, as interpreted at the time, a company had to value the assets on its balance sheet based on the market price for which they could be immediately sold. Some analysts believe that, in a market of declining real estate values, these mark-to-market rules led to a "death spiral" for companies holding mortgage-backed securities (because there was no one available to buy them). Others believe that FAS 157 is simply a convenient excuse used by poorly-managed businesses.

Short selling is, essentially, betting that a company's stock values will decline. For example, if you think that Lehman Sisters is holding too many securities backed by subprime loans, and is likely to lose value, you might execute the following scheme: Borrow some shares of Lehman Sisters today, sell them, and replace the borrowed stock with shares you will buy in a week or two, after the Lehman Sisters becomes more afford-able. "Naked" short selling, banned in the U.S. since 2008, takes a little more chutzpah. It is the same as short selling, except the sale is made before borrowing the stock and before even knowing if you can borrow the stock prior to the settlement day.

Many financial analysts believe that short selling — especially the naked kind — can lead to panic stock sales, and put corporations in fi-nancial jeopardy. Bear Stearns, Lehman Bros., Morgan Stanley, and AIG are a few of the financial giants that appear to have suffered from heavy short selling.

Model Part Four — Aggravating factors

The factors that have complicated the resolution of the crisis are outlined in Part Four (box on far right side of Figure 23). By now you have probably heard of the many crooked banks that forged documents so they could push unsuspecting home owners out of their residences. To some commentators, this was outright fraud, constituting a theft. A different perspective was offered by the Wall Street Journal in October 2010: "We're not aware of a single case so far of a substantive error." In Chapter 16 a detailed analysis is found.

Chapter 17 deals with bank capital reserve requirements. This dry and esoteric subject is of interest because, during the George W. Bush Administration, the Securities and Exchange Commission (SEC) made changes to bank capital reserve requirements, and the early reports said that the changes were deregulatory. Learned scholars were tripping over themselves to tell us how Bush's SEC threw out leverage limitations, causing bank debt-to-equity ratios to soar from 8-to-1 all the way up to 40-to-1. We now know that the scholars were wrong. The changes made by SEC, without partisan dispute, did not cause leverage to soar. That said, the net capital rules imposed on banks were deficient, and had been all along. They contributed to the crisis.

Chapter 18 addresses an issue that has been almost completely ignored during the aftermath of the 2007-08 financial crisis: state non-recourse (or "strategic default") laws. There are several very important reasons the crisis has lasted so long: One of them is the existence of obsolete non-recourse lending laws in many U.S. states. These laws, originating back in the 1930s, have enabled many prime borrowers to skip out on their mortgage obligations. The absence of non-recourse lending laws in Canada is often cited as a reason that country fared relatively well during the crisis.

Model Part Five — Class warfare politics

By beating the drums of class warfare, President Obama and some other politicians have tried to deflect blame away from failed governmental policies. They say the mortgage meltdown was caused by "Wall Street," by Bush's tax cuts for the wealthy, his deficit spending, and/or his deregulation of the nation's lending institutions. Did the wealthy really get a special break from George W. Bush, and did tax cuts contribute to the crisis? Did the crisis relate to Bush's deficit spending or to deregulation efforts of his administration? Exactly what did Bush deregulate? Did the financial crisis originate with Wall Street investment banks? Each of these questions is discussed and analyzed in Part Five.

Factors in the Environment

At the bottom of Figure 23 you will see a box that includes 3 additional factors that stimulated demand for mortgage loans and mortgage-backed securities. I call these "environmental factors": world-wide investment demand (the so-called "savings glut"), the collapse of the technology stock bubble at the end of the Clinton Administration, and tax policy in the United States that favors home-related debt over consumer debt. It is likely that these factors had a role in the crisis; however, they have been left for others to analyze.

Addendum B: Looney Logic

Silly arguments often spread and persist when they involve financial matters that are statistically confusing or rife with esoteric jargon. That is certainly the case with regard to the mythology surrounding the financial crisis of 2007/08. Here is a brief summary of some of the misconceptions and logical errors. Each of them is addressed in greater detail within other sections of the book.

Don't be tricked by a bogus definition of "subprime"

As pointed out on page 140 ("Stuck on stupid"), subprime lending is not the same as high-interest-rate lending, and subprime lending is certainly not limited to high-interest loans. A loan is subprime, depending on the characteristics of the borrower — not the terms of the loan. It is a loan given to a person who has a credit history that is substandard or who has assets or income that is inadequate.

Because most data bases do not track the credit histories of borrowers, or the amount of their assets and income, many analysts (including authorities in the U.S. government) use a crude and misleading proxy for subprime loans: high interest-rate loans. They believe that, if a borrower is charged a high rate of interest he must have a bad credit history, and if he is charged a moderate rate of interest his credit history is probably pretty good. If you want to exonerate affordable housing programs with respect to the growth of subprime lending, the high-interest proxy is perfect. That's because many government-endorsed affordable housing programs are, as a matter of policy, specifically designed to offer medium or low interest-rate loans to people who have lousy credit. If we use high interest rate loans as a proxy for subprime we will invariable understate the amount of subprime lending associated with HUD, CRA, Fannie, Freddie, or state/local affordable housing loan programs.

Affordable housing policies led to high-priced home foreclosures

Some people like to point out the high foreclosure rates that exist in some fairly pricey neighborhoods. They claim those foreclosure rates are evidence that the subprime mortgage loan crisis has little to do with affordable housing programs. What these people don't understand is that affordable housing programs are based on median level income and housing values *for a given locality*, and some localities have median incomes and values that are quite high. For example, in some areas of California, down payment subsidy programs were available for homes costing in excess of $800,000, as of 2007. (See page 55 for a listing.)

In addition, it can be shown that the quest for affordable housing led to an assault on all loan underwriting standards. Before long people who could afford $500,000 homes were stretching their finances to buy $800,000 homes, and so forth. These people effectively became subprime borrowers, due to the erosion of underwriting standards.

Businesses adapt to meet a competitive threat

Through encouragement or coercion, the government can influence business activity. Another way a business can be influenced is via competition, and this is true for the lending business. Traditionally, a borrower could get a slightly lower interest rate from a solid, community bank; however, he would generally find it easier and/or faster to get loan approval from a mortgage lender. Mortgage lenders stayed in business primarily by offering relatively flexible underwriting standards and good service. But, when the community banks that were subject to the Community Reinvestment Act (CRA) adopted underwriting standards that were even more flexible than those of the mortgage lender, he had to adapt to the threat or go out of business. The mortgage lender adopted even looser standards, and he did this despite his being (formally) excluded from the CRA. Remember this next time someone tells you that CRA affected only a small fraction of lenders.

Going to Las Vegas with lots of money doesn't help

In the opinion of some analysts, the crisis was caused by a lack of adequate capital reserves held by the investment banks. Capital reserves should have been higher for private banks as well as Fannie and Freddie, but there is another point to consider. The capital reserves of individual borrowers also should have been higher — much higher. For an individual the "capital reserve" is the cash he has in his bank account and the equity he has in his home, which is directly related to the size of his down payment and any home equity loans. A high percentage of foreclosures have related to mortgage loans held by borrowers who had no capital reserves whatsoever.

Here is a more fundamental point: Higher lender capital reserves would not have prevented the crisis. Investment banks were packaging subprime loans — an inherently risky activity. They were keeping many of those shaky securities on their balance sheets. If they had more funds at risk (i.e., more capital reserves) their behavior might have moderated, and the risk to taxpayers would have lessened. Those are both worthy goals; however, the only sure way to eliminate any risk is to stop the risky activity. Consider this analogy. Let's say your friend gambles heavily in Las Vegas and, afterwards, he often needs your financial help. You might tell him to take more of his own money on future junkets so that he won't need your assistance. However, the only way he can really decrease risk is through a cessation of the risky activity — gambling. Similarly, banks can not eliminate risk until they stopped the risky activity of subprime lending. Adding more capital would not, in itself, solve the problem.

Don't be confused by misleading statistics

There is a little game that is often played when reporting delinquency statistics. Members of the Blame-it-on-Wall-Street crowd like to compare the overall (company-wide) delinquency rates of Fannie and Freddie to the much higher, industry-wide rates for certain risky products, such as Alt-A loans (low-documentation loans) and subprime loans. This comparison invariably makes Fannie and Freddie look relatively prudent and respectable. However, it is an illusion. Consider this analogy: Fannie's Pharmaceuticals, a well-established drug maker, has produced and sold one very safe product — aspirin — for several years. It is now supplementing the aspirin with a small quantity of a new, much riskier product. To assess the safety of the new product, would we dilute its performance stats with those of Fannie's very safe aspirin? No. To do so would obscure any meaningful results. And, it would be even more misleading to compare the overall performance statistics of Fannie's Pharmaceuticals (aspirin and the new product, combined) with the performance stats for a smaller competitor that only produces the relatively risky product (i.e., no aspirin at all). For more information, see the discussion on page 78.

Business and liberalism are not mutually exclusive

The entertainment industry is big business, but it is also a stronghold of liberalism.[1] The two are not mutually exclusive. Likewise, the lending industry was not (and is not) a liberal-free zone. That explains why Goldman Sachs' employees gave nearly $1 million to Obama's 2008 presidential campaign — more than four times the amount given to McCain's effort.

In the case of the world's biggest subprime lender, Countrywide Financial, there is little doubt that its CEO, Angelo Mozilo, had deeply-held liberal beliefs, and these had an impact on the way he ran the company. In a biographical piece in the New Yorker, Connie Bruck described actions that may reflect Mozilo's liberal perspective:

> In 1992, shortly after Mozilo became chairman of the Mortgage Bankers Association, the Federal Reserve Bank of Boston issued a report stating that it had found systemic discrimination by mortgage lenders.... Mozilo was appalled. He ordered that all Countrywide records on rejected minority applicants be sent to him, and he retroactively approved about half of them. Then he dispatched African-Americans, posing as prospective borrowers ... to Countrywide branches....
>
> Between 1993 and 1994, the company's loans to African-American borrowers rose three hundred and twenty-five percent....[2]

Bruck concluded that "Mozilo always saw himself as providing mortgages to many who were like him — disenfranchised." His liberal point of view is also confirmed by a statement Mozilo once made in a speech at a housing conference. Declared Mozilo: "Homeownership is not a privilege but a right."[3] That sentiment is the epitome of liberalism.

Some people on the left think that Countrywide perfectly demonstrates that the quest for profits caused the crisis — not affordable housing programs. After all, Countrywide wasn't even subject to the Community Reinvestment Act (CRA).[4] Perhaps Countrywide and Mozilo

---

1 If you doubt this, I refer you to Primetime Propaganda by Ben Shapiro (Broad Side publisher), a book that presents the results of interviews with numerous corporate leaders in the entertainment industry.
2 Connie Bruck, "Angelo's Ashes," The New Yorker June 4, 2009.
3 Ibid.
4 Although Countrywide was not subject to CRA, CEO Angelo Mozilo signed a voluntary commitment pledging to HUD that Countrywide would lend as if it were subject to CRA.

were greedy; however, it is just as reasonable to conclude that the company's activities were a consequence of Mozilo's personal liberal lending philosophy.

A lemon is a lemon, no matter how it is financed

You buy this car, and it's a real doozy. It's a gas guzzler, it's noisy, it smells like a bus, and the heater doesn't work. You'd love to sell the car, but no one will buy it. What is your problem? Is it the finance terms you made with the bank, or is it the fact that your car stinks and has no resale value?

Today, there are lots of folks who could afford to make the payments on their loans, but they have chosen to walk away, instead. In many states, nonrecourse lending rules allow them to do this with impunity. To salve his conscience, the walk-away often justifies the action by demonizing the bank. It goes something like this. "I called my bank and they weren't willing to take anything off my loan. So, screw them!" Or, "I called the bank and they didn't return the call for a week. After that, I decided to send them the keys to the house, and just walk away." A walk-away may have a legal right to stiff his bank, but the effort to blame the bank (i.e., blame the victim) is just another example of loony logic.

Bad policy in one decade can cause grief in another

Some analysts try to exonerate government affordable housing policies on the basis of a time lag that took place between the ramped-up affordable housing policies of the mid-1990s and the explosion of subprime lending that started around 2002. However, the loose underwriting standards that sprang from the 1990 affordable housing policies were like timed explosive devices ready to go off. The only remaining requirement for an explosion of subprime was super-low interest rates. That was supplied, courtesy of the Federal Reserve, after 2001. Those two government policies, in combination, caused the financial crisis that became full-blown in 2007.

INDEX